Breaking the F
in Motor C

Breaking the Banks in Motor City

The Auto Industry, the 1933 Detroit Banking Crisis and the Start of the New Deal

DARWYN H. LUMLEY

McFarland & Company, Inc., Publishers
Jefferson, North Carolina, and London

All photographs from The Collections of The Henry Ford unless otherwise stated.

LIBRARY OF CONGRESS CATALOGUING-IN-PUBLICATION DATA

Lumley, Darwyn H., 1935–
    Breaking the banks in Motor City : the auto industry, the 1933 Detroit banking crisis and the start of the New Deal / Darwyn H. Lumley.
        p.   cm.
    Includes bibliographical references and index.

    ISBN 978-0-7864-4417-5
    softcover : 50# alkaline paper ∞

    1. Bank failures — Michigan — Detroit — History — 20th century.
    2. Automobile industry and trade — Michigan — Detroit — History.
    3. Financial crises — United States — History — 20th century.
    4. New Deal, 1933–1939.   5. United States — Economic policy —1933–1945.   I. Title
    HG2613.D6L86   2009
    332.109774'3409043 — dc22   2009019305

British Library cataloguing data are available

On the cover: President Franklin Roosevelt and the board of governors of the Federal Reserve System commemorating passage of the Banking Act of August 23, 1935 (Herbert Hoover Presidential Library); Guilloche border ©2009 Shutterstock

Manufactured in the United States of America

McFarland & Company, Inc., Publishers
 Box 611, Jefferson, North Carolina 28640
 www.mcfarlandpub.com

Table of Contents

Introduction   1

1. More Money Needed   11
2. "Wall Street Sees Ford as a Banker"   27
3. "In the Way Our Reports Were Being Made,
   It Never Was Material."   45
4. "It Is Going to Be Awfully Hard Work"   63
5. "Woe unto Those by Whom It Cometh"   82
6. "Your Friends Won't Hold It Against You"   102
7. The Banking System Ceases to Function   126

Epilogue   159
Chronology   171
Notes   177
Bibliography   187
Index   191

Introduction

In February and March of 1933, the "Motor City" of Detroit became the center of unsought public interest. Ordinarily the men who ran the auto industry would have welcomed, and even sought, free attention. But in the depths of the Depression, the imminent failure of their banking group was not supposed to be public knowledge. On the other hand, the auto men did seek attention and assistance from officials in Washington, D.C. The appeal of the auto industrialist bankers to federal governmental agencies was a measure of their desperation. As foremost industrial capitalists, inviting governmental involvement was contrary to their entire belief system.

By the first week of February, the critical state of banking in Michigan had come to the attention of President Herbert Hoover and others in the United States government. They, and all others involved, wished to keep the Detroit banking situation from becoming public knowledge. The concern was that a loss of confidence in the entire banking system would take place, causing depositors to withdraw their funds and to create a serious liquidity problem. A panic "run on the banks" was feared, with no one certain of the consequences. Nevertheless the grave situation could not be kept quiet and was not contained.

Direct attention was focused on Detroit from February 14 through March 4. Interest in Detroit banking problems continued through 1934, especially after testimony by officers of the failed Detroit banks in appearances before a United States Senate investigating committee.

On St. Valentine's Day, the 14th of February, the unresolved Detroit banking problems led to a temporary closure of all banks in Michigan, termed a "banking holiday." In turn, the problems in Michigan created a national crisis that, in a domino effect, led to the closing of all banks in the United States. The timing of the banking failure compounded the

1

nation's problem: Herbert Clark Hoover had been defeated for re-election on November 8, 1932, but would remain in office until March 4, 1933. The election results gave 472 electoral votes to Franklin Delano Roosevelt and 59 to Hoover. Forty-three of the then forty-eight states had majorities for Roosevelt. Reflecting the times was the nine percent popular vote for the Socialist candidate Norman Thomas. William Z. Foster, the Communist candidate, gained two and a half percent. Never before, and not since that time, have two minor party candidates who advocated radical change received such a large percentage of the popular vote.

During the 115 days between election and inauguration, the crisis grew with both President Hoover and President-elect Roosevelt unwilling or unable to find accommodation on policies and actions to lessen or ameliorate the situation. Also failing to take action that might have prevented the predicament were auto executives, in their dual roles as officers of the banking group that was on the verge of failing. The consequence was that the United States had both an economic and political crisis of the greatest magnitude.

Nineteen thirty-two had been a very bad year for most Americans. It appeared to many that the promise of American life and democratic ways no longer existed. Trust in the normal and orderly way of resolving issues was gone. Three examples of dissimilar groups in varied situations, all facing the effects of the Great Depression, point to the prevalent national mood. In March, a protest march of unemployed workers, led in part by Communist organizers, moved on the Ford plant in Dearborn. This action precipitated a violent response by Ford security forces, turning the event into a riot. A consequence was that four of the marchers were killed. Secondly, in the last days of a hot July summer, more than 40,000 veterans of the Great War marched on Washington, D.C. They were known as the B.E.F., or Bonus Expeditionary Force, a name patterned after the A.E.F. (American Expeditionary Force) of what we now term World War I. Violence again took place, with the U.S. Army called in to disperse the veterans. The goal of the Bonus Marchers was to seek immediate payment of a bonus due them in 1945. Lastly, in August, in the heartland state of Iowa, a "farm holiday" movement surfaced. In actuality, it was a strike by farmers to prevent the marketing of milk, grain, and livestock. Farmers had not shared in the boom years of the 1920s, and now in the Great

Depression farm products' prices had fallen to record lows. Farmers, normally conservative, responded with actions often associated with the labor strife of industrial workers. Highways were blocked, a train was stopped, a bridge was burned, crops were destroyed, and one person died. In a related event, a mob of Iowa farmers entered a courtroom and forcibly removed the judge. He was pushed and shoved and manhandled, with a noose put around his neck. Eventually, he was released after very rough treatment. There were many other instances where the social order seemed to have broken down. The nation was faced with a problem unique in the annals of all history; in the midst of plenty people were hungry and out of work, and many were homeless. Even those with sufficient food, work, and a home were uncertain of their fate. The nation was in despair.

In the formerly dynamic automobile industry, production declined precipitously from 1929 to 1932. General Motors Corporation production fell from 1,353,059 to 432,830, a loss of about two-thirds. Of the latter figure, the lowest-priced GM brand, Chevrolet, made up 306,716 units, or about 70 percent of the GM total. Ford and Lincoln numbers were even worse. In 1929 Ford and Lincoln production totaled 1,514,804. In 1932 their combined total was 290,683, or a loss of about 80 percent. The newly formed Chrysler Corporation also showed a decline, but not as statistically dramatic: 1929 production for Chrysler, DeSoto, Dodge, and Plymouth had reached 375,094, while that of 1932 was 215,056. The foremost independent automaker, Hudson, produced a total of 300,962 units in 1929 but fell to 57,550 in 1932. (Both years' figures include those of Essex and Terraplane, Hudson's lower-priced lines.) Decreased production meant fewer jobs for workers, more layoffs, and often shorter working hours for those who were employed. The effects of the Great Depression furthered the consolidation of the auto industry in Michigan, leaving fewer auto companies. Between 1929 and 1932, three Cleveland-based companies — Chandler, Jordan, and Peerless — all ended production. While none of the three was a large producer, closing down meant the loss of jobs for individuals and the community. For each failed company, as well as for the lowered production of the surviving firms, fewer workers were needed in the supply businesses such as steel, glass and other related industries.

When Franklin Delano Roosevelt took the oath of office and began

Introduction

his inaugural speech on March 4, 1933, the United States had reached a critical point in its history. Not since the inaugural speech of Abraham Lincoln on March 4, 1861, had Americans waited for the new president's words with such anticipation. Unfortunately, events in these critical times moved very quickly, faster than the authors of the Constitution of the United States could ever have imagined. The scheduling of the presidential election in early November with an inauguration in the first week of March perhaps was suitable for the eighteenth century. But by Lincoln's time in the nineteenth century, a new age had begun, with the patterns of life having quickened due to telegraphic communication and railroad transportation. By the twentieth century, telephones, radio, air travel and automobiles were added to the mix of communication and travel that combined to permit news and rumors to move about even more quickly than in Lincoln's time. A consequence was that policy makers, politicians, leaders of industry and finance, and other individuals in positions of leadership or responsibility had even less time to comprehend and attempt to resolve crises than in 1860 and 1861. In an interesting connection, some key automobile executives who had helped to speed up the pace of American life found themselves pressed for sufficient time to make decisions. They had helped to create a social environment somewhat like the relentless movement of an assembly line. That is, events moved with speed whether you were prepared or not. And nobody seems to have been prepared.

A comparison of the circumstances of 1933 with those of 1861 is not lightly made. The election of Abraham Lincoln on November 4, 1860, began a set of circumstances in which seven states of the lower South passed ordinances of secession. On the 9th of February, in the following year, Jefferson Davis was elected provisional president of the newly formed Confederacy. The president of the United States, James Buchanan, sent a message to Congress in December outlining the impotence of the federal government. By the time Lincoln had taken office, what had been known as the United States had ceased to exist. At least an entire geographic section held that belief. Four years of internecine warfare followed. At the end of the strife, the relationship between the national government and the states was forever altered.

The problem of the 115 days between an election in November, and an inauguration in the following March was a problem that had been considered. After the Civil War, much public discussion took place on how to prevent a repeat of the situation. When Lincoln was elected but not in office, the country experienced a time of drift, confusion, and national peril. But such matters take considerable time to work out. In fact a solution to the time gap, or interregnum, had been provided with the ratification of the 20th Amendment to the Constitution. While it was needed immediately, in the depths of the Great Depression, it was not due to become effective until October 15, 1933. So while a solution was in the offing, the problem of a discredited president remaining in office in the midst of an economic meltdown intensified the predicament. An issue that might have been stemmed in January or February seemed to be heading toward catastrophe.

The circumstances of 1932–1933 differed from those of 1860–1861, involving armies, battles and enormous numbers of civilian and military casualties. But in 1933, while the industrial, banking, financial, and political leaders wallowed about in futile attempts to prevent a crisis, one did take place. At the time, all memories turned to the terrible example of 1860–1861. In that critical period, regional and economic interests, taking advantage of a power vacuum, led to radical political decisions. Everyone knew how the crisis of 1860–1861 had led to horrendous consequences. The crucial question in 1933 was whether the national government could prevent a complete loss of faith in the basic economic arrangements of everyday life. Trust and faith, after all is said and done, are the fundamental requirements of any economic system. When the entire national banking system ground to a halt on March 4, there was no way to forecast what might take place. With banks closed, and cash money being hoarded and in short supply, some considered using scrip. This seemingly practical act might have had many consequences, including a greater loss of faith in the monetary system. This could have led to the possible fragmentation of the national economy. While the problems in 1933 stemmed from an economic depression, not secession, the lessons of 1861 were not forgotten. That is, the possibility that events could get further out of control was very real. What had been a banking disaster had widened into a currency crisis. The nation was headed into unknown peril, with the future looking worse still. Questions about the resiliency of the economic system remained unanswered.

Introduction

Had banks failed in St. Louis, New Orleans, Atlanta or many other American cities, the consequences would not have been the same. It was Detroit that counted. And Detroit mattered because it was the city in which the automobile industry had grown to both economic and psychological importance in American life. The American auto industry, centered in the Detroit area, had risen from a halting beginning at the end of the nineteenth century to the national economic driving force in about 25 years. But the social changes brought about by the use of the personally owned automobile added to Detroit's clout in American life. This is often described as an automobile revolution, arising from the social changes resulting when the nation became motorized. The city that is the center of any revolution always gains increased importance. Paris during the French Revolution and Moscow during the Russian Revolution both were the centers of substantial attention. So it was Detroit's association with the auto industry that gave it special significance and status in American life. In fact the social changes were so profound that any history of the period cannot be considered complete without at least a general summary of those changes.

The move toward urbanization, already in progress before the growth of the auto industry, was intensified. Land use patterns, formerly based on navigable waterways or rail lines, changed as roads and highways were developed and improved. The ease of mobility in going from the country into town or the reverse brought about a form of psychological mobility. One could take on a different persona in the various physical locations that were possible to reach in one's own motorcar. The impact of the auto on American life has been profound, and remains a continuous process. Historians, social critics, environmentalists, economists, journalists and others have opportunities without limit if they wish to explore the ways in which the personal automobile continues to alter and affect American life. But the political consequences of the auto industry are not often mentioned.

One subject that seems to have been neglected is the role of the leaders of the auto industry in a significant event in American history: the Detroit banking crisis of 1933. The Detroit banking crisis has been explored, but not the link between the banking crisis and the major executives of the auto industry, and the consequences of their involvement. By

1929 auto industry leaders had reached great heights in American life. Many had achieved enormous successes, and seemed to personify what was once proudly known as "American know-how." What they did not seem to comprehend is that with the rewards of their efforts went a measure of responsibility and accountability. Despite many opportunities to provide responsible leadership, auto industry leaders including Edsel Ford, Ernest Kanzler, Roy D. Chapin, and others, in their additional roles as bankers, failed. Their failures were many, frequent, and cumulative. As leaders of the auto industry the aforementioned had been accorded great esteem for their successes. But when they had an opportunity to demonstrate economic and political leadership on the national scene outside of the automobile industry, they failed to respond. Furthermore, once they were unsuccessful, they effectively shifted responsibility to Henry Ford and his old partner Sen. James Couzens. Both men were very much involved in Detroit banking crisis matters, and understanding their personalities is key to comprehending the events of the time.

The men who founded the auto industry are often given mythic status. This is especially true of the giants such as Henry Ford, William C. Durant, Alfred P. Sloan, and perhaps some others in what might be considered the first rank. James Couzens rightfully belongs among the men who might also belong to a select group of pioneers, innovators and organizers. His contributions to the growth and success of the Ford Motor Company have been acknowledged, and are part of the historic record. But it was the *Ford* Motor Company, and Henry Ford's successful efforts to eliminate many of the other founding and contributing men has resulted in those people being mostly neglected. The Ford Motor Company was a movie with the credits reading, "The Ford Motor Company, starring Henry Ford, produced by Henry Ford and directed by Henry Ford." Each of those credits would be in large type, probably in Ford blue. For the average person that's all the information required. However, for the person with a greater interest, there is always the list of the supporting cast, the music director, the cinematographer, the wardrobe consultant, and so on. That is where you might find the individuals who are profiled in *Henry's Lieutenants*, by Ford R. Bryan. The point is well made by the title of Bryan's book. Henry was in command, and he had a supporting cast who had no rank above lieutenant. We know now that others made significant and fundamental contributions to the success of the Ford Motor Company. The man who comes first to mind is James Couzens. But since Henry Ford continually rid himself of those who might have been considered his equals or threatened his dominance, Bryan's title echoes what Henry Ford intended the record to be.

The problem with James Couzens is that he did not fade into obscurity during his lifetime. Nor did he suffer failure in his post–Ford Motor Company life. Instead, after leaving the Ford Motor Company, Couzens went into Detroit municipal politics and charity endeavors. He did this with his customary energy, rising from what was supposed to be a figurehead position as police commissioner to mayor of Detroit. In his roles in Detroit city politics, Couzens said what he thought, and was as much of a news reporter's favorite as was Henry Ford. Both were available for newsmen with opinions on varying subjects, with reporters uncertain just what kind of men it was who would make such statements. Did Ford or Couzens believe what they said to reporters? Did they understand how others might interpret their remarks? It did not seem to make any difference. Both men continued to provide reporters with juicy quotations. One major difference, however, was that Ford had a well-oiled and diligent public relations department that distributed remarks attributed to him. Couzens, on the other hand, spoke directly to reporters, seemingly always on the record.

Ford had another advantage; it was his long-nurtured identification with the idea of progress. The production and successful sales of the Ford Model T tended to subdue criticism of his actions and instead assign oracle-like significance to his public remarks. Ford was continually promoted by the Ford Motor Company as one of the "greats" of the era. His well-publicized association with Thomas Edison assisted in his public persona. Edison occupied a place of honor unrivaled by anyone, and rubbing shoulders with him was significant. This was especially true after the founding of the Edison Institute in Dearborn.

Couzens created a special problem for Henry Ford. They had been partners, with Couzens being as co-equal with Ford as anyone ever became. They knew each other's shortcomings and strengths, as only partners do. Nobody else stood up to Henry Ford as did James Couzens, whose self-assurance was both problematic and advantageous.

Whenever Couzens and Ford had opposing views on any subject, neither shrank from publicly expressing his observations. For a newspaperman needing a good story, Ford and Couzens could each be relied upon to stir the pot. Over their lifetimes, after they had ended their Ford Motor Company partnership, Ford and Couzens publicly opposed one another over a number of issues. They were in opposition regarding streetcars in Detroit, over the power plant issue known as Muscle Shoals, over Ford's trial balloon for the U.S. presidency in 1923, over Ford's pacifism in World War I, and so on. Some writers believe that Ford and Couzens were feuding when the Detroit banking crisis took place and tend to put the banking crisis on their shoulders. But no evidence supports such a belief, and the history of both men indicates that if they had been feuding, it would not have been a secret. In fact, they tended to share some opinions about bank failures in the early years of the Great Depression. That is, both men believed that there were banks that were in such bad shape that no effort should be made to save them. Both also thought that government policies for supporting banks seemed to be heavily politicized. Furthermore, they had concluded that many of the banks in distress were in that condition due to bad banking policies. Attempting to save such banks, they thought, really was a means of publicly subsidizing banking practices that bordered on unethical or even criminal behavior. Ford was well aware of Couzens's views about letting some banks fail. In fact, he quoted Couzens in the fateful conference when emissaries of President Herbert Hoover met with Henry and Edsel Ford seeking support for a government funded loan to the failing banks in Detroit.

Focusing on whom to blame for the economic and political crisis that resulted is an interesting activity, as there are a considerable number of possible miscreants. But when individuals are singled out for blame, the focus is lost or diffused. The various individuals are primarily important as representatives or parts of a group. What must be understood is how the dealings of the individuals brought about the crisis, and how their actions led to the consequences of the bank closures. No matter who is blamed, the results remain the same: the banks were closed, leading to the dire situation on March 4, 1933. The facts also remain the same: the federal government assumed economic powers at the expense of those who previously had that power. Just as the election of 1860 presaged a growth in the power of the federal government, so also did the election of 1932, because of the banking crisis of 1933. A fundamental shift in American economic power took place that had immediate and long-lasting effects. This book studies the Detroit banking crisis of 1933 to explain how key individuals, as representatives of the automobile industry, responded in ways that led to fundamental changes in the distribution and use of American political and economic power.

1

More Money Needed

"We have to get considerably more money or the whole group is going to collapse."[1] These were the words Alfred Leyburn heard directed at him. Leyburn, chief national bank examiner from Chicago, was in a meeting specially scheduled for January 15, 1933, to which he was invited by the leadership of the Union Guardian Group. The Guardian was one of two banking organizations that controlled almost all banking in Michigan.

The speaker was Ernest Kanzler, then chairman of the executive committee of the Guardian Group. Leyburn was hardly surprised at the revelation; in June of 1932 he had met with Guardian Group to warn them about the financial condition of the group.[2] He had, in fact, been so concerned about the Guardian that he had written a very strong report on June 14, 1932. His report to the comptroller of the currency said, "The Guardian is sort of a promotion scheme." He further reported the Guardian's condition was "very unsatisfactory" and "we are forced to the conclusion that group banking is fundamentally unsound and dangerous and that it constitutes a menace to the general banking situation."[3]

Leyburn's only positive remarks were that he saw hope in Kanzler and Edsel Ford becoming more active in the management, and that they would dictate the policies to a greater extent than previously had been the case. His assumption seems to have been that neither man was actively involved at that time.

However, one day short of exactly six months after Leyburn's report, it became clear that his faith in the leadership of Ernest Kanzler and Edsel Ford had been mistaken. No improvement had been shown in the management of the Guardian Group, and it soon became clear to Leyburn that the purpose of the meeting was to get him to support the Guardian's loan application to the Reconstruction Finance Corporation.

The drama of the specially held Sunday meeting, and the blunt words from Ernest Kanzler, were indeed an attempt to influence Leyburn to back the Guardian Group's application, not an admission of mismanagement. Considering the importance of Detroit to the national economy, and the growing number of banking failures throughout the U.S., the implication was that a Detroit banking crisis would be the final blow in bringing about a national financial catastrophe.

Unfortunately, U.S. bank failures were frequent and nationwide. An underlying cause was that the United States had, at a minimum, 50 banking systems — one each for the 48 states and the District of Columbia, and another system under the national government. If the United States could be said to have a banking system, it was considered to be the worst in the world.[4]

Banks were organized based on the consequences of the early and continuous national political and social differences between those who followed what they believed were the precepts of Thomas Jefferson, and those who followed the percepts of Alexander Hamilton. Independent, small rural banks stemming from Jeffersonian politics were especially vulnerable to the agricultural fortunes of their local areas. A belief in the inherent virtues of local or state government, which placed few restrictions on banking, stood in contrast to the fear engendered by large-scale national banks, most of which were headquartered in the increasingly urban East. This political/economic debate began with the nation, and was the stated or underlying issue of election after election.

No person can better epitomize the divide in American life over banking than Henry Ford. Ford grew up on the farming frontier of Michigan and learned the economic prejudices of that time and location. The belief system included both a feeling of moral superiority on the part of the farmers and small town business people, and a distrust of the so-called "Eastern money interests." As the foremost innovator in mass production and mass marketing, Ford changed Michigan first, as he later changed the United States. His early-learned, deep-seated dislike of what came to be called Wall Street, or large-scale national bankers, never left him, even as he unknowingly worked to destroy the society which had formed his economic beliefs. The industrialized and urbanized America under development was at odds with the idealizations of the past. So were many organizations and institutions, including the banking system.

In the 1920s, 5,411 banks filed for bankruptcy in the U.S. Most of the failures were small banks in rural areas, reflecting the agricultural depression that followed the end of World War I. The continuous failure of banks created a loss of confidence as depositors sought to take out their funds before the bank failed, creating "runs" on the bank. As long as failures were small and localized, it was considered to be commonplace. But as the numbers increased, fear compounded.

And, the numbers increased. Bank failures in 1930 totaled 1,350, with 2,293 in 1931 and 1,453 in 1932. One reason that the number of banking failures did not increase after 1931 was that the supply of banks had dwindled significantly. In 1932, the Reconstruction Finance Corporation made loans of nearly $1 billion to over 5,000 banks. In the same month that Leyburn was meeting with the leaders of the Guardian Group, January 1933, another 273 banks failed.[5]

Failures and panic swept through Tennessee, Missouri, Indiana, Illinois, Iowa, Arkansas, and North Carolina in 1930. Each successive panic created a run as people rushed to withdraw both their time deposits and checking accounts. Everyone wanted cash: an accumulated $180 million in one month; $370 million another month.[6] The idea that a bank did not necessarily have sufficient quantities of cash was not fully comprehended.

Earlier, in 1907, in the midst of a brief financial recession, James Couzens tried to explain to his partner Henry Ford the difficulty of obtaining cash to carry out the business of the Ford Motor Company. Ford, in response, said he would simply go to the various banks and take out the money on deposit and bring it back to pay the workers. Couzens was incredulous. "But this money is not in the banks! You cannot think the money is in the banks?" Ford answered, "Certainly it is there."[7] Even after hearing an extensive explanation of banking operations, Ford persisted in his beliefs. Like Ford, the public tended to believe that banks should have cash on hand to meet any circumstance. The fact that banks could not meet all requests for cash during runs on the banks was considered as prima facie evidence of a banking weakness and/or dishonesty.

Even before a panic ensued in some areas, depositors began to withdraw funds. This created actual banking problems. As the stock market continued to fall, the values of assets held by the banks deteriorated. A decreasing market for securities prevented banks from gaining funds to meet depositors' demands. This often brought about steep discounts in security values, as banks needed to obtain cash. Loans that had been issued were now called in, resulting in a further downward spiral, especially in real estate values. In effect, a deflationary spiral began. By February and March of 1933 the vast attempt to withdraw funds from the banks was considered "without historical precedent."[8]

The loss of confidence in the banking system and the closure of banks is only one indicator of the intensifying depression that engulfed the United States. But the failed bank statistics are one of the few reliable measures of what was taking place. Nationwide unemployment or underemployment numbers are only estimates, as no system was then in place to gather such data. The reason was quite simple. There had been the underlying belief that it was no concern of the government. Until the consequences of mass unemployment were evident to all, the traditional belief was that the loss of a job was an individual matter.

Local governments such as the City of Detroit were well aware of the deepening economic predicament. Adding to the worsening situation was the shutdown of all Ford plants in August 1931. This was done to facilitate the changeover from the production of the Model A to the new V8. Ford did not reopen until March 29, 1932. The previous Ford shutdown, to change production from the Model T to the A, had caused huge unemployment in Michigan and throughout the nation. In the relatively good times of 1927 and 1928, one observer estimated that Ford employees lost fifty million dollars in wages.[9] The social effects were incalculable.

The closure of Ford plants in the midst of the economic crisis had disastrous consequences. One measure of the catastrophic situation was that by January 1932, every day in Detroit saw four thousand children standing in bread lines.[10] Statewide, the number of unemployed and their families reached 2.5 million people, approximately 40 percent of Michigan's population.[11]

Ford plants were primarily located outside the Detroit city limits, but most workers lived within the city, meaning that the social costs of industrialization were borne by Detroit without the tax base of the Ford factories in Highland Park and Dearborn. The mayor of Detroit estimated that his city would need at least $10 million to provide for the unemployed, hungry, and homeless in the winter of 1931. U.S. Sen. James Couzens, who had recently been reelected, requested that President Hoover call a special session of Congress to deal with the situation. Hoover declined, reflecting the orthodox view when he said, "We cannot legislate ourselves out of the Depression."[12]

As a one-industry city, Detroit was subject to great fluctuations in employment, riding on the successes or failures of the auto industry. From 1920 to 1930, before the impact of the Great Depression was evident, there were six instances in which employment in Detroit fell to less than 50 percent. Between 1920 and 1922 there were three such instances. Late in 1924, late in 1925, and late in 1927, employment fell to less than 60 percent. In 1928 and 1929, employment reached into the 90 percent area. In late 1931, employment never rose above 60 percent and fell to 20 percent in 1932. Putting it another way, unemployment in 1932 reached 80 percent.[13] The employment/unemployment fluctuations in Detroit were approximately twice that of the rest of the nation. After March 1933, conditions were even worse.[14]

Noting auto industry information, Alfred P. Sloan, Jr. of General Motors in 1941 wrote, "Between 1929 and 1932 car and truck production in the United States and Canada fell 75 percent, from 5.6 million units to only 1.4 million." He further pointed out that "in dollar sales the decline of the industry was even more precipitous — from $5.1 billion at retail to $1.1 billion, or 78 percent."[15] Reflecting the intensification of the financial situation, General Motors stock had been priced at 72¾ at the top of the bull market in 1929 but it had fallen quickly to 36. In 1932 it reached a low of 7⅝.[16] Hudson Motor Car Co. stock reached a peak of 93½ in 1929.[17] In 1932 it reached a low of 2⅞ and by December of 1932 it was at 4¼.[18]

As the auto industry faltered and unemployment increased, workers who had taken out mortgages to purchase homes were unable to keep up their payments. But there was no point in banks or other lending agencies foreclosing for resale purposes. There was no market. One Detroit bank held mortgages for 50,000 homes with a paper value of $150,000.[19] Many people simply abandoned their residences; among those that stayed, an increasing number became delinquent on their municipal taxes.[20]

Two days before Christmas in 1932, the City of Detroit was approaching financial ruin. The city had $5 million due on January 1, January 15, and February 1 of 1933. To meet the impending obligations, a plan was devised to ask the Michigan legislature to pass laws enabling the city to issue $20 million in bonds, to be paid by anticipated taxes. Of the total, it was expected that Detroit banks and the auto industrialists would back $15 million and see that the remaining $5 million was also subscribed. The City of Detroit already had short-term loans from Chicago and New York banks totaling $15 million and another $11 million with Detroit banks. To facilitate the matter, B.E. Hutchison, vice president and treasurer of the Chrysler Corporation; Hugh Ferry, treasurer of the Packard Motor Car Company; and Edsel Ford, president of the Ford Motor Company, were all slated to meet with New York bankers.[21]

It is clear that the City of Detroit had severe financial problems. It is unclear if the auto industrialists were being forthright about the groups they represented. The news reports stated that the City of Detroit would be backed by Detroit financial power, yet it less than a month later Ernest Kanzler would tell Alfred Leyburn of the dire situation facing the Guardian Group. It would soon be evident that neither of the two large firms that controlled banking in Michigan were solvent and could back or purchase any bond obligations. How does one account for public actions that promised financial support to Detroit, but privately acknowledged impending bank failures? It seems that the Detroit money interests were betting that loans would arrive and solutions would be found. That is, the possible failure of banks in Detroit was considered a very serious matter, and had unknown but possibly profound nationwide consequences of such enormity that failure would not be allowed to take place.

In the high-stakes wheeling and dealing, to gain support for their request for funds, the leaders of the Guardian Group attempted to gain political support. They went to Washington. In Washington, a shift in power was about to take place. The elections of November 1932 led to the Democrats becoming the majority party in both the Senate and House of Representatives. Both U.S. senators from Michigan, James Couzens and Arthur Vandenberg, were Republicans. Vandenberg had been elected in 1928 while Couzens had been reelected in 1930.

The president, Herbert Hoover, was also a Republican, who had been defeated by Franklin D. Roosevelt in the November elections. However, as eighteenth-century timelines remained in a twentieth-century world, Hoover would remain in office until March 4, 1933, as would all the defeated Republican congressmen. The Guardian leadership had two time constraints. The first was the urgency of obtaining funds due to the unraveling economic situation. The second was the need for a hearing before the Democrats controlled the Congress and presidency on March 4. If those who led the Guardian were to get a favorable hearing, it most certainly had to be before the shift in political power.

Even in defeat, as long as he remained in office, Herbert Hoover was still the president. The U.S. has a presidential system, highly dependent on the leadership qualities of the person who occupies that office. Widely admired by the nation and much of the world, in 1929 Hoover represented the qualities that were coming to the forefront in the automobile business: those of a professional manager. Relatively young at age 52, he was a proven management expert. Hoover, orphaned at an early age, was a self-made millionaire by the age of 40. His life experience seemed to create "a belief in heroic individualism, the self-reliant man expressing himself in technological mastery and personal accomplishment."[22] Personal accomplishment, of course, may be measured by the accumulation of wealth, which was not a new concept in American life.

Businessmen and industrialists admired Hoover, and for good reasons. During World War I, Hoover became known as "The Great Engineer" and also "The Great Humanitarian," for his outstanding leadership in three differing situations. As the head of the Commission for Relief in Belgium, an organization he founded prior to U.S. entry into the war, Hoover organized and directed a program to feed the Belgians, whose country had been occupied by the German Army. With his self-control, implacability, and his way of turning political controversies into technical problems, Hoover drove the Germans to distraction. In effect, he was responsible for saving an entire generation of Belgian children. When the United States entered the war, President Woodrow Wilson appointed Hoover as national food administrator. In this position he controlled the entire production of food and fuel within the United States. With the campaign "Food Will Win the War," Hoover gained the cooperation and further admiration of the whole nation. Through his efforts the United States was able to feed itself, supply the Allies with food, feed the military horses of the Allies, and save a significant part of central and south-eastern Europe from starvation after the war. This may seem strange, knowing that it was the contributions made by the auto companies that were decisive in World War II, but in World War I it was American food production that was a decisive contribution to victory.

Following the war, Hoover took on yet another extremely difficult task, and administered a plan to stem starvation in the war-torn, revolutionary Soviet Union. Hoover's personal qualities and characteristics confounded the Bolsheviks, as much as he had bedeviled the Kaiser's Army.

Following World War I, it is doubtful that any other man in the United States had the adulation and approval accorded to Herbert Hoover. It was unclear which political party he favored, even as an appointee of Democrat Woodrow Wilson, but both parties thought him presidential material. The question about his party affiliation was answered when Hoover accepted the position of secretary of commerce in the Republican Harding administration that succeeded Wilson. When Harding administration scandals later shook the nation following Harding's death, Hoover and a very small number of other cabinet officers remained free of any hint of scandal or corruption. As the sordid facts about the Harding administration came out day after day, the probity of Hoover and few others gave strength to the nation and to former Vice President Coolidge alike.

In keeping with the energy he had shown in his important roles during World War I, Hoover took a moribund part of the national government and made it into one of the most active and influential parts of the cabinet. Despite his popularity, Hoover had been relegated to what was an unimportant cabinet post, as he was both disliked and distrusted by the professional politicians in the Republican Party. When a disastrous Mississippi River flood occurred in 1927, President Coolidge remained inactive. Eventually, after public pressure, he named a special committee of five cabinet officers to oversee the flood emergencies. Hoover was named chairman and spent considerable time and effort in organizing the volunteer response. Once again, Hoover's efforts were well publicized and received great national approval, so that the professional politicians could not overlook his popularity. From the backwaters of the Commerce Department, Hoover rose to be the Republican nominee when Calvin

Coolidge chose not to seek a second term. His election to the presidency was the first time he had ever stood for political office.

Hoover's past and his previous successes are important in understanding his role in the banking crisis of 1933. From the pinnacle of success he had reached by 1929, his fall was precipitous. The great change in his popularity had to have an effect on a reportedly thin-skinned man who had previously been held in great public esteem. From the time during World

Light's Golden Jubilee: (From left to right) Thomas A. Edison at center in derby hat, Herbert C. Hoover, and Henry Ford. Taken on October 21, 1929, at the dedication of Greenfield Village in Dearborn. Ford had moved various structures to the site, including Edison's workshop, laboratory, and machine shop from Menlo Park, N.J. The celebration was of the fiftieth anniversary of Edison's invention of the incandescent light bulb. Other luminaries on hand included Jane Addams, Orville Wright, Marie Curie and Will Rogers. Among the hosts assisting Ford was Roy D. Chapin. This may be one of the last public photographs of President Hoover looking cheerful. Within the next ten days, the effects of the great sell-off on Wall Street would become apparent.

War I when "Hoovering" had a positive connotation, in the drive to save food and cut down on waste, his name became the basis for derogatory references. For example during the Great Depression shantytowns hastily built of cardboard, scrap lumber and tarpaper were known as "Hoovervilles." Usually located on vacant land near railroad tracks, the drab and dreary temporary housing indicated the public mood. Further ridiculing the president were "Hoover flags"— having one's trouser pockets pulled out to designate poverty, resembling small white flags of surrender. "Hoover blankets" were newspapers used to keep warm, while "Hoover hogs" were wild rabbits that were chased down and eaten. "Hoover Shoes" had visible holes in the soles while "Hoover leather" described the cardboard placed inside the shoe to cover the holes. In October 1932 on a campaign speaking tour, he was subjected to catcalls and boos from people in Detroit. As he drove through the streets of Detroit in limousines supplied by Henry Ford, Hoover was jeered and saw signs with the message "DOWN WITH HOOVER."[23]

In his last days in office Hoover was desperate to avoid what seemed to be the specter of a complete economic meltdown. He continued to believe that the "sole function of government" was to "bring about a condition of affairs favorable to the development of private enterprise."[24] Thus, when the Guardian officers went to Washington, they expected that Hoover would support their loan application.

However, among the complications in obtaining financial backing were some particulars about President Hoover. The first complication was that Hoover continued to believe that the American economy was fundamentally sound and not in need of change or reorganization. He had conference after conference with the industrial leaders of the nation, assuming that prosperity would return as confidence was restored. He further believed that voluntary cooperation was the proper means to restore confidence. All of his public successes had been based on volunteer efforts. Hoover seemed to believe the president's role was that of facilitator, in identifying common interests and gaining willing action from all who shared stakes in the situation.

So it was on the evening of Thursday, February 9, 1933, President Hoover invited a number of people to the White House to discuss the Guardian loan request. On hand were Secretary of the Treasury Ogden

Mills; his chief deputy Arthur A. Ballantine, undersecretary of the treasury; Roy D. Chapin, secretary of commerce; Charles A. Miller, president of the Reconstruction Finance Corporation; and both Michigan senators, James Couzens and Arthur Vandenberg.[25]

Both senators had learned of the precarious situation of the Guardian Group directly from Guardian representatives only on the afternoon of February 9. Coming to the Senate chambers to see Vandenberg and Couzens was a two-man Guardian delegation headed by Clifford Longley, then president of the Union Guardian Trust Company.[26] In 1919, Longley had become associated with the legal department of the Ford Motor Company and became legal counsel for the company from 1921 to 1929. During that time, he worked as attorney on the majority of consequential legal cases involving Henry Ford and the Ford Motor Company. After 1929, with his own legal firm, he represented the families of both Henry Ford and Edsel Ford.[27]

Two days earlier, on February 7, Jesse Jones of the RFC had informed Couzens of the Guardian loan application. Couzens was also informed that the Guardian Group had specifically asked RFC officials to keep the news from Couzens. As a member of the Senate sub-committee then investigating banking practices, Couzens was in a position to lecture the Guardian leaders about banking ethics.[28] Jones also told Couzens that there was no legal way for the RFC to make the loan requested by Guardian. Furthermore, under the regulating laws, the RFC board members could be held personally accountable for making a clearly illegal loan.[29]

At a February 6 meeting of the RFC to review the Guardian application, John McKee, chief appraiser of the RFC, said that Union Guardian Trust Company, a part of the Guardian Group, was insolvent. The trust company had deposit liabilities of $20.5 million but only $8 million available to pledge for a loan. Without some intervention, the trust company would fail and bring down the entire Guardian Group, and probably all of Michigan. McKee further said that the banking situation was only part of the problem. The City of Detroit was, in essence, bankrupt, and in danger of rioting by the vast numbers of the unemployed.[30] Alfred Leyburn, the chief national bank examiner who had been working closely with the Guardian Group, agreed with McKee's assessment and added that if Guardian were left to fail, the effect would be nationwide.[31]

Ernest Kanzler representing the Guardian Group at the meeting, admitted that there was a sizable gap between the value of the collateral that could be pledged and the amount of the loan that was requested. However, Kanzler pointed out the situation was very serious and was approaching a crisis. If left to fail, the demise of the Guardian Group would affect not only the State of Michigan, but the nation.[32]

As Leyburn later testified, after discussing the Guardian Group loan application for some time, the members of the RFC came to the conclusion that another means was available to resolve the problem. In the meeting they asked, "Why should we bail out Mr. Ford?" As Leyburn went on to say, the people in the meeting "figured he should come to the rescue up there."[33] Near the end of the meeting the RFC group also told Ernest Kanzler and Clifford Longley, the Guardian representatives, that they should get the backing of James Couzens for the loan. That advice is what led to the meeting in the Senate chambers with Vandenberg and Couzens three days later, on February 9.

In between, on February 8, Edsel Ford arrived in Washington to confer with Secretary of the Treasury Ogden Mills and later with Charles Miller of the RFC. Miller told Edsel Ford that it was his duty, and that of his father, to step in and resolve the impending banking crisis in Detroit. Edsel Ford seemed agreeable, but he gave the impression that his father had a contrary view. Furthermore, Edsel Ford seemed to say that other people needed to persuade his father. Miller concluded that the person who needed to contact Henry Ford was President Hoover, and he called the White House and made that suggestion.[34]

For whatever reason, Hoover decided he would not call Henry Ford. Instead, he convened the meeting on the evening of February 9. When the group met, Hoover told them he had earlier met with Alfred P. Sloan, Jr. of GM and Walter Chrysler of the Chrysler Corporation. Both agreed that GM and Chrysler would deposit $1 million each in the Guardian Group and agree to back the RFC loan. This was based on Hoover's belief that Henry Ford was still agreeable in subordinating $7.5 million in the Guardian.[35] In practical terms, subordination would mean that the Fords, and the Ford Motor Company, would give up rights and control of the $7.5 million deposit. This action would provide the Guardian Group with sufficient funds to become eligible for an RFC loan. In effect, it would be a loan of immense proportions without any conditions or collateral.

Just why Hoover thought the Ford funds would remain untouched is not known, as Edsel Ford, on the day before, had clearly told Miller of the RFC that his father would not subordinate his deposits. Nevertheless, without giving any advance notice to Senator Couzens, Hoover, in the presence of all the others at the meeting, asked Couzens to contribute $2 million of his personal funds.[36]

Hoover was acting on the advice of Treasury Secretary Ogden Mills, Undersecretary of the Treasury Arthur A. Ballantine, and RFC Chairman Atlee Pomerene. They had concluded that a pool plan, in which the most important figures would be Henry Ford and James Couzens, was the way to provide the security necessary to obtain an RFC loan. Henry Ford's position was already known, but nobody had discussed the matter with Couzens.[37]

Couzens's response to Hoover's request that he contribute $2 million in a scheme either to make possible an RFC loan, or as a means of substituting for the RFC loan, was disbelief. He had just heard Charles Miller state that the RFC had rejected the Guardian request as both illegal and immoral.[38] Since April of 1932, Couzens had been an active member of the Senate subcommittee investigating banking and stock exchange practices. He was thoroughly fed up with the revelations made to that committee. Couzens had heard about all manner of banking practices, from shady to clearly illegal. As a consequence he had come to doubt the wisdom of loaning any more money to save banks. It seemed to be a case of throwing good money away while individuals and others with clear needs were not provided with government assistance.

Having been blind-sided by Hoover and in the frame of mind he had developed from the Senate investigations, Couzens then made the statement that has been used time and again to place responsibility on him for the Detroit Banking Crisis. He said he "would scream from the housetops, and on the floor of the Senate" if an inadequately secured RFC loan was made to the Guardian Group.[39] Couzens went on to reject Hoover's idea and to state that the Guardian Group situation was one that Henry Ford should resolve.[40]

There is no record that any of the other participants in the White

House meeting spoke in favor of an RFC loan. As has been noted, the meeting was an attempt to find a way to resolve the immediate crisis in Detroit by having Henry Ford and James Couzens provide the necessary financial guarantees, with some assistance from General Motors and the Chrysler Corporation. Couzens's statement about "shouting from the housetops and on the floor of the Senate" was colorful and is revealing of the senator's personality. It's a great quotation, but not a key factor leading to the banking failure in Detroit.

Before the meeting there were ample opportunities, through responsible management of the Guardian Group, to prevent the circumstances that led to the need for funds. In the five days between the White House meeting the evening of February 14, when the banks were closed, there were many other chances to prevent the impending disaster. And from February 14 to the inaugural day, March 4, there were seventeen days to contain the effects of the Detroit bank closures. Many people were involved in meetings and negotiations, but no solutions came about. In this time of need, none of the foremost industrial managers in the United States stepped forward.

In a spirit of acrimony, Hoover responded to Couzens by lecturing him about his "duty" as a Detroiter who was being asked to give up less than 5 percent of his personal fortune to save his home area and state. In the meeting, Hoover was "visibly perturbed" at Couzens, "feeling that the Detroit collapse might precipitate a national calamity."[41] Hoover never forgave Couzens for his response.[42]

Couzens, whose personality was such that any lecture to him about "duty" was likely to result in a furious and intense response, was certainly innocent of neglecting the Detroit area and the State of Michigan. After leaving the Ford Motor Company in 1915, Couzens went into local politics. He successfully brought about public ownership of the streetcar line in Detroit, and purchased the municipal bonds to facilitate the matter.[43] As first police commissioner and then mayor, he refused to accept any salary. In 1929 he created The Children's Fund of Michigan, donating a cumulative amount of around $30 million.[44] In the summer of 1931, he offered to contribute $1 million to private relief in Detroit if nine other wealthy men would follow suit, but nobody responded to his offer.[45]

When Hoover asked Couzens for a contribution of $2 million, the men were not on good terms. That Hoover invited Couzens to the White House at all is an indication of a very desperate situation. While both Hoover and Couzens were members of the Republican Party, in the most recent presidential election, Couzens gave no support to Hoover. While he did not actively campaign for Franklin Roosevelt, Couzens had stood up in the Senate to defend a speech that Roosevelt had made.[46] Hoover and Couzens had first met in 1921 when Hoover was secretary of commerce. At the time, Couzens was impressed with Hoover's views and later hosted Hoover in the Couzens home.[47] But during the Depression Hoover disappointed Couzens, beginning with the retention of Andrew Mellon as secretary of the treasury. In contrast to Couzens's own view of himself as a man of action who was blunt spoken, he saw Hoover as being "ponderous and authoritative."

Hoover in return did not care for Couzens and once described him as "a very dangerous man."[48] The mutual dislike of Hoover and Couzens is only one unfortunate example of how the temperaments of key individuals played an important role in the events of February and March of 1933. While they differed in many ways, both Hoover and Couzens believed in their own rectitude. In regard to individual honesty, they were both correct. But both Hoover and Couzens, each with his personal sense of righteousness, closed off possibilities of discussion and cooperation.

While Couzens responded with great vehemence during the discussion of Guardian's need for funds, Vandenberg is not reported to have said anything. "Overwhelmed by the whole matter, and not wishing to antagonize either Couzens or Hoover, the junior senator remained in the background during the conference."[49] Considering the importance of the matter, and Vandenberg's equality with Couzens as a U.S. senator, it is surprising there is no record of Vandenberg taking an active part in the banking crisis.

It is especially puzzling, as there is at least one record of Vandenberg interceding on behalf of another Michigan applicant for RFC funds in September 1932. In that instance, he wrote a letter to both President Hoover and Pomerene of the RFC.[50] Vandenberg's inaction may be more understandable when you realize that he was facing reelection in 1934. Among those present at the White House meeting on February 9 was Secretary of Commerce Roy D. Chapin. In his campaign for reelection in 1934,

Vandenberg enlisted his close personal friend, Chapin, to prepare the groundwork for his campaign.[51] Chapin, whom we will see had many interests in the looming crisis in Detroit, was by 1934 back in Detroit as head of the Hudson Motor Car Company.

After Couzens and Vandenberg had left, participants decided to send a delegation to Detroit to meet with Henry Ford.[52] Again, Hoover refused to call Ford and speak to him directly. After some discussion, Secretary of Commerce Roy D. Chapin and Undersecretary of the Treasury Arthur A. Ballantine agreed to go to Detroit to meet with Henry Ford.

As the situation was becoming increasingly critical, Ballantine and Chapin left via train for Detroit as soon as arrangements could be made. They arrived in Detroit on Saturday, February 11. Since Abraham Lincoln's birthday was on Sunday, February 12, the legal holiday fell on Monday, February 13. This gave an extra day to resolve the crisis, as banks would be closed on Monday and would not reopen until Tuesday. The Guardian Group needed an immediate fix and the time for a decision was slipping away daily. On February 10, Alfred Leyburn had convened a conference in Detroit and invited the leading financiers and industrialists of Michigan to attempt to hammer out some means of averting the crisis.

Both Walter P. Chrysler and Alfred P. Sloan, Jr. attended, but neither Henry nor Edsel Ford. Instead, Ernest Liebold represented Henry Ford while Ernest Kanzler had his own interests at stake and presumably those of his partners in the Guardian Group.[53] Such a meeting could not be kept secret or confidential very long. If word of the likely financial crisis leaked out, a run on the banks was a certainty with the consequences being what the conference was attempting to prevent.

Since 1929 the Guardian had been involved in questionable banking practices, but to avoid immediate failure the participants in the Detroit meeting had a timeline of no more than four days to reach an agreement for at least a temporary fix. Time was short and solutions lacking. Leyburns conference produced no adequate or workable solutions, which conferred even greater importance on the Monday meeting that Ballantine and Chapin had scheduled with Henry and Edsel Ford.

2

"Wall Street Sees Ford as a Banker"

As a personality in the history of the United States, Edsel Ford is usually marginalized. If his name is known at all to most Americans it is in connection with the ill-fated Edsel automobile, named after him, which had only three model years, from 1958 to 1960. Yet he was president of the Ford Motor Company from 1918 to his death in 1943. During that period of time the Ford Motor Company loomed large throughout the world, with assembly plants in 11 foreign nations and 23 locations in the U.S. outside of Michigan.[1]

Nationally, Ford was the largest producer of vehicles, with 45 percent of total U.S. sales in 1920, 60 percent in 1921,[2] 57 percent in 1923 and 45 percent in 1925.[3] Thereafter, Ford went from being first in production to second and sometimes third place behind General Motors and the Chrysler Corporation. The fall in rank was not due to negligence on the part of Edsel Ford, nor a lack of ability. Instead, as automotive historians know, the Ford Motor Company lost its dominance due to the intransigence of Henry Ford.

Henry Ford had stubbornly persisted with his vision of a simple-to-operate, inexpensive, and very utilitarian car, that began successfully with the Model T, introduced in 1908. The dominance of the Ford Motor Company until the mid 1920s had, Henry Ford believed, proven his vision. And despite the urging of Edsel Ford and others, Henry Ford did not intend to change. The decline in Model T sales brought out a basic conflict between Henry the father and Edsel the son. The often-contentious father-son relationship between the two Fords was a dominant and continuous theme during the 25 years of Edsel Ford's presidency. One overriding factor regarding the two men and the Ford Motor Company cannot

The Big Three: (From left to right) Edsel B. Ford, Alfred P. Sloan, Jr., and Walter P. Chrysler. Taken outside the U.S. Senate in April 1934 when the three were in Washington, D.C., on business. Befitting his office as president of the Ford Motor Company, Edsel, and not his father, represented the company. Neither Sloan from GM nor Chrysler from the Chrysler Corp. looks any more pleased than Edsel. All three were unwilling to adjust to the interventionist business ideas of the New Deal.

be disregarded: while Edsel Ford was president, he did not have the real power.

Instead, his father Henry Ford retained it. As the only child of Henry Ford, Edsel "was not a chip off the old block, and in many ways was the antithesis of his father."[4] Henry Ford, for his own purposes, appointed his son as President, but retained the ultimate decision making — often making decisions contrary to decisions of Edsel, and after the fact. As David Lewis has written:

> In retrospect, Edsel emerges as one of the most tragic figures in American business history. He was more than talented, he was creative. He was more than hardworking; he had an extraordinary sense of responsibility to his company and community. He was an excellent administrator, and he commanded the affection, respect, and loyalty of his associates.[5]

Edsel is often characterized for his qualities of "modesty, gentility and goodness, civic-mindedness, and exemplary family life."[6] Involved in civic affairs in Detroit, especially in supporting the Detroit Institute of Arts, Edsel Ford was the sponsor and economic supporter of the famed murals created by Diego Rivera. With an apparent artistic flair, he played a critical role in the styling of all Ford Motor Company products and is generally given credit for leading the designers of the classic Lincolns of the late 1920s and 1930s.

In deference to his father, Edsel was non-confrontational when second-guessed or when his decisions were countermanded. Instead, he sought paths in which he could use his abilities and talents apart from his father. The relationship between Henry Ford the father, and his only child, Edsel, is one that could very well become a play or movie, with no need to add drama or crisis. And crisis they did have in February and March of 1933. But it was not just a crisis within the Ford family; it was one that shook the entire nation during a period of great vulnerability. It has become known as the Detroit banking crisis, which came to the forefront of national attention on February 14, 1933.

Edsel Ford was at the center of the banking crisis. He was involved in the crisis from its inception, in the midst of the crisis during a fateful meeting, in attempts to resolve the crisis, and finally afterward in an investigative period. Actions he took, and did not take, had significance in American economic and political history.

Before the Detroit banking crisis and the subsequent domino effect in which banks throughout the nation were closed, economic decision making and power primarily resided in New York City, especially in the banks, brokerage houses and other economic forces which are collectively known as Wall Street. There were other regional locations of economic power, less powerful than New York City, which were generally seats of a Federal Reserve District. Detroit, despite its status as the center of the increasingly important automobile industry, was not the seat of a Federal Reserve District. The cities chosen to be seats of Federal Reserve District banks were identified around 1912 as Detroit was in the process of growing. Detroit's not having its own Federal Reserve District and being subordinated to Chicago was an annoyance to the leaders of the auto industry. Nevertheless Detroit, as the nation's fourth largest city[7] and center of the auto industry, had real economic muscle.

Despite his lack of fundamental authority within the Ford Motor Company, Edsel Ford had great name recognition, especially with his title as president. Those outside the Ford Motor Company and the automobile industry assumed that the title had real meaning. So when he was involved in an activity, the assumption was that the great Ford Motor Company was also involved. This was especially true because, since 1919, ownership of the Ford Motor Company was within the family. Henry Ford owned fifty-five percent, Edsel forty-two, and Mrs. Henry Ford (Clara) had three percent.[8] Auto industry insiders treated Edsel Ford with respect and when he chose to branch off into the world of banking, many were willing to follow him. Many were personal friends, but it is very probable that they too believed that the enormous financial power of the Ford Motor Company would support any venture of Edsel Ford. In this judgment they proved to be both right and, when it counted most, quite wrong.

In May of 1925 a *New York Times* article announced, "Wall Street Sees Ford as a Banker."[9] The report noted that "despite denials" from Detroit that Henry Ford himself was involved in the opening of the Guardian Detroit Company in New York City, the involvement of Edsel Ford in the Guardian venture led to contrary conclusions. The report went on to note "the general opinion in the financial district yesterday was the automobile manufacturer "had moved closer to the banking world than he had been before." Of course Henry Ford and the Ford Motor Company had been involved in banking in Detroit. The enormous amounts of money from the sales success of the Model T led to Ford-owned banks for use in the direct business of the company. The Guardian Detroit Company announcement, however, was the first indicator of an investment banking interest that was assumed to be connected to the Ford Motor Company. From its inception, the Guardian name, in the various iterations that evolved, was identified with the Fords. The Fords themselves largely disregarded any nuances separating the interests of Edsel Ford from the Ford Motor Company or from his father, Henry Ford. There was no concern about pesky shareholders; the funds of the Ford Motor Company belonged to Edsel and Henry Ford.

However, there were still opportunities for others to share in the wealth production of the Ford Motor Company through associated investments. The formation of the Guardian Detroit Company as a subsidiary of the Guardian Trust Company of Detroit was seen as one such means. First, the new organization took over the bond selling business of Keane-Higbie and Company.[10] Higbie, the president, was a close associate of Edsel Ford, being part of an investment consortium known as KFH. The K was for Ernest Kanzler, the F for Edsel Ford and the H for Carlton Higbie. All three were residents of the exclusive Detroit suburb of Grosse Pointe.[11]

Secondly, there was speculation that the Guardian Detroit Company in New York City would handle the huge volume of business that derived from the Ford export market. Enormous cash balances were kept in New York City for the export market as well as for financing dealers and sales of Ford products. While Henry Ford insisted on having no owners outside of his own family, and eventually had complete vertical integration from transportation of the raw materials on his own ships and via his own railroad, his antipathy toward banking made it possible for other investors to ride the Ford success. The key to share the Ford success, it seems, was a connection with Edsel Ford.

Subsequent newspaper articles in June and July of 1925 confirmed the association of the Guardian Trust Company and the New York correspondent, the Guardian-Detroit Company, with Edsel Ford and the Ford Motor Company.[12] One article stated that the formation of the trust company "has been regarded as the entry of the Ford interests into Wall

Street."[13] Edsel Ford, president of the Ford Motor Company, and Ernest Kanzler, vice president of the Ford Motor Company, were both identified as directors. But so were other men from the auto industry, which added a second connection to the Guardian Trust Company. In the public mind it was associated foremost with the Ford Motor Company, but secondarily with the auto industry. The connection was not difficult to comprehend as can be seen from the following list of directors identified in the same news reports. Included were: Robert Wilson, formerly president of the Maxwell Motor Corporation; Fred J. Fisher, president of Fisher Body Corporation and vice president of General Motors; Alvan Macauley, president of the Packard Motor Car Company; Lewis Mendelsohn, treasurer of the Fisher Body Corporation; Roy D. Chapin, chairman of the Hudson Motor Car Company; James R. Murray, president of the auto body building Murray Manufacturing Company; Carlton Higbie, later to be a director of REO Motor Car Company; and Henry Bodman, counsel, director, and sometimes vice president of Packard Motor Car Company and also counsel to the Automobile Manufacturers Association. Also listed were Frank Couzens, son of Henry Ford's old partner Sen. James Couzens; and Phelps Newberry, son of Truman H. Newberry, director and early investor in the Packard Motor Car Company.

To further identify the Guardian name with the auto industry, prominent stockholders were named as well. They included brothers-in-law Henry Joy and Truman H. Newberry. Joy, like Newberry, was a Packard director and early investor in Packard. From the Hudson Motor Car Company, prominent Guardian stockholders were R.B. Jackson, cofounder and sometime president and general manager; W.J. McAneeny, Hudson vice president, and Howard Coffin director and also one of the cofounders of Hudson.

Ostensible competitors in the marketplace, the above named auto executives were often considered as a group. They bonded together to forward their common interests in organizations such as their lobbying organization, the National Automobile Chamber of Commerce, as well as in varying organizations that made up the "good roads" movement. Various business relationships, as well as many personal relationships which transcended business, united them in many ways. Many of the leaders of the '20s and '30s were the pioneers of the auto industry and had years of working with one another in what originally was a very small industry. Early business connections abounded, as when Alfred P. Sloan, Jr., later of General Motors, wrote to Henry Ford in 1899 in an attempt to obtain his business for the Hyatt Roller Bearing firm that Sloan then controlled. Further, Charles Stewart Moss, vice president of General Motors, who was later to play an important role in Guardian matters, was the godfather of Walter Chrysler's children, a relationship stemming from their working together in General Motors.[14] Roy D. Chapin and Ransom E. Olds maintained a close relationship, one that evolved from 1901, when Olds gave Chapin his first entry into the auto industry. Many other personal connections existed, sometimes based on lodging, as was the case when Roy D. Chapin and Charles Sorensen of the Ford Motor Company lived in the same Detroit rooming house when they were both starting out.[15]

The many relationships between and among the auto industry leaders need to be considered in the perspective of that era. Many of the men of the industry were, in a way, proprietors. As has been stated, the three members of the Henry Ford family were sole owners of the Ford Motor Company. Roy D. Chapin was a founder and major stockholder in the Hudson Motor Car Company; Ransom E. Olds was a major stockholder in the REO Motor Car Company, which, like Ford's was named for him. (The initials of Olds's first, middle, and last names are the origin of the name.) Walter Chrysler was a major stockholder in the company that bore his name. Even General Motors, which had many stockholders, had significant ownership by executives, including Alfred P. Sloan, Jr., Charles Kettering, and the largest individual shareholder of GM, Charles Stewart Mott.[16]

The present day corporate model, in which a CEO is salaried and provided with stock options, is considerably different from the model in the '30s. Those men were founders of the automobile industry and their success and personal wealth were tied up in the long-term success of the firms that they led. The sense of personal ownership, and the privileges which accompany ownership, gave the auto leaders of the '30s a much different perspective than most present-day top auto executives. Did they discuss industry matters informally? Probably so, but in doing so they were always conscious of representing their personal interests, which were intermingled with the success of their corporations. In their world, minority stockholders were fully aware of their mostly powerless status and no consumer advocacy groups, or Securities and Exchange Commission, existed to protest real or imagined collusion. Being successful pioneers of an industry further solidified a group identity.

Many of the auto men also belonged to the same social organizations. One example is Charles Sorensen, longtime Ford executive, who noted that he knew Walter Chrysler from their common memberships in the Bloomfield Hills Country Club and the Detroit Athletic Club.[17] Taking charge as first membership chairman of the Detroit Athletic Club was Roy D. Chapin, who nominated his former associate, Hugh Chalmers, of the Chalmers-Detroit Motor Car Company, as the first president. Chapin was also in charge of the committee to select charter members for the D.A.C.[18]

Perhaps one of the most interesting connections is in the founding of the Hudson Motor Car Company. The man who supplied the capital for the firm was J.L. Hudson, a very prominent Detroit department store owner. Two nieces who lived with the Hudsons became Mrs. Edsel Ford and Mrs. Ernest Kanzler. This led to the long-standing, but not quite accurate, newspaper identification of Ernest Kanzler as being Edsel Ford's brother-in-law. Two of Edsel Ford's best friends were Ernest Kanzler and the prime mover in organizing the Hudson Motor Car Co., Roy D. Chapin. The Chapin and Edsel Ford friendship, however, developed after the formation of Hudson in 1909.

Both Kanzler and Chapin, along with Edsel Ford, were also involved prominently in the 1927 formation of the Guardian Detroit Bank, formed under Michigan state charter, which included an investment affiliate and a trust company.[19] The establishment of the Guardian Detroit Group, Inc. in 1929 is often used as the beginning date of that organization. However, this was really a recapitalization and start of an exchange of stock that brought in banks throughout the State of Michigan.[20] At the same time, the Guardian Detroit Group, Inc. acquired another holding company, the Union Commerce Corporation, creating the new Guardian Detroit Union Group, Inc.[21] If this sounds confusing it is, and perhaps it was meant to be that way. But the key point to remember is that the Guardian Group was a holding company.

Holding companies began with the formation of the United States Steel Corporation in 1901. In the '20s and '30s, the holding company was a very popular form of business organization. In banking, A.P. Giannini led the way with the San Francisco based TransAmerica holding company, to control the Bank of America throughout California. Samuel Insull was the leading proponent in the use of holding companies in the electric utility business, starting in Chicago but spreading to include many northeastern states. But the example evident to the auto leaders was the formation of General Motors, a holding company started by William C. "Billy" Durant. The method by which holding companies were formed became the key for rapid growth as a well as a possible source of weakness. During the Great Depression, the potential weakness in the holding company structure became very evident. No holding company failure generated more publicity than that of the one held by Samuel Insull. But it may be that the failure of the Detroit Union Guardian Group, Inc., with Detroit as a base but encompassing all of Michigan, had the greatest significance and, at the same time, is the least understood calamitous event of the 1930s.

The significance of the Guardian Group in Michigan came from the totality of its involvement in Michigan banking. Just as Billy Durant had exchanged shares of General Motors for those of firms he added to GM, the Guardian group exchanged shares for its acquisitions. For example, in 1913, Durant added the wheel manufacturing Weston-Mott Company to GM on a straight exchange-of-stock basis. GM used no funds; instead Charles Stewart Mott received GM stock.[22] In the formation of the Guardian Group, all parts were added by exchange of stock.[23] So it was that Charles Stewart Mott became involved in the Guardian Group when his bank, the Union Industrial Bank in Flint, was added.[24]

The word group is also important in understanding the issues that led to the banking crisis in Michigan. Through the exchange of stock, the local bank retained its name, and the personnel continued to be those that were known in the local community. But it became a part of a larger group with common ownership in a holding company. The supposed benefits to the general public of group banking were the managerial and financial resources available in case of need. The banking system of the United States had not kept pace with the forces of industrialization and urbanization, but giving up a personal relationship with a local banker in a hometown bank, and fear of decisions made by far-off corporate offices led many to oppose banking chains. The group bank organization was a supposed compromise. It allegedly brought the benefits of chain banking, but with the same familiar face in charge even after the local bank became part of a group.

"Holding company" is the other key term. A holding company exists only to hold, own or control the stocks or securities in other companies. Since the shares of most large companies are often widely distributed, a holding company can control a business by having a block or percentage of shares well short of a majority of the total shares in existence. In actual practice, six or nine percent of the total number of shares may be sufficient to exercise control of a company, even less if differing types of stock give voting rights to some and not to others. As a corporate entity, a holding company may sell shares but the only income it obtains is that paid by the corporations in which it holds stocks or securities. One may readily understand that there are opportunities for irregularities when a holding company, dependent for income on the corporations whose stock is held, holds a minority but controlling interest.

The formation of differing organizations with similar sounding names was one of the characteristics of the holding companies of the 1920s and 1930s. In some cases the identified subsidiaries actually produced revenue by engaging in some business activities. In other instances, the name might identify a holding company whose primary function was to receive income from a subsidiary, sell shares in it, distribute some of the income as dividends and pass the remaining funds up the line. Holding companies often held shares in other holding companies. Each holding company, of any size, also had a board of directors and officers, all of whom received payment for their services.

Some believe that Edsel Ford's association with the Guardian Group was a conscious attempt to separate himself from his father, an attempt to be a success on his own terms. His Guardian Group activity was also considered a "gesture of defiance"[25] towards his father, as Henry Ford was known for his negative view of bankers, often lambasting a general "Wall Street crowd."[26] Harry Bennett, in charge of employment at the Rouge plant, which led him to be close to Henry Ford, believed that Henry permitted Edsel to go on with some projects without overt criticism, but he used clandestine means to gain information. Then, at a critical moment, the senior Ford would destroy his son's plans.[27] Bennett also stated, "Nothing ever happened at the Ford Motor Company without Mr. Ford's knowledge."[28] Edsel Ford's involvement in the Guardian Group, however, was not kept secret from Henry Ford. In fact, for a time, Henry Ford owned 1,188 shares of Guardian stock,[29] while Edsel, as the largest stockholder, owned 50,000 shares.[30] Using his position as president of Ford, Edsel Ford actively sought deposits from corporations that did business with the Ford Motor Company.[31] He also gave instructions for Ford Motor Company deposits to be made in the Guardian Group at strategic times, followed by withdrawal of the same deposits within a short timeframe.[32]

To the auto men of Michigan it seemed as if the great Ford Motor Company was firmly behind the Guardian Group. Its success seemed certain, with Edsel Ford as president of Ford assisting the banking group in differing ways, and Henry Ford going along with the relationship linking his name, his son's name, and that of his company to Guardian. In effect, the auto men from other companies had found a way to share in the success of the Ford Motor Company. Chapin of Hudson, Macauley of Packard, Mott of General Motors, Olds of REO and others had a good arrangement: If their auto companies did well, they prospered, and if the Ford Motor Company did well, they also prospered. The ties of the Universal Credit Corporation (UCC), which was the Ford Motor Company financing arm, with the Guardian Group provided an additional income source. (The UCC is discussed in the section about Ernest Kanzler, the prime mover of the UCC.)

To be sure, a central motivation for investing in, and providing leadership for, the Guardian Group was to make more money. But the development of a statewide financial giant was also indirectly beneficial to the auto executives. For example, instead of profits flowing outward from Michigan, the money would stay home. This could mean more funds for expansion of the auto industry or to otherwise invest in Michigan. At the same time, having funds readily available in Michigan could eliminate dependence on Eastern banking interests. While Henry Ford was the most outspoken critic of Wall Street, or eastern banking interests, there was a general antipathy toward bankers that came with being a resident of the areas west of the Hudson River. Farmers and other rural interests had long felt that Eastern bankers had too much power, and all who were in need of investment capital shared this feeling. With large sums of money pouring into Michigan from the rapid development of the auto industry, the idea that the money should stay in Michigan seemed very good.

Scale was another consideration. The auto industry by 1929 created at least three organizations that later became known as the "Big Three"— Ford, General Motors and the relatively new Chrysler Corporation. By 1930, 83.3 percent of the new passenger car registrations were from cars produced by the three companies.[33] In turn, the industrial giants needed giant financial institutions. The other issue of scale was in the State of Michigan itself. We speak of "Detroit" in a shorthand way, describing the auto industry. But the auto industry was in many cities including Flint and Lansing, plus other cities and even small towns throughout Michigan. Only the consolidation provided by group banking offered the required financial services needed throughout the state.

Another factor was competition. In effect, a duopoly in banking existed in Michigan. The rival of the Guardian Group was the Detroit Bankers Company. The two groups "controlled 87 percent of the banking in Detroit, and held 57.5 percent of all loans and investments in the state."[34] Once the consolidation of banking using the group banking structure began, both organizations sought to keep up with the other.

The auto men had seen what capitalization and a large organization meant in terms of profitability, and they intended to be the most powerful group. Their intent was to replicate the growth and profit of the auto industry in the financial sector, through group banking. Since group banking was a new concept, complicated by the use of the holding company organizational format, supervision by state or federal agencies was slight. In an era when government intervention in economic matters was considered improper, those who ordinarily audited banks found they had serious issues to overcome. One factor was the heroic or folk-legend status accorded to many of the auto men who had survived the pioneer years. Operating from positions of power and national esteem, the auto-bankers paid little heed to reports of bank examiners. The Guardian Group investors believed they were in on a good thing at the right time.

But timing was of great importance. It was December 16, 1929, when the Guardian Detroit Group and the Union Commerce Corporation of Detroit merged to form the Guardian Detroit Union Group, Inc. On

October 24, 1929, the New York Stock Exchange went into a "wild panic" of selling and on October 29 the worst day of selling took place.[35] Events leading to the Great Depression had begun, but that was not readily apparent at the time. However, by the middle of November an understanding of the enormity of the problem began to be evident. The amount of money lost in the market crash equaled approximately $30 billion. That amount was about equal to the entire cost to the U.S. of fighting World War I. It was also greater than the entire national debt, and about ten times as much as the cost to the United States government for the Civil War.[36] The immediate effect of the market crash was felt most directly by the rich and prosperous, after all, they were the people who had been investing in and speculating on stocks and bonds.

One consequence was the seemingly strange behavior of corporations, which continued to pay high dividends to the stockholders, even as production was being curtailed and workers were being laid off. In the face of declining stock values, it seemed that one way to reestablish the value of a corporation was by paying dividends. This may have been to shore up declining values, but it also may have been to bring stock prices high enough so that stocks could be sold at a profit. At the same time the directors and officers of corporations were putting money into their own pockets, possibly to offset the losses they had experienced in the stock market crash.

In the auto industry no greater example can be found than the actions of Albert Russell Erskine, president of the Studebaker Corporation. In 1930, Studebaker declared a dividend of $7.8 million and in 1931, Studebaker paid out about $3 million. The first amount was nearly five times the profits of 1930, while the second amount came out of capital.[37] Erskine, like many others of his time, believed, as President Herbert Hoover had repeatedly said, business conditions were "fundamentally sound." Hoover went on to advise that business should be conducted as usual. "Prosperity is just around the corner," was a catchphrase, one in which Erskine and others seemed to believe. The problem is that Erskine paid for his beliefs with his life. Despondent over conditions and in ill health, Erskine committed suicide in March 1933.

In retrospect, his personal tragedy mirrored events of the time. March of 1933 saw the fallout from the Detroit banking crisis, the psychological bottom of the Depression, and was the month in which political power was transferred from Herbert C. Hoover to Franklin D. Roosevelt. At the same time, Erskine's death symbolized the powerlessness of industrial management, especially in the auto industry, in the face of the conditions of 1933.

This was a far cry from the esteem in which the auto leaders had been held by the American public. The Roaring Twenties were real enough. While speculation may have been a root cause of the market crash on Wall Street, there was a real boom or growth that was built on the new technology of the time. The automobile industry was especially central to the economic growth, one author saying, "Numerous other industries surged forward in the twenties, holding on to the rear bumper of the automobile."[38] It seemed as if the automobile was driving the industrial destiny of the United States. Statistics are one measure of the drive of the auto industry. From 1919 to 1929, rubber sent 85 percent of its output to the auto industry, while 80 percent of gasoline, 75 percent of plate glass, 25 percent of lead and 18 percent of steel went to support auto growth.[39] Using an interesting metaphor, another writer has said, "The new automobile industry, with the slabs of cement it had created that stretched across the countryside, had imparted a dynamic urge to the whole economy."[40]

The increasing importance of the automobile in the United States even influenced U.S. foreign policy. Roughly three-fourths of the world's petroleum was used in the United States. This increased consumption began to cause worries about the known petroleum reserves in North America and, based on the knowledge of the time, geologists mistakenly forecast that in twenty-five years the North American reserves would be exhausted. This opinion precipitated a search for supplies elsewhere, notably in Iran, Iraq and Indonesia. The British and Dutch had already secured those areas, so American companies using various means, including some involvement by the national government, persuaded the British and Dutch companies to allow an American presence.[41] American corporations' involvement in the aforementioned areas, and the continued increase in the usage of petroleum products within the U.S., have had many consequences. But until December of 1941, the general public had little reason to be concerned about the location of such natural resources.

Many other products, such as radios, electric irons, refrigerators and washing machines were part of the same move toward mass consumption. But the basic prosperity of the time was built on automobile production and sales. In the ten-year period from 1919 to 1929, the number of motor-cars in the U.S. increased to 23 million, from fewer than 7 million.[42] In the same timeframe, 320,000 filling stations, 51,200 garages, and 56,300 car and truck dealers had come into being.[43] The automobile industry was responsible for the employment of approximately four million people in the industry itself and in many indirect ways.[44]

As Morison and Commager have written, "For Many Americans the automobile was a symbol of freedom, a badge of equality, useful for trans-portation but essential for social intercourse and self respect."[45] In the 1920s, businessmen in general were highly regarded. But no group had greater public acclaim than did the auto industrialists. In 1918, at the behest of President Woodrow Wilson, Henry Ford was the Democratic candidate for Senate from Michigan and was narrowly defeated. In 1924, he was considered as a possible candidate for the Presidency of the United States. It was said about him that his public statements commanded as much attention as did those of the U.S. president.[46]

Ford, in fact, was the foremost symbol of the industry that was build-ing a better America. Despite making enormous errors in judgment out-side of the auto industry, Henry Ford was the de facto leader of the industry. By far the most serious and long-lasting Ford issue was his long anti–Semitic campaign in his own newspaper. It is perhaps a commentary on the times that the anti–Semitic diatribes were accepted by the general population, and no public statements seem to have been made by Edsel Ford to distance himself from his father's views.

While Henry Ford was the most popular auto leader, others were also identified in glowing terms. For example, Walter P. Chrysler, a "dynamo," was characterized as going from "prodigious" activities to the higher plane of "fabulous" accomplishments, as *Time* magazine identified him as the "outstanding businessman of the year."[47] People in the 1920s were well aware of the enormous changes that personal ownership of a car had cre-ated in their lives and in the entire nation. The changes were considered as progress, and the men who had built the auto industry were accorded high esteem. "In the position of honor rode the automobile manufacturer. His hour of destiny had struck."[48]

At first, the Guardian Group grew quickly. The growth took place in the addition of more banks to the group, in the totality of the funds deposited in all branches of the group, and in the amounts that were loaned for various purposes. Speculation on the stock of the group took place as soon as it was listed on the Detroit Stock Exchange. The initial price range was from $250 to $300 per share, but at one point it reached a high of $350.[49] Within a short time it became evident that the ideas on which the Guardian Union Group had been formed were root causes for weakness, especially as Detroit was a one-industry town. When the auto industry was booming, the idea of retaining the profits in Michigan seemed like a good idea. But when the auto industry faltered and started to lay off workers and cut production, the self-perpetuating money machine began to dry up. Investments within the state, such as home loans to autoworkers, became a huge problem, as workers' hours or even their jobs were cut. By 1930 the value of Guardian Group stock was in the $75 to $80 range.[50]

The precipitous fall in the price of Guardian Stock brought on a number of actions by the principals of the group. One attempt to restore the value of the Guardian stock price was the formation of a pool. In the latter part of 1929, Edsel Ford, Roy D. Chapin, Charles Stewart Mott, and other directors of the various Guardian companies agreed to purchase a total of 60,000 shares, with the stipulation they would hold on to the shares for a year.[51] The idea was that this action would not only increase the individual share price, but also perhaps show price stability and thus lead to confidence in the banking group. This arrangement, as previously noted, was called a pool, which was commonly used at the time in many other sectors of the economy. There were two other considerations in being a part of the pool. The first was that participants in the pool were not to engage in trading the stock within the time period. Secondly, pool members hoped that after the year ended the pool manager could sell the stock at a profit.

At least two other Guardian Group pool arrangements are found in various references, but the dates are uncertain. One other pool purchased 93,000 shares for $4 million, or about $43 per share. Yet another pool bought 18,000 shares at a per unit price of $19.97, for a total of $3,384,000.[52] The per share price indicates the chronology of the pools even without specific dates, and also provides evidence that all was not well with the Guardian Group.

The pool efforts, however, did not provide the desired results. So about one year after the Guardian-Union merger in 1930, and concurrent with the first pool effort, Edsel Ford loaned $6 million to the Guardian Group. The loan consisted of one million dollars in cash and five million in Liberty bonds that were owned by the Ford Motor Company.[53] The government bonds were used as collateral for a $4.5 million loan from the Bankers Trust Company of New York.[54] In December of 1931, Edsel Ford secured a loan on his own credit of $2.5 million from the Continental Illinois Bank and Trust of Chicago that was also loaned to the Guardian Group.[55] Then, in December of 1932, the Ford Motor Company loaned another $3.5 million to the Guardian Group.[56]

These were not the only loans being made to the Guardian Group in the years 1929 through 1932. It was obvious that the Guardian Group was not doing well. Considering what took place later, and the general views of the Guardian Group's failure, the ties between Edsel Ford and the Ford Motor Company on one hand, and the Guardian Group on the other, were real and substantial. Note that funds from the Ford Motor Company were used in differing ways to support the Guardian Group. With the loan of December 29, 1932, came a memorandum of agreement between the Ford Motor Company and Guardian Detroit Union Group, Inc. Two provisions of the agreement ceded decision-making of the Guardian Detroit Union Group, Inc. to the Ford Motor Company in all matters of further borrowing! The third provision specifically stated that the group "agrees it will make no further or additional borrowings nor pledge the capital stock of its subsidiary companies without the consent of the Ford Motor Company, so long as the obligation hereby created remains unpaid." The fourth provision was that no sale of the bank holdings could be made without consent of the Ford Motor Company, unless the proceedings were used to pay off the loan, and that no dividends could be paid without the consent of the Ford Motor Company.[57]

It is now clear that the Guardian Group was dependent on the Ford Motor Company, through Edsel Ford as president. Not only did he make the various loans to the Guardian Group either himself or on behalf of the Ford Motor Company, but also deposits of the Ford Motor Company were used to give financial clout to the bank. One practice was to move Ford Motor Company funds in and out of various subsidiaries to improve deposit statements.[58] On February 14, 1933, when the banks in Detroit closed, the Ford Motor Company had $32.5 million on deposit in various Guardian Group banks

The memorandum of agreement between the Ford Motor Company and the Guardian Detroit Union Group, Inc., of December 29, 1932, came to light only during the U.S. Senate investigation into the Detroit banking crisis. At the time of the crisis in February and March of 1933, the full connections between the Ford Motor Company and/or Edsel Ford, and the Guardian Group were believed to be real, but the facts were not known until January 1934. Despite the disclosure of the Ford Motor Company/Edsel Ford investment in, and control over, the Guardian Group, this information has been neglected or dismissed by many writers. However now that the control of the Guardian Group by the Ford Motor Company is known, new light is cast on the subsequent events. The new light provides for differing perspectives on the entire banking crisis, as we shall see as the entire story unfolds.

3

"In the Way Our Reports Were Being Made, It Never Was Material"

Ernest Kanzler was deeply involved in all Guardian Group matters. Immediately after leaving Ford in 1926, Kanzler became executive vice president of the Guardian Detroit Bank.[1] In January 1932 he was elected chairman of the board of directors of the Guardian Detroit Union Group, Inc., where, as we know, his best friend Edsel Ford was the largest individual stockholder.[2]

But there seems to have been more to Ernest Kanzler than his relationship with Edsel Ford. As previously noted, before he left Ford, while he was production manager, second vice president and director,[3] Ernest Kanzler, Edsel Ford and other automobile executives started the Guardian Trust Company.[4] Kanzler appears to have been fully accepted by leaders of the auto industry including the driving force of the Hudson Motor Car Company, Roy D. Chapin; the leaders of Packard, Alvan Macauley and Henry Bodman; Fred J. Fisher and Lewis Mendelsohn, executives of the General Motors subsidiary Fisher Body Corporation, as well as other foremost auto men. The associations in the auto industry continued throughout his career. That may be interpreted as positive evaluation of Kanzler's abilities.

Ernest Kanzler began his business association with the Ford family in August of 1916,[5] and was pushed out in 1926.[6] Despite being compelled to leave the Ford Motor Company, Kanzler had a continuing relationship with the Fords that lasted for 51 years, ending with his death in 1967. Ernest Kanzler was uncle to Henry Ford II and influential in making recommendations after Henry II took over as president of the Ford Motor

Company.[7] As a member of the War Production Board in the early years of America's entry into World War II, Kanzler is believed to have used his influence to have Henry II released from Naval service to enter the Ford Motor Company, with the successful intent to replace his grandfather as president.[8]

While he left the direct employment of Ford in 1926, he did not leave the indirect means that led to his continued economic benefit. While still involved in the Guardian Group as vice president of the Guardian Detroit Company (later to become the Guardian Union Group) and executive vice president of the Guardian Detroit Company, Kanzler headed up the creation of the Universal Credit Corporation (UCC). This was to finance the new Ford Model A.[9] The ownership of the UCC was divided, with Ford Motor Company owning 7,501 shares, the Guardian Detroit Union Company, Inc. with 5,000 shares, and 2, 499 shares held by Kanzler as trustee.[10] In May of 1933 the partnership was dissolved and control of the UCC went to the rival Commercial Investment Trust (CIT). Kanzler stayed on as chairman.[11] When CIT gained complete ownership, Kanzler continued and, after retiring from executive duties, remained on the board of directors.[12]

Henry Ford recruited Kanzler to his new tractor company, Henry Ford & Son, in 1916.[13] Henry Ford also caused him to leave, subsequent to Kanzler's move to the Ford Motor Company. The proximate cause for Henry's displeasure was a six-page letter Kanzler wrote to Henry Ford, stating the reasons why the Ford Motor Company needed to move beyond the Model T.[14] However, the underlying problem was that Ernest Kanzler and Edsel Ford were close friends, and Henry Ford resented Kanzler's influence. Both of Edsel's parents believed that Kanzler was coming between them and their only son.[15]

It seems that Henry Ford actually did have reasons for concern about the relationship between Edsel Ford and Kanzler; there is some evidence that they had a plan to supplant him, with Kanzler actively involved on Edsel's behalf in an attempt to gain control of the company.[16] Edsel and Kanzler wanted to keep the Ford Motor Company competitive, not only in the products it produced but in the way it did business, by instituting professional management methods and procedures. Henry Ford resisted such ideas and was apparently opposed to rational business methods. Perhaps the most significant illustration is the action he took in the 1920s when

Kanzlers and Fords: (From left to right, front row only) Ernest Kanzler, Josephine Clay Kanzler, Edsel Ford, Eleanor Clay Ford. The others are not identified. Taken November 15, 1922, in Los Angeles. Sisters Josephine and Eleanor share some resemblance in appearance, including their clothing. At the time Ernest Kanzler was a top executive in the Ford Motor Company, providing support to his good friend Edsel Ford.

Edsel started a new office building to house a number of departments, including accounting. When he found out about the construction, which was underway, Henry Ford ordered the destruction of the accounting building and the termination of the accounting department, thus removing the need for a new building. This was done overnight, so that when the employees reported for work in the morning they found everything removed, and all employees fired.[17] This shows not only Ford's contempt for accounting, but also his disregard for Edsel's position as president, and is an example of the irrational manner in which he often acted. No discussion was possible in such situations, and he took abrupt actions without concern for the human consequences.

Henry Ford's suspicions about Edsel and Kanzler were reinforced by the many connections between the two men. They were of the same generation, with a different world outlook than the elder Ford. They shared a common vision of the direction of the Ford Motor Company. They spent much time together. At Ford they worked in adjacent offices, at home they lived near each other, and they had vacation homes close together. Having married sisters who were very close to one another, the Edsel Fords and Ernest Kanzlers had many family events that reinforced their close relationship. To Henry Ford, the residences in luxurious Grosse Pointe and vacation homes in Maine near the Rockefellers and other wealthy Easterners were all signs of moral decadence, further evidence of Kanzler's corrupting influence.[18]

First at Henry Ford & Son, and later at the Ford Motor Company, Kanzler proved to be a good executive and introduced a greater degree of rationality into production.[19] Even Charles Sorensen, Ford's right hand man for production, had some good words to say about Kanzler's work. Sorensen noted that despite Kanzler's law degree from Harvard and lack of manufacturing experience, he did a "good job" and was willing "to do anything."[20]

In 1923, Edsel Ford's bid for autonomy resulted in Kanzler being elected a director and vice president of the Ford Motor Company. Charles Sorensen, in his authorized biography, sees this as defying Henry Ford,[21] while another source says Henry Ford considered it a "betrayal."[22] Edsel's cause was not helped when Kanzler made an "unrestrained tirade against Mr. Ford and the way he held Edsel down," directly to Charles Sorensen.[23]

Sorensen immediately went to Henry Ford with the information. In doing so, Sorensen was certainly not a disinterested party. He and Kanzler had both proven their abilities in production, and seemed to be vying for the same position at Ford, with Kanzler being supported by Edsel. Having worked for Henry Ford since 1904, Sorensen made his choice to remain true.[24] The attempt by Edsel Ford to be president in fact as well as in name forced employees to choose sides, with most deciding to remain loyal to Henry Ford while ignoring Edsel.[25]

Henry Ford did not respond directly to the letter Ernest Kanzler wrote to him about the Model T and the need for new Ford products. Ford's only evident business response was to order prices on the Model T reduced one more time. His personal response was to treat Kanzler with public rudeness,[26] ignoring his presence at meetings, interrupting Kanzler when he spoke in group settings, and subjecting Kanzler to ridicule. When Raymond Dahlinger, Henry Ford's driver, personal helper and general factotum, observed that Kanzler was a Jew, it was clear there was no place for Kanzler at the Ford Motor Company.[27] It was no matter that Kanzler was not Jewish; Dahlinger was only jumping in with the well-known anti–Semitic bias that was a part of Henry Ford's worldview.

Kanzler was forced to resign as Edsel Ford was on his way to Europe. It was left to Edsel, as president of the Ford Motor Company, to announce Kanzler's departure.[28] His reaction to this duty is unknown, but in effect he was announcing the end of his attempt to gain control of Ford, and his loss of his best friend and confidante. The news article stated that having severed connections with the Ford Motor Company, Kanzler was going to "look after some private investments of Henry Ford and Edsel Ford." It also noted that Kanzler was "especially fitted for this particular work."[29]

When interviewed in the 1950s, Harry Bennett saw the ousting of Ernest Kanzler as a defining event. He saw it as marking "the parting of the ways between Mr. Ford and Edsel." Furthermore, Bennett saw a change in Edsel, who had been and continued to be embarrassed by his father's actions. With Kanzler gone, Edsel developed an attitude of "cynicism."[30] Considering the close personal and business relationships between them, it is reasonable to assume that Edsel knew of Kanzler's actions, including the fateful letter to Henry Ford. In effect, Kanzler took the risk and paid the price, being a surrogate for Edsel.

Henry Ford is quoted as having said, "Both Edsel and Kanzler should have been bankers."[31] That statement may have been meant as an insult, considering Ford's oft-quoted dislike of bankers. Nevertheless, becoming bankers is what both Edsel and Kanzler did in the Guardian Detroit Union Group, Inc., with Kanzler taking the lead in the executive ranks of the Guardian Group.

As befitted the largest individual stockholder, Edsel Ford served on a number of committees. He was a member of the board of directors of the holding company, the Guardian Detroit Union Group, from the time it began and also the boards of two major subsidiaries. He also was a member of the advisory committee of the group, commencing approximately when the Ford Motor Company caused the Guardian Group to sign the memorandum of Agreements.[32] The timing of his becoming a member of the advisory committee indicates that he was especially interested in the Guardian Group being accountable for debts to the Ford Motor Company. Involved as he was, Edsel Ford was certainly knowledgeable about the financial condition and situation of the Guardian Group.

In the spirit of the times, the Guardian Group expanded, with the intent to become the dominant financial organization in Michigan. Using the aforementioned technique of adding banks by the swapping of stock, Charles Stewart Mott, a vice president of General Motors, became a major player in Guardian Group matters when his Union Industrial Bank of Flint became a Guardian subsidiary.[33] In the same manner, Sen. James Couzens became a shareholder in the Guardian Group when two banks he had founded, the Bank of Detroit and the Highland Park State Bank, were added to the Guardian Group.[34] The shareholder relationship of Senator Couzens with the Guardian Group is not mentioned in many accounts of the events of the time. This neglect lessens the understanding and complexity of the many relationships between and among the individuals who were involved in the Detroit banking crisis of 1933, the attempts to forestall the crisis from becoming national in scope, the investigation of the banking crisis, and the many attempts to assign responsibility for the crisis.

The relationships will be explained in due course, but in regard to Couzens here are some basic points to consider at this time:

- Couzens was a cofounder of the Ford Motor Company, and is given credit for having established the business practices of the company which contributed to its dominance in the ten-year period from 1909 to 1919.
- Henry Ford and Couzens had a business relationship that succeeded during Couzens's time at Ford, despite their mutually strong-headed ways.
- Subsequent to Couzens leaving Ford, the relationship between the two men varied from reciprocal criticisms to grudging respect.
- After entering politics and holding elective offices in Detroit, including that of mayor, Couzens was appointed to the United

States Senate. The seat he took had been occupied by Truman Newberry of the Packard Motor Car Company. Newberry had defeated
Henry Ford for the seat, but private investigative pressure brought
about by Ford eventually caused Newberry to resign.
• Following the bank crisis in Detroit, which spread into a nationwide emergency, a U.S. Senate subcommittee investigated banking
in Detroit. James Couzens was an important member of the investigative committee.

The sprit of the times provided the context in the formation of the
Guardian Group. The Harding, Coolidge, and Hoover administrations all
encouraged the growth of large-scale combinations in business and industry. One impetus to continued growth was the reputation of the well-
known auto leaders, whose names were prominently mentioned in
association with the Guardian Group. Through their daring and energy
the auto men had built an entirely new industry in a very short time period.
Their success, it was commonly believed, was evidence of their wisdom
and leadership. When a bank became a part of the Guardian Group it
meant an association with known winners.

Other men in the auto industry whose successes were well known
added to the imposing list of Guardian Group officers and investors. One
additional director listed in 1929 was Albert Kahn,[35] the prominent archi-
tect who designed and built both factories and mansions for the automobile leaders.[36] Other directors included W. Ledyard Mitchell, general
manager of Chrysler Motors; Hiram H. Walker of the Canadian liquor
firm as well as GM of Canada; Howard Bonbright, treasurer of the Briggs
Body Company[37]; William A. Fisher, of the GM subsidiary Fisher Body
Company; Ransom E. Olds, founder and head of REO; and Clifford Longley, counsel to the Ford Motor Company and the Ford family.[38] Working at the Guardian Detroit Bank, as assistant cashier, was Alvan Macauley,
Jr.[39]

The experienced auto industry men who built Guardian knew that
consolidation was taking place in their industry. The Guardian Group and
its rival, the Detroit Bankers Group, led the trend toward consolidation
by together controlling most of the banking in Michigan. In the industrial setting, efficiencies of scale worked, a fact the auto executives under-

stood quite well. It was thought that the benefits of a large-scale organization could be applicable in banking as well. For example, the Guardian Group could obtain better discount rates, loan arrangements, and terms and scopes of loans than separate banks with limited deposits, where each needed to apply individually to the varied sources from which banks obtained their funds.

However, the Guardian Group also grew for other reasons that were problematic. One was insider knowledge. Controlling a segment of the economy, especially in the days before regulatory organizations, gave officers and shareholders of businesses the ability to profit from buying and selling stock at especially opportune times. It also provided them with numerous other advantages, which at the time were considered to be the prerogatives of ownership. As the Guardian Group established statewide domination of banking and a duopoly with the Detroit Bankers Company the concentration of power in a group of men who were at the same time the industrial and banking leaders in a regional economy based on one industry, was subject to exploitation. Without an active competitor seeking market gains, or a countervailing authority to question their actions, self-serving decisions were possible. In addition, the auto men were creatures of their background as promoters. From the earliest days the men of the auto industry attempted to gain venture capital through advertising hyperbole and various forms of publicity. Promotion of their brand, introduction of new models, or advertising alleged improvements were part and parcel of the automobile business from the beginning of the industry.

But banking was a different type of business in which conservative values were paramount. No one embodied the stolid banker more than J.P. Morgan, who twice came to the rescue of the American economy. In 1895, when the gold reserve of the United States was eroding, Morgan assured the other bankers that they could safely lend funds to the United States government. Without the loans, U.S. currency would have been worthless, and a great crisis would have ensued. In 1907, when a loss of confidence in New York banks led to a panic and a run on the banks, Morgan brought all of the bankers together, and through use of his strong personality and reputation again averted a potentially disastrous event.[40] Emerging as an unlikely hero, he embodied the reputation of solid, safe, and conservative bankers everywhere.

"Until the Depression, bankers had commanded great admiration according to Susan Estabrook Kennedy."[41] When Edsel Ford, Ernest Kanzler, Roy D. Chapin and the other auto executives went into banking, the auto business was a great success and their reputations as successful executives were without blemish. At that time they could have reasonably assumed that as bankers their already high reputations would be greatly enhanced.

However, events were to lead to lessened reputations. In contrast to the storied banker J.P. Morgan using his influence to loan money to the government, the Guardian Group borrowed money from the government. Soon after the Reconstruction Finance Corporation was established, a subsidiary of the Guardian Group, the Union Guardian Trust, applied for a loan. On May 24, 1932, the RFC responded with a loan of $4.25 million, and in July 1932, another $8.73 million was added.[42]

The RFC was authorized on January 22, 1932, when President Herbert Hoover reluctantly signed the necessary legislation. Hoover had unsuccessfully attempted to resuscitate the economy through exhortation, continued reassurances in the basic strength of America, and through voluntary organizations and efforts.[43] He stated that the RFC was to "stop deflation in agriculture and industry," leading to increased employment. He further stated that the RFC was "not created for the aid of big industries or big banks."[44] However the very first loan of $15 million was made to the Bank of America, which, by any measure, was a very big bank.[45] This loan, like all RFC acts for about five months, was secret.

The RFC took a hit when in June of 1932 it authorized a loan to a Chicago bank headed by former U.S. Vice President Charles G. Dawes. Dawes had, only three weeks before, been the president of the RFC![46] Circumstances in Chicago were desperate. It seems that the Dawes bank had made enormous loans to the failed utility holding companies run by Samuel Insull.[47] Aside from the financial situation in Chicago, politics entered the issue, as Chicago was also the site of the Democratic National Convention, which nominated Franklin D. Roosevelt for president. President Hoover could ill afford to have an economic disaster in Chicago, and so he took a great interest in preventing a financial panic, supporting the Dawes loan.[48] As the news came out, it seemed to many that insider favoritism and political considerations were what determined approval of RFC loans. All of this had significant impact on the applications made by the Guardian Group to the RFC.[49] One immediate result was that open disclosure was required. By February of 1933 the Democratic majority in the House of Representatives ended the secrecy and divulged the previous actions of the RFC.[50] So the furor over the Dawes loan and all previous RFC actions took place at the time that the Guardian Group was actively seeking a third RFC loan.

Thus, the RFC loans made in May and June of 1932 greatly influenced the later decision of the RFC, when the Guardian applied again in February of 1933. Federal law banned any loan that was not fully secured, and given the findings of the bank examiners, it appeared that perhaps the RFC had not practiced due diligence in making the earlier loans. The RFC was feeling pressure to be completely in accord with all regulations and to avoid favoritism. Furthermore, a *Harper's Magazine* article in December 1932 charged that the RFC had earlier succumbed to political influence exerted by Roy D. Chapin to make the 1932 loans.[51] Chapin, of the Hudson Motor Car Company, was a founding member and director of the Guardian Group. He was also active in Republican Party matters, close to President Hoover, and in August of 1932 was appointed by Hoover to be secretary of commerce.

The RFC loans came in addition to loans already supplied by Edsel Ford. It was after the RFC loans that the Ford Motor Company followed with the December 1932 loan that resulted in the memorandum of agreement. Nor were these the only loans obtained by the Guardian Group. Charles Stewart Mott guaranteed a loan of $2.5 million[52] and also covered an employee embezzlement of over $3.5 million from the Union Industrial Bank of Flint, a Guardian Group subsidiary.[53]

Another $8.4 million was obtained in exchange, with other banks, for slow or undesirable assets in Guardian Group institutions.[54] Directors of the group, to carry loans of distressed officers and employees, also lent $1.6 million in credit. The loans were in addition to the previously mentioned pools used in attempts to prop up the stock price. In testimony before the Senate subcommittee, the president of the Guardian Detroit Union Group, Inc. stated that the total help provided to the various entities of the Guardian Group came to at least $27 million.[55]

At the same time as the Guardian Group was securing loans it failed to follow good business practices. For example, in 1930 the group had a deficit of $39,000 and paid $86,000 in salaries. In 1931 the deficit was $288,930, and the salary total expanded to $131,624. The next year the deficit was higher, and salaries had increased to $181,280, with $375,134 paid in dividends and $722,000 owed as interest on loans.[56] Apparently following the same logic used by Albert Erskine at Studebaker in paying large dividends in a declining economic situation, from 1929 to 1932 the Guardian Detroit Union Group, Inc., paid $9.3 million to its stockholders. These funds had come to the holding company from member banks that paid $9.7 million in dividends.[57] The major sources of income for the Guardian Detroit Union Group, Inc., were money paid by the twenty-five banks in the group and proceeds from the sale of Guardian Group stock.

While the deficits were mounting, one bank, the Guardian National Bank of Commerce, loaned directors $4.4 million in direct loans and $3.3 million in indirect loans. Other banks in the group made proportionate loans.[58] Ernest Kanzler received a direct loan of $382,191 and an indirect loan of $350,989.[59] At the time of the loan he was serving as chairman of the Guardian Union Group executive committee. That is, while the Guardian Group found it necessary to obtain loans from the United States government via the RFC, its executives were lending money to themselves.

In many instances, the only collateral the officers and directors put up was stock in the Guardian Group. The National Bank of Commerce, a member bank, had over 48,000 shares held as collateral in September 1930. By March 1931 the number had increased to over 57,000, and in May 1932 the number of shares held as collateral was nearly 150,000. There were 61 directors of this bank. Fifty-two had received loans, while 33 of the 43 officers in the main office also received loans. Thirty-four percent of the total capital of the Guardian National Bank of Commerce had been loaned to officers and directors, as reported on December 31,1931.[60] Another bank had made loans to 122 junior officers and employees for a total of $1 million, on the basis of collateral booked at a value of $15,000.[61] The same type of activity took place in other units of the Guardian Group. Directors used the group for their own enrichment, without regard to the situation in the group, nor the situation in their home state.

Dividends from the member banks supported the price of the group stock. The member banks of the group were forced to accept Guardian

Group stock as collateral for the loans made to the officers and directors. The practical fact was that member banks could not then sell the stock to realize any income, as putting it on the market would cause the share price to drop. Any such fall in group stock price would then lead to a further loss of confidence by the general public, and perhaps lower stock prices even further. A further decrease in the stock value would, at the same time, lessen the value of the collateral held by the unit banks. No matter the actual circumstances, the group, as the holding company, determined the dividends that member banks were to pay to the Guardian Group. The subsidiary Union Guardian Trust Company was directed to pay a dividend of 20 percent. At least one unit president had the courage to object, saying that no dividend had been earned and should not be paid.[62] While average corporations were paying a six to seven percent yield on stocks, the Guardian Group was paying sixteen to seventeen percent.[63]

To review, the Guardian Group found it necessary to attempt to shore up the price of the its stock by having stock pools formed by the officers, directors, and shareholders. The funds used to purchase the stock were often borrowed from the member banks of the group. The collateral used to borrow the money was shares of the Guardian Group! Had the Guardian Group actually been a bank, rather than a holding company that owned banks, the use of its own stock as collateral for loans to officers and directors would have been clearly illegal. As it was, the Guardian Detroit Union Group, Inc. was a holding company whose officers were more attuned to the automobile industry than banking.

When Ernest Kanzler was called to testify before the Senate Subcommittee on Stock Exchange Practices in January 1934, he was questioned about the loan and dividend practices of the Guardian Group. He was identified as "chairman of the board of the Detroit Union Guardian Group, Inc," with his testimony and cross-examination taking more than three hours.[64] When asked by Committee Counsel Ferdinand Pecora if the policy of declaring dividends was "shaped partly, if not entirely by a consideration of the effect upon the public mind," Kanzler answered affirmatively. He said, "Quite certainly that had a substantial effect upon the minds of the individuals declaring dividends." Pecora followed up asking if it was "fair to infer or conclude" that the directors periodically declared dividends "at a figure that was designed to bolster up public confidence in the banking units of the group?" Kanzler would not agree to Pecora's conclusion, and turned the cause and effect around, saying, "I would put it the other way." In speaking of the actions of the directors, of whom he was one, in declaring dividends, Kanzler said, "They declared dividends in such a way that they would not destroy the institutions by reason of the runs that might be incited by lack of confidence."[65]

When asked if he was a founder of the Guardian Group, Kanzler would not agree. Instead, he provided the names of twenty-three other men, adding that this was not a complete list. Of course this was dissembling on Kanzler's part as the public records clearly identified him as a key force in the founding of the Guardian Group. Evidence was presented to the investigative committee that a decision was made by a Guardian Group committee Kanzler headed to publish the consolidated group statement in "standard" form rather than what was known as an "understandable" form.[66] The implication, of course, was that there was an attempt to keep the true nature of the Guardian's precarious financial situation from becoming known. On the same general subject, Kanzler was asked about the apparent discrepancies in what he reported to the stockholders. In January 1933 he reported that the year 1932 was one of "notable improvement," which was in contrast to the information he provided to the RFC in the February application for the third loan. The report Kanzler made to the stockholders was verbal, no written statement was provided.[67] Pecora asked if Kanzler knew in January 1933 that the group "as a separate corporate entity had incurred a deficit of $714,331, which included a carryover of $288,080" from 1931.[68]

Kanzler's response was: "In the way our reports were being made, it never was material and I do not know whether I ever saw a sheet showing a deficit or not, because of the manner of the keeping of our books."[69] One must grudgingly admire the sheer gall of Kanzler's response. It is astonishing what he admitted to in his reply. First, he stated that as chairman of the board he did not know the true state of the finances of the group. He further admitted that his apparent lack of knowledge was due to the inefficient or inept way in which the financial records were kept. Nevertheless, one month after making his verbal report to the shareholders, he had requested a loan from the RFC for the purpose of paying off the $20.5 million debts of the subsidiary Union Guardian Trust Company of Detroit.

Pecora then asked him "which was the truer picture," the one he had presented to the stockholders in January or the one he presented to the board of the RFC on February 6, 1933? The response was mind-boggling: "I cannot tell today, which was the truer picture. There was a corps of people inspecting the assets and there was a difference of opinion and whose opinion today is correct, I do not know. And I do not think anybody else knows what those assets were worth. They would have had to be appraised by the rule of reason."[70]

Kanzler thus evaded directly answering Pecora, and did not admit to having made a false statement, or being certain of the real values of the assets of the Union Guardian Trust Company of Detroit. Even as of January 1934, eleven months after the request for the RFC loan, he did not have correct information. Or so he said. This response was from a man of high financial experience, as evidenced by his many successful years heading the Universal Credit Corporation. In responding to questions, Kanzler stated that he simply did not know. When his good friend Edsel Ford was called to testify, Ford could not remember. Edsel was reticent. Kanzler was audacious.

It was not as if the Guardian Group had not been warned. The comptroller of currency issued warnings to the group and bank examiners chimed it.[71] In testimony before the committee, Alfred Leyburn, chief national bank examiner of the Fourth Federal Reserve District, testified that he was amazed that the Guardian banks were in such poor condition after starting up in 1929. In June 1932 Leyburn met with Guardian representatives and told them that only two of the twenty-five banks were justified in paying dividends. In fact, some banks had gone into the accounts of depositors to obtain funds to pay dividends. He further testified that he advised them to stop paying dividends but to take care of their losses and bad assets. The problem was that Guardian Group had obligations of $14.5 million in loans with an annual interest of $850,000. The group meeting with him argued with him and rejected his advice. Among those representing the Guardian Group were Edsel Ford, Charles Stewart Mott, and Clifford Longley.[72] Leyburn's evaluation was that the Guardian Group had "bad management," and its dividend policy was "absolutely unwarranted both from a legal and business standpoint."[73]

The bank examiners who were assigned to review the accounts of the

Guardian Group units did not have an easy job. Various member banks issued false and misleading reports, which did not follow normal accounting practices. Instead, certain accounting practices were used in an attempt to deceive the auditors. For example, government securities owned by a bank under audit, but pledged to other units for payment, were shown as assets. Securities of customers, kept for safekeeping, were added to the assets of member banks and also shown as liabilities in such a way as to cover the true financial status of the unit being examined. Actual losses of member banks were not provided in annual reports, and a conscious policy of issuing consolidated statements in incomprehensible language began in July of 1931.[74]

The bank examiners also had to carefully evaluate the timing of large deposits. Evidence was presented that various subsidiaries of the Guardian Group engaged in the swapping of deposits, with an apparent intent to make the assets appear greater.[75] As noted previously, funds of the Ford Motor Company were used in this manner at the direction of Edsel Ford. Appearing before the Senate subcommittee, Ford was asked if this procedure was ethical or fair. His response was, "No, I don't suppose it is."[76]

Pressure, attempts at intimidation, and offers of employment were brought to bear on the examiners investigating the Guardian Group. Four former national bank examiners became vice presidents of various subsidiaries.[77] As usual, politics was also in the picture. One auditor discovered an unsecured loan of $100,000 to the incumbent Michigan state treasurer. Officers of banks objected to having any examination and one officer, who was a former Michigan governor, was reported by name as attempting to prevent an audit.[78] But one reason to suppress the findings of examiners was the enormity of the financial problems that were discovered. In May of 1932 an examiner reported that one member bank, the Guardian Detroit Bank of Commerce, had taken a $1.2 million loss. However, he noted that this was a "nominal" amount, as the actual loss was so great that authorities did not believe they dare make the information public. Notwithstanding the enormity of the problem, the bank paid out a dividend of $200,000 in the first quarter of 1932. In November 1932, another examiner found that the "doubtful loans" of the same bank exceeded the entire capital funds of the bank. Once again a dividend was paid, this time of $150,000.[79] The Guardian Group continued its policies headed toward failure and bankruptcy, despite having full knowledge of the actual financial situation.

In testifying about the pool arrangements, Kanzler said that in October 1930 the Guardian Union stock price was beginning to be a concern. All 110 or 112 directors agreed that they should purchase 60,000 shares and hold them for a year. The board of directors believed that it was necessary to purchase the shares to stabilize the price of the stock. However, despite the agreement, only 35,000 were purchased.[80] The reasons some directors didn't take part are probably varied, but one cannot help concluding that some may have thought that it was not a wise use of their investment capital. It may be that some of the shareholders did not comprehend the actual condition of the Group, as positive and optimistic statements were regularly provided to shareholders.[81]

Kanzler further testified that the chairman of the pool committee was Charles B. Warren, an influential Michigan Republican Party leader, and former U.S. ambassador to Japan. Warren had once been a Calvin Coolidge nominee for United States attorney general during a time when he was under indictment for alleged "sugar trust" misdeeds. One of the persons who had led the opposition in the Senate to Warren's appointment was Sen. James Couzens. Warren was considered to have been the person who originated group banking in Michigan.[82] Other members of the pool committee included Roy D. Chapin and Ernest Kanzler. Kanzler further testified that the Guardian Detroit Company was made the agent on behalf of the directors. Considering the other financial methods used by Guardian Group officials, it is probable that the shares held for the pool had other Guardian Group shares used as collateral for the loans made to artificially support the price of the Group stock.

A 1931 newspaper article revealed that twenty-two men in the U.S. had $3 million or more in life insurance policies. Of those, two, Charles Stewart Mott and Carlton Higbie, were associated with the Guardian Group. Fred Fisher had a policy of just over $2 million while Albert Kahn, Ernest Kanzler, and group President Robert O. Lord had policies of no less than $1 million each. The corporate practice of purchasing fully paid, whole life insurance for executives is a normal way of enhancing executive benefits. But this is an example of how tall the Guardian Group officers stood in the realms of U.S. business. Kanzler and Lord were the two highest executives in the Guardian Group and they were in the same insurance league as Powel Crosley, Jr. (then of radio and appliance renown); war hero, aviation entrepreneur, and Indianapolis Speedway owner Eddie Ricken-backer; entertainers Mary Pickford, Will Rogers, and Al Jolson; and financier Bernard Baruch.[83]

We do not know the financial losses, if any, incurred by Kanzler and his partners when the Guardian Group failed. Through brazen responses, apparently insulated from legal consequences by their positions in Amer-ican society, the auto industry bankers spread the consequences of their actions among the rest of society just as they distributed the financial prob-lems to trusting depositors. They remained very rich, and many prospered, but they had lost their aura of omnipotent success. Who could value a man who headed a large financial institution but said he did not know its true worth? Edsel Ford, Ernest Kanzler, Roy D. Chapin, and the other automobile men associated with the Guardian Group had been honored as men who had built a giant industry that was a basic economic force in American life. But in attempting to become bankers, they were found to be similar to the other bankers whose shady dealings were previously exposed by the Senate subcommittee.

One might have concluded that the leaders of the Guardian Group, involved as they were in an industry that was national and even interna-tional in scope, would have had an understanding of the effects of their banking decisions. But it seems that while their auto businesses were con-ducted with one mindset, their decisions in the Guardian Group were self-serving, narrow, and limited in scope. Perhaps some of the Guardian executives believed the misleading and incorrect information that was pub-lished. Some may have thought that if they simply hung on long enough, the circumstances would change and all would be as it had been. How-ever, it is difficult to comprehend that some of the most effective men in the United States, as evidenced by their auto industry successes, failed to come forward with the truth and forthrightly deal with the seriousness of the matter. Instead, their actions that brought about the crisis, and their subsequent responses attempted to absolve them of responsibility. In effect, they came close to bringing down the social system in which their busi-nesses had thrived.

Edsel Ford and Ernest Kanzler had gone into banking and failed to achieve a powerful banking organization replicating the success of the Ford Motor Company. The Guardian Group stock that had sold as high as $350 per share in 1929 had declined within a year to between $75 and $80.[84] By 1931 the price had dropped to $30. I was worth $10 in 1932, and had no value thereafter.[85]

4

"It Is Going to Be
Awfully Hard Work"

Roy D. Chapin, like Edsel Ford and Ernest Kanzler, was profoundly involved in the Detroit banking crisis of 1933. However, unlike Kanzler, Chapin represented diverse and contradictory interests in the crisis. Aside from his personal interest, Kanzler officially represented the leadership of the Guardian Detroit Union Group and a main subsidiary, the Universal Credit Corporation. Chapin represented much more.

At the time of the crisis in February 1933, Roy D. Chapin was secretary of commerce in the last days of the Hoover administration. As the crisis in Detroit intensified, President Hoover sent Chapin and Undersecretary of the Treasury Arthur Ballantine to Detroit to meet with Henry Ford. At the time it seemed there was only one way to avoid a complete financial meltdown in Michigan. That way was to gain Henry Ford's approval to use Ford Motor Company deposits in the Guardian Group to guarantee a loan from the Reconstruction Finance Corporation. Otherwise, the Hoover administration feared correctly that the collapse of the Guardian Group would trigger a failure of the entire banking system in the United States.

As the representative of President Hoover, Chapin had an official role in meeting with Henry Ford. But in addition to his official status, Chapin had a personal relationship with Herbert Hoover, and was a good friend of both Henry and Edsel Ford. The meeting with the Fords, while discreet, was not a secret and was known to Ernest Kanzler and other banking and automotive interests in Detroit. In effect, Chapin represented the interests of the power elite in Detroit while at the same time he was a major investor in the Guardian Group. Chapin brought to the meeting personal financial interests, his reputation in Detroit, his loyalty to Hoover and his status as a cabinet member, his friendships with both Fords, his mutual financial interests with Edsel Ford, his concerns about conditions in Detroit, and a friendship with Arthur Ballantine.

Thus Chapin's attempt to be a mediator or diplomat in meeting with Henry and Edsel Ford was full of complications and conflicts. One additional factor affecting Chapin's perspective was that he knew that in less than a month he would be returning to Michigan and the auto industry. The presidential election had already been held, and Hoover and the Republican Party had suffered a crushing defeat.

Herbert Hoover most certainly knew of Chapin's connection to, and involvement in, the Guardian Group. News reports had described Chapin's Guardian involvement since 1925.[1] If Hoover had missed the connection then his aides, or Chapin himself, had failed to inform him. If Hoover did know of Chapin's Guardian interests, questions arise as to Hoover's decision-making. To meet with Henry Ford, the president of the United States had chosen an emissary who had varying and conflicting interests instead of being solely the representative of the president and responsible to the American people. Even as a lame-ducks, Chapin and Hoover had both power and responsibility. Both men were highly motivated to prevent the failure of the Guardian Group. Herbert Hoover feared, correctly as it turned out, that he would become the political scapegoat for any failure. For generations his name was invoked by orators of the Democratic Party as a Republican symbol of indifference to human suffering. What Hoover had attempted to prevent happened anyway. Why was it then that with such high stakes, Hoover selected Chapin for the critical meeting with Henry Ford?

The most likely conclusion is that the ethical standards of the time conflicts of interest and the duty to represent the broad interests of the American people differed markedly from what is now expected. In fact, it may be that President Hoover believed that Chapin's own interest in Guardian matters made him an excellent envoy. After all, Chapin stood to have considerable losses if his mission failed. And Chapin's standing with both Henry and Edsel Ford was considered advantageous. Furthermore, Chapin was fully informed of the situation of the Guardian Group. He was in communication with Ernest Kanzler,[2] Charles Stewart Mott, and Ransom E. Olds[3] on Guardian Group matters as the crisis was unfolding. Hoover may have reasoned that Chapin was the only person who could speak to Henry Ford, having the shared experiences as an automobile executive, and being the representative of the president of the United States.

It is no secret that the meeting failed. Henry Ford refused to subordinate the deposits of the Ford Motor Company and the crisis ensued. How was it that a meeting of three automobile leaders (Henry Ford, Edsel Ford, and Roy D. Chapin) on non-automotive matters could have such importance? Henry Ford and the Ford Motor Company at that time were giants worldwide. As president of the Ford Motor Company and by association with his father, if for no other reason, Edsel Ford also had importance. But what about the importance of Roy D. Chapin? What led to his involvement in the meeting?

By all rights there should have been a car named after Roy D. Chapin. He was a true automotive pioneer and may be the only person to have been involved in the successful start of four different automobile companies. Chapin began with the Olds Motor Works in 1901, and except for a brief time as secretary of commerce in the last year of the Hoover administration, he was in the auto industry until his untimely death in 1936. To be sure, the Olds Motor Works was in business when he joined the firm. Chapin's initial work involved a variety of tasks; he filed gears, used his interest in photography to enhance Olds advertisements, and tested newly constructed cars. To demonstrate that the Olds light runabout model, which we now call the Curved Dash Olds, was more than a city car, Chapin drove from Detroit to New York in October 1901.[4] His photo at the tiller of an Olds appears in many automotive references due to the significance of his trip. It was one of the first of many endurance trials that helped to increase acceptance of the motorcar as a useful and reliable product. Olds sales went from 425 vehicles in 1901 to 2,500 in 1902,[5] some of the increase attributable to Chapin's Detroit to New York run.

By 1904, at age 24, he was named sales manager for Olds.[6] Sales increased to around 5,000 cars in 1904 and 6,500 in 1905,[7] making Olds the world leader in production and sales. However, the majority shareholding Smith family and Ransom E. Olds, founder, general manager and chief designer, had differing opinions as to the direction that Oldsmobile should take. R.E. Olds left the firm, causing concern to Chapin and other key executives. Chapin and his friends felt their interests would be served best by leaving Oldsmobile, and through some maneuvers created a partnership to build the Thomas Detroit automobile. Though successful, Chapin and his partners wanted more control and a greater financial return. The consequence was to end the Thomas Detroit arrangement and phase into what became the Chalmers Detroit firm. Again successful in sales, Chapin and his partners still did not have what they sought in decision-making, control and compensation. This led to the formation of the Hudson Motor Car Company, the third company Chapin helped to found and the fourth in which he was key to initial success.

The Hudson Motor Car Company began in 1909, which means that in eight years Chapin had ascended in the auto world from a general employee at Olds, through successful enterprises with Thomas and Chalmers, to the founding of the Hudson Motor Car Company. What seems amazing is that the various business arrangements seem to have been managed without recrimination or lasting animosities. It may be a measure of Chapin's personality and character that no one ever had anything negative to say about him. In fact, quite to the contrary, he received praise, as when E.R. Thomas sent a telegram to President Hoover in support of Chapin's nomination to be secretary of commerce. Twenty-four years after the business relationship in the Thomas-Detroit Company, E.R. Thomas said "divine providence" led Hoover to select Chapin.[8]

In 1912, only three years after the formation of the Hudson Motor Car Company, Chapin's status in Detroit was such that he was selected to determine who would be charter members of the Detroit Athletic Club (D.A.C.),[9] which developed into the exclusive club of movers and shakers in Detroit. Here again, a positive previous business relationship was evident as Hugh Chalmers accepted the first presidency of the D.A.C.[10] A year later the Lincoln Highway Association was formed with Chapin on the executive committee.[11] Also on the board with Chapin was his friend Carl Fisher, in whose Prest-O-Lite Company he had invested.[12] Others with whom Chapin associated on the Lincoln Highway Association included the presidents of Goodyear, U.S. Rubber, Firestone, Packard, and Willys, in addition to William Randolph Hearst and T. Coleman Dupont.

The Lincoln Highway Association was part of the "good roads" movement in which Chapin had been involved since 1905.[13] During World War I, Chapin became one of the "dollar-a-year-men" of American industry and commerce who gave vital assistance in planning and organizing the U.S. war effort. His particular involvement was as chairman of the Highway Transport Committee. In that role he was a successful proponent of the use of truck transport and convoys, helping to develop the concept of logistics.[14]

By 1918 he became a contributor to the *Saturday Evening Post* magazine, then a popular and respected national publication. His pieces generally expressed a vision of the benefits of good roads and the use of motor vehicles in enhancing the lives of everyone. At the time, the future he projected seemed quite distant. He remained active in promoting improved roads, and found that going to Washington, D.C., as a lobbyist had significant benefits in creating a means of national coordination and planning.

In 1920 he met Herbert Hoover, then secretary of commerce, when Chapin helped to form a group to promote American exports.[15] Since 1903, when he began national sales work at Oldsmobile, Chapin had actively sought out and met men of influence in various parts of the nation and in varying capacities. He knew bankers from Wall Street to Main Street, presidents of large corporations, politicians from the state house to the shadow of the White House, and virtually all of the leaders of the automobile industry. His temperament, connections, and experience on the national scene, combined with his status as a pioneer in the industry, led him to be selected as a spokesman for the auto industry in 1927.[16] He was, it seems, an ultimate insider.

Having been in the industry almost from its beginning, Chapin was a target of opportunity for disparaging remarks. In his first work at Olds, he had contacts with many other automotive pioneers. For example, Chapin was on the scene in October of 1901 in the race which brought Henry Ford to prominence. He and Jonathan Maxwell both drove Oldsmobiles in a race for light cars associated with the big race where Ford bested Alexander Winton. "Detroit's pioneer auto dealer," William E. Metzger, who was later involved in various automotive manufacturing efforts, promoted the race.[17] At Olds, other men who later went into auto manufacturing took part, including Robert Hupp.[18] And Charles Sorensen and Chapin shared a rooming house in Detroit.[19] The number of people with whom Chapin dealt was extensive, and most left some records of their activities in which Chapin was a coworker or competitor, but his reputation is unblemished. The one recorded incident, in which he and James Couzens engaged in some written exchanges in 1912 and 1913,[20] dealt with Hudson advertising hyperbole. Chapin's biographer, J.C. Long, uses the incident as a means of characterizing James Couzens and infers that it was a motivating factor for the Senate investigation of the Guardian Group in 1934, in which Couzens played a significant role. Couzens's biographer, Harry Barnard, relates the episode as one in which Couzens was trying to appease Henry Ford. In any case, Chapin was not called to testify during the investigation.

The reality is that Chapin managed to have good relationships with many, if not most, of the men of the auto world. At Olds, when the dispute for control of the company led R.E. Olds to leave, Chapin was promoted by the Smith family,[21] who controlled the company, while he maintained a lifelong positive relationship with Ransom Olds. When Olds

left for a long oceanic cruise, Chapin, while serving as secretary of commerce, took the time to write to the steamship line to inform them of Olds's presence on one of their ships, and to stress Olds's eminence and historical importance in the auto indus-

Roy D. Chapin, circa 1920. The original of this photograph has an inscription from Chapin which says, "TO HENRY FORD — WHO TAUGHT SOMETHING TO US ALL. Roy D. Chapin." At the time of the Detroit banking crisis, Chapin was U.S. secretary of commerce. He had been, and would soon return to being, the top executive of the Hudson Motor Car Co. He was also a major investor in the Detroit Union Guardian group and good friend of both Henry and Edsel Ford.

try.[22] In January 1933, when funds were needed for the Guardian Group, Charles Stewart Mott and Chapin were engaged in correspondence. Mott asked Chapin to communicate with Olds and have him "do his duty" by supplying the amount that Mott believed was Olds's responsibility.[23]

Chapin even managed to be on good terms with both Edsel Ford and his father. Henry Ford generally was suspicious of any friend of Edsel, but Chapin seems to have been an exception. The exchange between Chapin and James Couzens that centered on a Hudson Motor Company advertisement claimed that Hudson co-founder Howard Coffin was the "foremost engineer" in the automotive industry.[24] Couzens took exception, loyally maintaining that Henry Ford was the "foremost automotive engineer." The apparent dispute obviously had no effect on the relationship between Chapin and Henry or Edsel Ford. In fact, Chapin served as a witness in a 1926 Ford tax case, giving very positive remarks about Henry Ford, correctly noting that Ford's ideas about standardization of design to lower costs per unit produced" had created a precedent ... now being followed in all American businesses."[25] On October 14, 1929, when Henry Ford held his celebratory inauguration of the Edison Institute and the Henry Ford Museum and Greenfield Village, Chapin was one of the hosts. This was a very important event for Henry Ford, with President Herbert Hoover presiding over the ceremonies. Ford was clever in linking himself to the fiftieth anniversary of the light bulb, honoring Charles Edison. For such a significant event, Ford invited only guests and hosts of whom he approved, Chapin being one.

In the following month, Chapin wrote a letter to Henry Ford recommending a *Saturday Evening Post* article about Albert Einstein, and also included a booklet, which he thought Ford would find agreeable.[26] It was a habit of Chapin to send articles with which he agreed to associates. Considering all that has been written about Henry Ford it seems that he was not likely to receive an article about Albert Einstein with any great enthusiasm. Chapin's presumption of Ford's interest, and the forwarding of suggested reading materials, seems to indicate a high degree of familiarity between the two men.

The relationship between Roy D. Chapin and Henry Ford is further substantiated in an exchange of letters between Chapin biographer J.C. Long and Arthur Ballantine. Ballantine was undersecretary of the treasury and, along with Chapin, was a special emissary of President Herbert Hoover to meet with Henry Ford to seek his support in preventing the impending banking collapse in Detroit. Ballantine, refers to Henry Ford as a "very good friend" of Chapin.[27]

In his friendship with Edsel Ford, Chapin bridged the gap between Edsel and Henry Ford as industry spokesperson when Chapin headed the National Automobile Chamber of Commerce.[28] Henry Ford refused to join the organization, contrary to Edsel's inclination. But Chapin, realizing that leaving the Ford Motor Company out of any issue relating to the auto industry would have been foolhardy, always touched base with Henry Ford and often included Edsel Ford as a member of a delegation.[29] When the Chapins moved into a larger home in 1927, among the friends who temporarily loaned furniture and accessories to the Chapins were the families of Edsel Ford and Ernest Kanzler.[30] Among those present at the railway station to welcome him home after Chapin had been nominated to be secretary of commerce were both Edsel Ford and Ernest Kanzler.

Given his personality and friendships, and as a prominent auto industry pioneer and successful entrepreneur, it is not surprising to find that when the Guardian Group was in its formative stages, Roy D. Chapin was very much involved.[31] This association was public knowledge and Chapin's name was listed along with other automotive leaders in news stories about the Guardian Group,[32] and also later when the Universal Credit Corporation was formed to finance the sales of Ford Motor Company vehicles.[33] Considering the enormous success and profitability that Ford had achieved from 1908 to 1927, the investors in the Guardian Group no doubt anticipated that the use of the UCC to finance Ford dealers and consumers would result in significant earnings for their banking organization. In this they were correct, at least until the spring of 1933, when Henry Ford ordered the sale of UCC.[34]

The resolution of Henry Ford to sell the UCC is one more example of how he, and not Edsel, was the ultimate decision maker for the Ford Motor Company. It also confirms the relationship of the UCC to the Ford Motor Company. The UCC, upon its founding, had been publicly identified as "an affiliated special organization controlled by the Ford Motor Company,"[35] meaning that Roy D. Chapin, Alvan Macauley, C. Ledyard Mitchell, Charles Stewart Mott, R.E. Olds and the other non–Ford auto executives' relationship with the Ford Motor Company was a matter of public record.

At its peak, "the UCC is reported to have had a gross business of $200,000,000 in installment sales of Fords, Fordsons, and Lincolns."[36] The use of a financing arm to provide for consumer installment purchases of Ford products and financing for dealer purchases from Ford was very important. The sales resistance to the continued production of the Model T, which had necessitated the introduction of the Model A, occurred at about the same time that most first-time buyers of vehicles had made their selections. From 1927 onward, new car sales were replacement sales, when young people qualified to buy, or when the new "two-car family" began to emerge.[37] It was also when used cars, having been accepted for trade-in credit on new cars, began to affect automobile sales.

Despite the fact that the Ford assembly line was capable of producing one car "every 10 seconds, for a total of 9,575 in a single day,"[38] Henry Ford had resisted the idea of installment buying. But economic forces had created the need for "a social invention no less novel than the assembly line,"[39] which was the installment purchase plan. A significant change in personal finances was in the process of taking place. Previously, a family might have considered debt as a limiting factor. Unlike a society dependent on the vagaries of agricultural income, the concurrent changes of urbanization and industrialization provided people with the opportunity to count on a regular source of income. Being able to forecast a likely income over a period of time led to an enormous shift in thinking. Now an individual or family had credit, not debt. With the advent of installment buying, and the acceptance of credit, cars began to be sold on the ability of the purchaser to make a monthly payment rather than his ability to pay immediately the total sales price.

Chapin's involvement in the Guardian Group, and thus by extension in the Universal Credit Corporation, brings up an interesting issue. His own company, Hudson, used the Commercial Investment Trust (CIT) to finance sales of Hudson and Essex vehicles. Today, Chapin's personal investment in the Guardian Group, which was closely associated with the Ford Motor Company, and his indirect investment in the UCC, were obvious conflicts of interest with his responsibilities at Hudson. While he was in a position to profit from sales of Ford products, the minority stockholders of Hudson did not have the same advantage. Did the others who had invested in Hudson, perhaps due to Chapin's reputation, know that as a founder of the Guardian Group, his interests and energies were not totally devoted to Hudson Motor Car issues? As previously mentioned, Chapin was actively involved in Guardian Group stock pool arrangements. Family employment is a further indicator of interest and influence. Like Alvan Macauley of Packard, whose son was assistant cashier of the Guardian Detroit Bank,[40] Chapin's younger brother-in-law, Carsten Tiedeman, was employed at the Universal Credit Corporation.[41]

Chapin was also an investor in the REO Motorcar Company, Ransom Olds's second company that was a direct, but mostly inept, competitor with Chapin's own company.[42] This is not to say that Chapin had a unique ethical problem. His activities are representative of the period. Alfred P. Sloan, Jr., of General Motors, for example, was an early investor in the Nash Motor Car Company.[43] The other automotive Guardian Group directors had the same the same conflicts of interest as did Chapin. For instance, Charles Stewart Mott, a vice president of General Motors, benefited from the sale of Ford products via the Universal Credit Corporation, while his own company financed sales through the General Motors Acceptance Corporation. Alvan Macauley and the others from Packard, and C. Ledyard Mitchell from Chrysler gained from their firms' sales through the Commercial Credit Corporation, and also from Ford sales via the UCC.[44] Clearly the partners in the Guardian Group had a clubby arrangement. In the auto industry they were supposedly competitors, but in the Guardian Group and its subsidiary the Universal Credit Corporation, they were partners.

While greatly involved in matters outside the Hudson Motor Car Company, Chapin exhibited successful leadership of that firm. As Hudson had moved upward in pricing, Chapin formed a separate company to produce a lower-priced car, the Essex. This proved to be a success and led to Hudson's change from a closely held corporation to one listed on the stock exchanges. This move resulted in a great financial return to Chapin and his fellow executives at Hudson. But the most significant innovation for which Chapin was responsible was the introduction of the low-priced closed car in 1922.[45] As Alfred P. Sloan, Jr., of General Motors later wrote, "Such a development was no doubt inevitable."[46] But innovative ideas

Not every innovative idea looks revolutionary. The famed Ford Model T, ungainly in appearance, with profound effects in countless ways, was a case in point. So too was the box-like Essex Coach. While less significant than the Model T, it was an important product that affected automobile production and marketing. The $100 price differential between the Coach, a closed car, and the open touring car at $1,045 was much less than had formerly been the case. The simple lines of the Essex Coach lowered production costs and created a market for a moderate priced closed car. In turn, the season for selling new cars could become year-round. This improved employment stability and provided a more economical use of auto production facilities. Combined with the possibility of financing auto purchases by companies established for that purpose, the less expensive closed car changed the automobile market. Hudson and Essex production increased from around 28,000 in 1922 to almost 89,000 in 1923. An increase took place each year through 1927. Roy D. Chapin, as the leader of Hudson and Essex, personified the innovative idea of the automobile industry. His standing in the auto industry and national prominence led to his appointment as secretary of commerce in the last days of the Hoover administration (*The Saturday Evening Post*, 17 February 1923).

often seem that way once they have been introduced. Sloan went on to admit that the introduction of the Essex coach, as it was called, influenced General Motors as it was developing plans to introduce its new car, the Pontiac.[47] But the Essex coach had a much wider impact on the auto industry, and consumer trends. As Chapin's friend Edsel Ford noted: "That changed the public's buying habits. In the days of the open car, most of the selling was in the spring and summer. A good many plants closed down for half the year, but people would buy the closed car in any season. It stabilized the industry, and put us on an all-year basis."[48]

Coming at the same time that installment purchases became popular, the effect for Detroit and other auto producing areas was very beneficial. Year-round work meant a steady source of income for a community, while for the individual worker it meant both a steady income and wage, and fewer periods spent in the uncertainties of reemployment. As Harry Bennett noted: "It was the custom in the industry, when changing models, to pay everyone off and close down the plant. Upon reopening, all the men would be rehired at the flat rate. Thus, a man who might have worked his way up to $8.00 or even $10.00 per day, would be rehired at the wage of a beginner."[49]

The ability to produce and sell cars throughout the year put an end to the winter layoffs that had been the industry practice. The introduction of the Essex two-door coach, when combined with the advent of installment payments for cars, had a multiplier effect in increasing both the availability and the demand for a totally new product — the low-priced, closed car. The introduction of the Essex coach in 1922 followed a sharp period of deflation and recession in 1920–21. The opening of a totally new market, on a year-round basis, fueled by easy payment plans helped to create a large expansion in the purchases of durable goods.

Of course, Chapin simply wanted to gain market share for his company, but his actions had many substantial effects, which enhanced his already growing reputation. Adding to Chapin's reputation was the introduction of a new car line, the Terraplane, during the doldrums of the Depression summer of 1932. Amelia Earhart, the famed aviator, was engaged to assist in the introduction, while pioneer aviator Orville Wright took delivery of the first production Terraplane. The connection with aviation, both with the name and the involvement of Earhart and Wright, were purposeful. The name Terraplane was copyrighted and said to refer to "the plane that skims the earth."[50] The aviation connection was considered, at the time, to have been an innovative and successful advertising gimmick by Chapin. One month after the introduction of the Terraplane, Chapin agreed to become secretary of commerce in the Hoover administration.

Smoothing the way for Chapin was Arthur Vandenberg, junior U.S.

senator from Michigan. He approved of Chapin being in Hoover's cabinet. In the process, while he agreed that Chapin would be great for secretary of commerce, he actually suggested Chapin to head the Reconstruction Finance Corporation![51] Had Hoover followed that suggestion, the possible complications are mind-boggling. The first thought that comes to mind is that Roy Chapin, a partner in the Guardian Group, would have received a request from his partners to provide another loan underwritten by the U.S. government via the RFC. A political firestorm would have resulted. Fortunately, Hoover selected Chapin for the commerce position. Even as Secretary of commerce, Chapin did not escape a key role in the significant economic and political crisis culminating in the closure of all banks throughout the U.S. Had he been head of the RFC, and the Guardian Group had requested a third loan from that organization, it is difficult to exaggerate the enormity of the consequences. As it was, only Abraham Lincoln, inaugurated 72 years earlier on another March 4, faced a graver crisis than did Franklin Roosevelt.

Chapin's appointment as secretary of commerce recognized the importance of the automobile industry. John North Willys, appointed as U.S. ambassador to Poland in 1930, was the only previous president of an automobile company elevated to a significant government post. But Willys was posted off in Warsaw in a largely ceremonial position. In contrast, Chapin was taking over the cabinet position which Herbert Hoover had helped to define. He was also taking over at a crucial time, only months before the U.S. was to choose between the incumbent Hoover and his main challenger, Franklin D. Roosevelt.

As Chapin knew, the reelection of Hoover was not a certainty. All around the nation, 1932 was the year in which Depression conditions seemed to be getting worse. In his home area of Detroit, on March 7, 1932, only ten days after the new Ford V8 had come off the assembly line, violence had taken place at the huge River Rouge Ford plant, resulting in the deaths of four men and injuries to many others. The trouble had flared as several thousand men, led by Communist organizers, had staged a march for jobs and relief.[52] With no work and no assistance available, radical ideas had begun to sound plausible.

Taking advantage of poor working conditions in the auto industry and weak efforts by national union organizations, beginning in 1928 Communist organizers began publication of the *Ford Worker, Packard Worker, Dodge Worker, Fisher Body Worker*, and *Hudson Worker*.[53] The conditions were ripe for exploitation throughout the nation but in Detroit the Depression hit about twice as hard as elsewhere in the nation.[54] By the beginning of 1933, one-third of all wage earners in Detroit had been totally or partly unemployed for over four years in succession, while 200,000 dependents were on the city relief rolls and another 154,000 abandoned everything and left Detroit.[55]

Chapin was certainly well aware of the conditions in Detroit. However, it is doubtful that he was prepared for what he found in Washington, D.C., when he met with President Hoover on August 3 to discuss the commerce position. In the capital city the situation was extremely unsettled. Conditions were only beginning to return to some type of normality following the use of U.S. Army infantry, cavalry, and tanks to disperse about 2,000 veterans of World War I. During late May and early June of 1932, over fifteen thousand veterans had arrived in Washington in what was called "The Bonus March." The self-styled "Bonus Expeditionary Force" had petitioned Congress for immediate payment in full funds that were due its members in 1945. Congress split on the issue, the Senate defeating a bill for immediate payment. The throngs of veterans, some with families, had camped out in tidal areas of the Potomac River and in some abandoned World War I buildings. The despair of the veterans, the usual heat and humidity of July in Washington, D.C., and the conditions in the mud flats where they camped created a very touchy situation. Fear of potential problems found realization when in the evening of July 28 and the morning of July 29, Communist agitators, looking for a situation to exploit, provoked the police. In panic, the police shot into a crowd and killed two people. Within hours President Hoover ordered the army to suppress what appeared to be a riot. Under the leadership of Army Chief of Staff Douglas Mac Arthur and his aide Major Dwight Eisenhower, the soldiers advanced on the veterans with bayonets and tear gas. In the confusion that followed, one seven-year-old boy had his leg pierced by bayonet and one three month old baby died of tear gas inhalation.[56]

Violence in Detroit and violence in Washington, D.C., were representative of the crisis in social order in the United States during the summer of 1932. Despite, or perhaps because of, the conditions of the time,

Chapin accepted the position of secretary of commerce. There is no record of how the events in Washington affected him, but Chapin did write to his father-in-law, "It is going to be awfully hard work, but if I can help I want to give what I can."[57]

There was no doubt that Chapin's appointment was due to his leadership at the Hudson Motor Car Company. The economic power of the auto industry was evident to all, and Hudson, as an independent firm not directly allied with the mega corporations of Ford, General Motors or Chrysler, demonstrated the outstanding leadership of Chapin. The very fact that Hudson existed, while many other firms had failed, was a measure of success.

The importance and power of the auto industry, when combined with the fantastic growth it had demonstrated in a period of about thirty years, seemed to imbue auto executives with almost-mythological qualities of leadership and foresight. In commenting on Chapin's appointment, one writer said:

> Mr. Hoover showed great political sagacity of the broader sort in naming an automobile man to the post. Businessmen are apt to feel that automobile men as a class are live wires. The motor makers have been consistent exponents of international trade. In domestic trade they stand for the newest and best in production and sales.[58]

Chapin was said to have "put the sex in Essex," and "was a welcome symbol of a still vigorous American industry [that] would build a new model car at the very bottom of the Depression."[59] *Time* called Chapin "breezy, bustling, ambitious," as well as "compact, kinetic, [and] quick-spoken,"[60] all meant as positive qualities. The same article went on to say:

> The President needs a more active, hustle-bustling figure to dramatize any business recovery, no matter how small, which might come before the election. Mr. Chapin's appointment not only seemed to clinch Michigan for the Hoover-Curtis ticket but, of more importance to open the automobile industry's moneybags to the G.O.P. campaign.[61]

Hoover certainly had his reasons for appointing Chapin to the position of secretary of commerce, some of which were just noted. In addition, Chapin's predecessor had simply worn out, and had used up his relevance by continued optimistic statements about business recovery in the third year of the Depression. Chapin, in contrast, was an actual producer of consumer goods for the mass market. While Hudson sales were faltering, the introduction of the Terraplane was a bold move that lent credence to Chapin's opinions regarding the economy. His leadership of Hudson had demonstrated management and organizational skills and he had significant business contacts beyond the auto industry and throughout the nation.

As early as 1930 Hoover had attempted to get Chapin to enter the cabinet. In fact, he was offered the post of undersecretary of war.[62] This was an important post but perhaps being an undersecretary was not appealing to Chapin. However, being undersecretary of the Navy had been beneficial in the political careers of both Theodore and Franklin Roosevelt. A cabinet position was important, as Chapin's friends had long known of his political ambitions and interest in public office.[63]

Being secretary of commerce, even in the midst of a Depression and for an increasingly unpopular president, was another matter. President Hoover, after all, had risen from secretary of commerce to the presidency. If Hoover was reelected, Chapin might take some credit, as his major function was to speak on behalf of the administration in attempting to make up for Hoover's well-documented deficiencies as an orator.[64] If, as did happen, Hoover lost, then Chapin had done his duty as a good Republican, and might find his commerce duties qualifying him for other political positions.

Chapin was sworn in on August 8, 1932, while Congress was in recess. Approval by the Senate did not come until December 15, approximately one month after the defeat of Herbert Hoover. Despite the rancor of the times and Senate opposition to other Hoover appointments, Chapin's appointment was by unanimous consent,[65] including, of course, the vote of Sen. James Couzens of Michigan.

As previously noted, Chapin's major task as secretary of commerce was to support Hoover's campaign for reelection. The only major initiative, in one of the worst years of the Depression, that seems to have been cosponsored by Chapin was the "share-the-work" program. This voluntary plan was designed to have employers hire more workers, but split the amount of work. The plan went nowhere. Carrying out his real duty as a spokesperson for the administration, Chapin started out by meeting with reporters. He spun some platitudes with a positive viewpoint, but did not go out on a limb in making predictions.[66] In the months leading up to the presidential election, Chapin pursued the theme that economic conditions were improving. In September he authored a *New York Times* article that said, "The downward tendency has been checked and the general picture is favorable."[67] In October he noted that "indications of improving business were visible in many lines,"[68] and that there were "indications the worst of the depression has passed."[69]

In an October 1932 interview, a *New York Times* columnist returned to Chapin's connection with the auto industry. The auto industry was described as "one of the greatest in the country," and Chapin as "one of its outstanding figures."[70] Chapin was described as "tall, well-built, with a face round and ruddy," having a "make-up and manner ... [that] typifies the successful business executive.... He exudes energy and purpose, he instills confidence, he displays enthusiasm."[71] In one of the last newspaper articles, appearing the Sunday immediately preceding election day, Chapin's article "Winning the War on Hard Times" continued on the theme that conditions were improving.

> The significant fact, for us today is that the trend is no longer downward. We have passed the stage of fear-struck bewilderment that until a few months ago handicapped every effort to progress. We have regained a sense of consideration in our destiny and are in a position to hasten the working of natural forces in our behavior.[72]

Chapin's prediction was to prove completely incorrect. But he was being the good cabinet and Republican Party man, probably having his name placed on articles he did not actually write, but containing views that he approved. The articles that appeared with his name, the interviews he gave to reporters, and the speeches he made to groups and over national radio networks were addressed to the conservative and business core of the Republican Party. Chapin's role was not to convert, but to keep a particular constituency from staying home, or voting for Franklin Roosevelt.

Loyalty to Herbert Hoover and the Republican Party were evident in all of Chapin's official pronouncements, except about Prohibition. As a resident of Michigan, Chapin could witness the ease by in getting liquor from Canada and for that reason, as well as for the practical, vote-getting reason, he advised Hoover to revise his position.[73] Chapin could feel free to make such a suggestion to Hoover, for in every other way Chapin was a conforming member of the Hoover cabinet. No Catholic, Jew, or South-erner was to be found in Hoover's cabinet. All of the members tended to have had experience in administration, and most of them were self-made millionaires.[74]

Within the Hoover administration was the "athletic group," which met three or four mornings each week at the White House and took part in "Hoover Ball," which involved tossing a large medicine ball over a net, somewhat in the manner of volleyball. This activity was followed by a breakfast in the White House. Chapin became an immediate member, which signified his close relationship with the president.

Whatever Chapin's motivations in becoming secretary of commerce, it seems that he had not factored in the continuing decline in auto pro-duction and sales. In 1929, Hudson corporate profits reached approxi-mately $11.5 million. In 1930 the profit had slipped to about $325,000. By 1931, Hudson reported a loss of almost $2 million. The next year the company lost almost $5.5 million and for a third year in a row Hudson lost money again in 1933, this time about $4.4 million.[75] Responding to the problems at Hudson, Chapin resumed the presidency only eleven weeks after leaving Washington, D.C.[76] He immediately faced the prospect of suppliers threatening legal action over payments, a bank loan of $800,000 being due, and an ominous announcement by the Commercial Investment Trust that it might refuse to finance new car sales. Chapin even believed that some competitors were attempting to close down Hudson, or to take advantage of the situation by gaining control of the company.[77] All told, Hudson needed about $6 million to continue in operation. From the time he returned to Hudson in May 1933 until May 1935, Chapin was involved in using his many business contacts and his personal and business repu-tations, to put his company back on track. But the long hours, constant travel, and nonstop negotiations took a toll. When Hudson returned to profitability in 1935, Chapin's role in the industry in representation and lobbying in Washington, D.C., resumed. He was once again a determined advocate for the auto industry. On February 16, 1936, he died of pneu-monia.

No doubt Roy D. Chapin accepted the position of secretary of com-merce with mixed motives. Certainly he was a believer in the policies of the Republican Party, and was a loyal member. He seems to have harbored some political ambitions, and he was not alone in thinking that Hoover's policies would solve the business slump and end the Great Depression. In his single most important assignment as secretary of commerce, Chapin certainly had many reasons to secure Henry Ford's cooperation to prevent the failure of the Guardian Group. While he and many others thought they understood the seriousness of the situation, the scope of the resulting nationwide bank failures and the political consequences were beyond all of their known experiences. As a result, the failure of the Guardian Union Group in February 1933 affected the balance of power between the private and public sectors. At the same time, the consequences of the bank closures changed the expectations and fortunes of many Americans, including those of Roy D. Chapin.

5

"Woe unto Those by Whom It Cometh"

When the February 9 meeting at the White House failed to enlist Sen. James Couzens in the proposed pool arrangement, there were still some possibilities of preventing the Guardian Group failure in Detroit. Secretary of Commerce Roy D. Chapin and Undersecretary of the Treasury Arthur A. Ballantine headed to Detroit to meet with Henry Ford.[1] President Hoover was scheduled to make a Lincoln Day address in New York City on the February 12, and before leaving Washington he phoned Henry Ford to arrange for the Ballantine and Chapin meeting. Ford agreed to see both men, but would not agree to any more than that.[2]

On the 11th, President Hoover met with Atlee Pomerene, the chairman of the RFC. He told Pomerene that the funds necessary to prevent the panic were insignificant compared with the serious consequences likely to result if Guardian folded. He asked that an emergency loan be made and announced on Tuesday, February 14.[3] This was never done, and no adequate explanation can be found to explain the inaction. It is possible that the RFC board members did not wish to open themselves up to personal liability for a loan. They had previously been told such a loan would be clearly illegal.[4] Furthermore, circumstances leading to the bank failure were taking place at a greater speed than the responses of private individuals, government representatives and agencies. The situation was without precedent, and no mechanism was in place for unified action. At this point in United States history, the role and responsibility of the federal government in such situations had not been assumed or assigned.

Meetings to prevent a financial crisis had resumed in Washington on February 10. The Federal Reserve Board, the RFC, the secretary of the treasury, and the comptroller of currency met separately and together as they attempted to come up with ideas to support the Guardian Group. On the 11th, Jesse Jones of the RFC introduced a motion to make a full loan to the Guardian, but the other RFC board members voted it down. Jones's action seems to have been independent of, and without knowledge of, Hoover's request to chairman Pomerene on the same day. Earlier on the 11th, Walter P. Chrysler of the Chrysler Corporation and Alfred P. Sloan of GM had a breakfast meeting with President Hoover and reiterated their earlier million-dollar pledges. By themselves the pledges of Sloan for GM and Walter Chrysler for his firm were insufficient to resolve the crisis. The pledges were symbolic and conditional. That is, both Sloan and Chrysler would assist in preventing the Guardian closure, but they would not take on the risks of leadership. It is probable that both men were fully informed of the relationship between the Ford Motor Company and the Guardian Group, knowing that Edsel Ford was the majority investor in the Guardian.

Meanwhile in Detroit at the February 10 meeting called by Alfred Leyburn, were representatives of the Guardian Group, and executives from Detroit Edison, the Packard Motor Car Company, the department store J.L. Hudson Company, General Motors and the Chrysler Corporation.[5] On hand during part of the two and a half days of the meeting were GM Chairman Alfred P. Sloan, Jr. and Donaldson Brown, vice president and chief financial officer. Walter P. Chrysler and B.E. Hutchison, the vice president and treasurer, represented the Chrysler Corporation. The Ford Motor Company was represented by Ernest Liebold. Ernest Kanzler was also on hand for the Guardian Group,[6] along with Clifford Longley, his law firm partner Henry E. Bodman, and others.[7] At the time, Longley was president of the Union Guardian Trust Company. Bodman was present in a dual role. He was chairman of the board of the Union Guardian Trust Company and also general counsel and a director of Packard.[8]

The meeting was fluid, with people entering and leaving. At least three top executives representing New York banks arrived on Monday February 13, while two Chicago banking executives were also present. Among those on hand were executives of the banks from which Edsel Ford had borrowed money to support the Guardian Group. Nobody seemed to know who invited the out-of-town bankers, or how they had learned of the meeting.[9] One additional dynamic of the meeting, was that communications with people outside of the meeting were constant, including calls to and from Washington, D.C. Other calls were local. One source has reported that the Ford representative, presumably Ernest Liebold, called Henry Ford and informed him of Sen. James Couzens's remark of February 9 about "shouting from the housetops."[10]

It is evident, from the importance of those attending, that the seriousness of the Guardian Group's financial status was fully comprehended. But the participants had to consider the entire situation in Detroit. The banking problem, while of immense importance, was only one element of the worsening conditions in Detroit.

If those involved in the meeting had turned on their radios, each Sunday afternoon and evening they would have heard the Rev. Charles Coughlin fulminating against "banksters." Coughlin had a radio broadcast emanating from a Detroit suburb with a large national audience, and he spoke about the social, political, and economic issues of the day. At the height of his popularity he received 80,000 letters a week.[11] Known popularly as "Father Coughlin," Coughlin spoke in opposition to the same Eastern money interests as Henry Ford, in favor of silver inflationary economic policies, and against both the gold standard and an alleged conspiracy involving international banking.

If you missed Coughlin's radio broadcasts, newspaper accounts, especially in the *Detroit Free Press,* were frequent. That paper carried on a running editorial critique of Coughlin, partially in defense of the paper's publisher, who was also involved in the Detroit Bankers Group, the other half of the duopoly that controlled Detroit banking.[12] Coughlin did not let any criticism of him pass without a strong response, and in his verbal battle with the Detroit Bankers Group he lumped all banks into the same category. Jesse Jones of the RFC noted Coughlin's effect and concluded that each Monday morning there were an increasing number of withdrawals by small depositors in Michigan banks,[13] evidence of a declining lack of trust in the banks and banking.

By February 1933, Detroit had been suffering for a number of years. In the fall of 1931, it was estimated that one person was dying of starvation every seven hours and fifteen minutes in Detroit. Additionally, four people per day whose starvation symptoms could not be reversed were accepted at Receiving Hospital. Mayor Frank Murphy stated that around

200,000 persons had been out of work since 1932, "with large number of suicides not being reported in the newspapers."[14]

To further increase the difficulties in Michigan, on January 11, 1933, a strike had started at the Briggs Manufacturing Company,[15] where 43 percent of Ford Motor Company auto bodies were produced.[16] By the end of January the strike had spread to the Hayes Body plant in Grand Rapids and additional Briggs plants. Six to ten thousand men were on strike in response to disregarded safety regulations and forced pay reductions. The Murray Body Company, where a strike had been threatened, was abruptly shut down. One effect of the strike was the shutdown of the assembly lines at Ford, putting another 45,000 men out of work and stopping the delivery of new cars. The Auto Workers' Union led by the Communist Party, not to be confused with the later United Auto Workers, claimed to be leading the strikes. The same leadership was behind a strike at Hudson on January 30, along with strikes at nine other Detroit auto plants in the same time period. After negotiations, the Hudson strike ended February 13.[17] Despite labor unrest in other auto related plants, Henry Ford chose to focus only on his own problems and believed the Briggs strikes were caused by rival industrial interests.[18] This was a claim he would make again when he and Edsel Ford met with Ballantine and Chapin.

Like Roy D. Chapin, Arthur A. Ballantine, who accompanied Chapin to meet with Henry and Edsel Ford, was an insider in the Hoover administration. He belonged to the breakfast and exercising group that met informally with President Hoover several times a week.[19] His relationship with Hoover led to direct communications with the president, often bypassing the protocol of going through the secretary of the treasury, Ogden Mills. Ballantine was among those who had suggested that Henry Ford and James Couzens form a pool to support a third RFC loan to the Guardian Group.

Whether Henry Ford knew of the pool proposal is unknown. Considering the widespread distribution of Couzens's remarks at the White House meeting "to scream from the housetops," it is quite possible that other information from the White House meeting of February 9 might have reached the attention of Henry Ford. If so, that would have negatively predisposed Henry Ford's views of Arthur Ballantine. Henry Ford already knew that Roy D. Chapin was not just a representative of President Hoover, but was also a partner in the Guardian Group, with great financial interests at risk. No doubt his suspicions were aroused at Chapin's involvement. What he might have known about Arthur A. Ballantine would have greatly fueled Ford's penchant for imagining in conspiracies.

Ballantine, a Wall Street lawyer, represented much that Henry Ford seemed to dislike. Ballantine's professional life included connections with

Arthur A. Ballantine, as undersecretary of the treasury during the last years of Herbert Hoover's administration, was very well connected. A graduate of Harvard, Ballantine did not think highly of Franklin D. Roosevelt, who had been a staff member on the Harvard *Crimson* when Ballantine was editor. According to his descendants, he later admitted he had underestimated FDR's political skills. In government service, he was known as an expert on taxes. The law firm in which he was a partner had one two-time candidate for the U.S. presidency (Thomas Dewey), and another who was secretary of war in both a Republican (Taft) and Democratic (FDR) administration, and secretary of state for Herbert Hoover. An earlier partner was secretary of war (for McKinley and T. Roosevelt) and later secretary of state for T. Roosevelt, and then awarded the Nobel Peace Prize. While serving as undersecretary of the treasury, Ballantine was in the close group of advisors who met with President Hoover for breakfast. Arthur A. Ballantine was involved in the banking crisis of 1933 into the administration of Franklin Roosevelt (Herbert Hoover Presidential Library).

the Eastern establishment, beginning with his graduation from Harvard University. At Harvard he was editor of *The Crimson*, while Franklin Roosevelt was a member of the staff.[20] But Ballantine's World War I work as a special adviser to the U.S. Treasury on the collection of special war taxes from industry would have been important to Henry Ford. No industrialist had welcomed the special war taxes imposed during the Great War, least of all Henry Ford. Ballantine then became a solicitor of what was then known as the Bureau of Internal Revenue, and served as counsel to a congressional committee on taxation.[21]

Henry Ford could have learned about Ballantine from a number of sources, including Harry Bennett or Ernest Liebold. Sometime prior to the Ballantine and Chapin meeting, Bennett had informed Henry Ford that he had learned of the impending banking crisis. The consequence was a meeting, at Ford's insistence, of Ford, Ernest Liebold, Clifford Longley, Bennett and a state bank examiner. In this meeting Ford found out the worst — his deposits were unavailable.[22]

Deeply involved as he was, Longley certainly knew who Ballantine was. Bennett would have relished the task of providing information, but the key informant was probably Ernest Liebold. He had been assigned the job of representing Henry Ford and the Ford Motor Company in the February 10 meeting called by Alfred Leyburn.[23] When Ballantine and Chapin arrived in Detroit on February 11 they reported to the Leyburn meeting underway in the Guardian Group building. In the meeting, as well as through other sources, Liebold had ample opportunity to get relevant information about Arthur Ballantine.

In fact, keeping Henry Ford informed was one of Ernest Liebold's duties. Liebold maintained an office in the Ford Motor Company, but he was actually a personal employee of Henry Ford.[24] Around 1910, Liebold had been hired by James Couzens and was soon assigned to keep Ford's personal finances in order, which he did with great efficiency. After Couzens left, Liebold's authority is said to have increased.[25]

Along the way, Liebold gained power of attorney for both Henry and Clara Ford.[26] Representing Henry Ford at the February 10 meeting was not new for Ernest Liebold. He had regularly been assigned to various high-level meetings and missions on behalf of Henry Ford or the Ford Motor Company. Liebold was considered to be an efficient and competent financial manager. Henry Ford placed great trust in the judgment of Ernest Liebold and their professional relationship lasted for thirty-four years.

In gathering information, Liebold could also have found that Arthur A. Ballantine had been a member of the very prestigious Wall Street law firm headed by Elihu Root.[27] In an extraordinary career, Root was a Nobel Peace Prize winner who served in three administrations, both Republican and Democratic. He had been secretary of war for William McKinley, secretary of state for Theodore Roosevelt and ambassador extraordinary to Russia for Woodrow Wilson. Furthermore, Henry L. Stimson, a partner in the Root and Clark law firm, served as secretary of state in the Hoover administration. Stimson had previously been secretary of war for two years under William Howard Taft, and governor-general of the Philippines from 1927 to 1929 for Calvin Coolidge. (Stimson would later serve as secretary of war from 1940 through 1965, for Franklin Roosevelt and Harry S. Truman.) When Herbert Hoover selected Arthur Ballantine for the Treasury Department he was obtaining direct and influential connections with the international finance wing of the Republican Party. Even though he was successfully involved in foreign trade and finance, Henry Ford's belief system led him to suspect people who had the connections of Root, Stimson, and Ballantine.

Ballantine's background also included connections to the auto industry. While at the Root law firm, Ballantine had represented the Dodge Brothers auto company when the Chrysler Corporation purchased Dodge from the New York investment firm Dillon Reed.[28] The process by which Chrysler had obtained Dodge was quite complicated, requiring considerable financial deftness by all of the parties involved. The entire agreement was contrary to the favored Ford notion of paying or demanding cash in large transactions. The complexities of the Dodge deal were such that Henry Ford's suspicions of Wall Street and investment bankers would have been aroused and confirmed.

If Ford knew of Ballantine's role in Chrysler's acquisition of Dodge it would have provoked great concern about the man himself. After all, here was a Wall Street lawyer who had helped to arrange the growth of the rival Chrysler Corporation, sent by the president of the United States with the intent to seek funds to back what was clearly a banking operation in distress. In Ford's conspiratorial world-view, evil machinations were always at work attempting to seize or ruin the Ford Motor Company. With the creation of the Chrysler Corporation, which now included the respected Dodge line, Ballantine had helped to create a direct competitor of the Ford Motor Company. In 1932, Ford production totaled 290,773 vehicles. General Motors led at 306,716 and the new Chrysler Corporation had a significant 204,416.[29] By contrast, the Hudson Motor Company did not represent a threat to Ford, having a production total of 25,202 Essex and Hudson vehicles in 1932.[30] To Henry Ford, Roy D. Chapin was both known and familiar, but Arthur A. Ballantine was quite a different matter.

There is no doubt that the situation in Detroit was extremely serious. This was confirmed on February 12 when the head of the Detroit Bankers Group put a call in to the White House. The other half of the banking duopoly had just been informed of the financial problems of the Guardian Group. The call to the White House was a call for assistance. The premise was very simple. If the Guardian folded, the run on the Detroit Bankers Group banks would be immediate and disastrous. To respond to this possibility, the Detroit Bankers Group was asking for an immediate RFC loan of $200 million in cash.[31] The RFC board refused the loan application but gave no reasons for its actions.[32]

Meanwhile, the two days of meetings called by Alfred Leyburn had not come up with sufficient funds or a workable plan to prevent the Guardian Group from failing. No help seemed to be forthcoming from Washington, so increased importance was placed on the meeting scheduled with Henry and Edsel Ford for the 13th. If Henry Ford would subordinate $7.5 million on deposit in the Guardian Group, a plan could be enacted to solve the immediate crisis. The president of the Ford Motor Company, Edsel Ford, was not asked to make the decision. Instead, it was Henry Ford, the majority shareholder and a founder of the company who was asked to take action.

Before Chapin and Ballantine could meet with Henry Ford, a significant series of events took place that eventually destroyed the belief that the automobile executives worked in concert to support mutually beneficial decisions. Old friendships were tested, and suspicions within the automobile industry increased to the point that interested outside observers began to take notice.

The Guardian Group was an example of how executives from Ford, Packard, REO, Hudson, Chrysler, General Motors and the major body manufacturers had been partners, further cementing social relationships that had begun in the earliest days of the industry. This concert of interest situation had given the appearance of a solid and unified industry. Now, the problems of the Guardian Group gave opportunities to the growing industrial union movement. As cracks and fissures developed between and among the various auto companies and their executives, the leaders of the industrial union movement watched carefully. Within several years they would institute a new strategy to gain recognition by targeting one auto corporation at a time.

Edsel Ford's loans to the Guardian Group were the cause of the difficulties. The impending failure of the Guardian Group put great stress on each investor, and on their partnership. The largest individual investor in the Guardian Group was Edsel Ford, and a commensurate amount of pressure fell on him. He was the first to take action for his own protection, leaving his partners to develop their own solutions.

Ernest Liebold is quoted as saying that Edsel Ford, fearing a personal financial disaster, had confided his situation to him. In the process, Edsel broke down crying, saying, "Well, I'm cleaned. All the Continental Bank has to do is to call me on my note and that will clean me of all I've got."[33] What he was talking about was the $2.5 million loan he had obtained on his own credit, which he then loaned to the Guardian Group.[34] He had also provided other loans to the Guardian of $1 million in cash and $5 million in U.S. government Liberty Bonds.[35] Richard Bak, in his book *Henry and Edsel*, states that Henry Ford gave orders for Liebold to take Ford Motor Company funds and make up Edsel's losses.[36] Available evidence supports this view: In his second day of testimony before the Senate subcommittee, on January 12, 1934, Edsel Ford revealed that the Ford Motor Company had repaid him a total of $7.5 million, covering the two loans he made to the Guardian Group.[37]

For Edsel Ford an important precedent had occurred: his father would assist him to cover some of his losses. No matter what took place with the Guardian, the resources of the Ford Motor Company would prevent Edsel from being "cleaned." His friends and partners, who had believed that the enormous financial power of the Ford Motor Company would support any venture of Edsel Ford, were proven correct, but it was Edsel alone for whom this was true when the crisis came.

There is no evidence that Edsel Ford informed his friend and partner Roy D. Chapin of his changed circumstances. Without advance information from Edsel, that his father had taken steps to keep Edsel from financial ruin, Chapin would have had every reason to believe that Edsel would support the subordination of the Ford Motor Company deposits in the Guardian Group, for his own benefit if for no other reason. Chapin and Ballantine may have been counting on Edsel to be a moderating influence on his father. Instead, the only written account of the meeting does not indicate that Edsel contributed in any way to the discussion.[38]

The written account of the meeting is eleven pages long. The report concludes that the account is not verbatim, but does give "the general tenor and effect of the discussion."[39] In the report Ballantine and Chapin clearly explained the situation, the plan, that they hoped Henry Ford would accept, and the probable consequences if he did not agree to the plan. Equally clear is Henry Ford's unyielding refusal to respond as Ballantine and Chapin requested.

Ballantine and Chapin arrived to find that Henry and Edsel Ford had Ernest Liebold present. Liebold had earlier been at the Guardian building meeting, representing Henry Ford and the Ford Motor Company, so it is very likely he had communicated the tenor of that meeting to Henry and Edsel Ford. Nevertheless, Ballantine started the meeting by laying out the situation of a specific Guardian subsidiary, the Union Guardian Trust, which was facing financial ruin, and a plan that had been devised to keep the trust company open.[40]

Liebold seems to have fulfilled his responsibilities, as Henry Ford stated at once that he "knew about the plan."[41] He went on to say that he would not agree to what was proposed to him, but he would talk about the situation.

Ballantine attempted to convince Henry Ford that the situation was critical. They spoke of the possibility that if the trust company failed it would take the Guardian Group along. In addition, Ford was warned that the failure of the Guardian Group could lead to the closure of the Detroit Bankers Group along with all other banks in Michigan. Further, Ballantine said, it was probable that the banking problem would eventually encompass the entire nation. He appealed to Ford to consider the three million people in Michigan who would suffer great losses if the banks failed.[42]

In response, Ford concluded that it seemed strange to him that the government should permit such terrible consequences to come about for $6 million. Ballantine said the amount was not the critical element, it was the necessity for Ford to subordinate $7.5 million. Ballantine reported that "in effect" Henry Ford responded, "All right, have it that way, I think that Senator Couzens was probably right in saying, 'Let the crash come.'" Ballantine immediately responded that if Couzens had said that in the past, he had since changed his mind. Ford chose to believe Couzens's opinion was as originally stated.[43]

Henry Ford went on to reveal his old concern. Ford stated his belief that only he understood the real situation: other forces were at work to destroy or harm the Ford Motor Company. He referred specifically to the strike at the Briggs plant that had shut down Ford production. In the continued discussion Ford maintained that his competitors, or those who supported his competitors, were responsible. In short, Henry Ford saw a conspiracy at work. It may be that Ballantine's earlier mention of General Motors and Chrysler Corporation had triggered this response. These two major rivals of Ford were willing to support the plan to prevent the Guardian failure, but they thought the Ford Motor Company should take the lead.

Ballantine attempted to reason with Ford, saying that it would be "suicidal" for any competitor of Ford to do as Ford suggested.[44] In addition, Ballantine argued that a "crash" was not inevitable. Not only would many people be hurt, but the Ford Motor Company also would suffer. Ford held fast to his belief that neither Chapin nor Ballantine really understood what was going on. Ford said it would take three or four days to explain it all to them. He said he believed in the cleansing power of a crash, and didn't care how soon it took place.[45]

Chapin then played his card, addressing Henry Ford as a "fellow-manufacturer with whom he had been on friendly relations for thirty-two years."[46] Chapin was appealing to the mutual interests and long-term friendship they had shared since 1901. He explained how the probable bank failure would affect their auto sales. Chapin did not mention the investment he had in the Guardian, and how a banking failure would affect him personally. He also failed to mention that his company, Hudson, was experiencing labor problems at the same time Ford was being shut down by the Briggs strike. He didn't use these arguments against Ford's belief in a conspiracy solely directed at him. But Ballantine and Chapin were attempting to persuade Henry Ford, not to argue with him.

Chapin reminded Ford of his great contributions to the development of Detroit, and said it would be strange for Ford now to act contrary to what he had spent years building.[47]

Ford agreed that he and Chapin had mutual interests as auto manufacturers, but he could not resist identifying what was a major difference in their two companies. Chapin's company was listed on the stock exchange. Ford believed the family ownership of the Ford Motor Company was superior. Implicit in Ford's view was that having shareholders meant having to succumb to Eastern money interests.

Time and again Ford returned to his belief that a crash, a failure in the banking system, was inevitable, and that it would be a very good thing and bring about some needed changes. Even if it destroyed the Ford Motor Company, he said he still felt young and would start a new company.[48]

Both Chapin and Ballantine pursued every idea that came to their minds in an attempt to find something that would get Ford to reconsider his refusal to subordinate the $7.5 million, on which any rescue effort was based. Chapin spoke about possible civil disturbances. Ballantine quoted a Biblical passage. "If needs must be offense come, but woe unto those by whom it cometh." Both pointed out that the banking problem would likely spread throughout the nation. They even used a historical analogy to the events leading to World War I, when inadequate discussion of probable events was believed to result in the war.[49]

Ballantine and Chapin continued to return to the situation as they saw it. Henry Ford became irritable and suggested they were making threats. Ford did relent somewhat, and said he would subordinate his deposits in the trust company, but only if he received "endorsed notes which would be absolutely good."[50] This was clearly not possible. If such guarantees could be made, there would have been no need for Ford to subordinate the $7.5 million.

Quite early in the meeting, Ford had stated that if the Union Guardian Trust Company was to be closed, he would immediately withdraw Ford deposits of $25 million in the First National Bank, a subsidiary of the Detroit Bankers Group. When Ballantine and Chapin returned to the meeting at the Guardian Group building and reported their discussion with Ford, the others were astounded. To make certain he had understood Henry Ford, Ballantine phoned Ernest Liebold. Liebold confirmed Ford's intent. In their report of the meeting, Ballantine and Chapin concluded, "That message appeared to entirely end the hope of any support for the plan to save the trust company by Mr. Ford."[51]

After the confirmation from Liebold, news of the situation in Detroit was transmitted to those waiting in Washington, D.C. The Ballantine and Chapin meeting with the Fords and Ernest Liebold had been scheduled for 10 A.M., Central time.[52] The return call, made by Liebold, took place at about 4:30 P.M. Central time, or 5:30 P.M. in Washington, D.C. At 6:45 P.M. Eastern time, Sens. James Couzens and Arthur Vandenberg, along with RFC members Charles Miller, Jesse Jones and Atlee Pomerene, met in the nation's capital to discuss the Detroit situation as they knew it.[53] One source notes that representatives from the Federal Reserve and the comptroller of the currency were also in the meeting.[54]

It really was not important who was in the meeting, as the key person became James Couzens. Whatever else was discussed, it was decided Couzens should place a call to his old partner, Henry Ford. Those who overheard the conversation have reported that Couzens was very diplomatic, "dropping sweetness into the phone at every word," and did not criticize Ford's position.[55] Vandenberg's biographer has the same view. "Couzens used charm and diplomacy."[56] This was despite Couzens's anger with Ford after he learned the results of the Chapin and Ballantine meeting. Both sources note that once Couzens had Ford on the phone, he changed his tone. In fact, Charles A. Miller of the RFC volunteered that nobody could have faulted Couzens, and that if any errors had been made in negotiating with Henry Ford, Couzens was not responsible.[57]

After hearing Ford go on about the alleged conspiracies of his rivals, Couzens decided there was no use in attempting to talk about details. Instead, he asked Henry Ford to have Clifford Longley call him. Longley, like most others involved in the Guardian situation, had conflicting inter-

Clifford Longley and others, April 10, 1934: (Left to right) Clifford Longley, unidentified, Harvey Firestone, and B.J. Craig, Ford Motor Company treasurer. Longley was president of the Guardian Detroit Union Group and an attorney for the Fords. He seems to be the first person to have alleged that James Couzens was responsible for the RFC loan being denied to the Guardian Group.

ests, being "Henry Ford's lawyer"[58] as well as president of Union Guardian Trust. Longley called Couzens at about 8 P.M. Eastern time on February 13. Couzens went over the situation with Longley, who of course knew it very well from his deep involvement in the Guardian Group, and all of the meetings in Detroit. But most importantly, Couzens asked Longley to convey an offer to Henry Ford. It was quite simple: Couzens would go fifty-fifty with Ford in putting up the collateral needed to make an RFC loan to the Union Guardian Trust Company.[59]

The amount Couzens was offering was "at least $6.9 million" of his own money.[60] When Longley returned the call after presenting Couzens's offer to Henry Ford, Ford's answer was, "No!"[61]

Henry Ford's achievements are many, and more easily understood than his blunders and misdeeds. The anti–Semitic campaign of his own newspaper, with the resurrection of the discredited so-called "Protocols of the Elders of Zion," had an enormous and murderous effect worldwide, notably in Nazi Germany. An association with Henry Ford gave credence to such calumny. Sadly, the ominous influence continues into the twenty-first century, most recently being quoted by Iranian leaders. Ford made huge positive contributions, and at the same time took others actions that were contrary to human welfare. Henry Ford was a human being with contrary impulses who operated on a worldwide scale. His decision to refuse to support the Guardian Group resulted in serious consequences. But the failures of many others contributed to his being in a critical, decision-making position. Unfortunately, he and other leaders continued to fail even after he refused to support the Guardian Group. No rational economic decision making system should have allowed a man like Henry Ford in effect to determine whether the United States should suffer the consequences of bank failures.

President Hoover, officials of the RFC, and many other responsible persons in the federal government failed to step forward and exercise leadership to prevent a national calamity that they foresaw. However, the political and economic beliefs of the day did not assign such responsibility to the federal government. That would soon change. But until March of 1933, what we now call the private sector was expected to provide economic leadership. Based on the operative and belief system of the time, there is no excusing Edsel Ford, Ernest Kanzler, Roy D. Chapin, Charles Stewart Mott and other automobile executives entwined in the Guardian Group for their leadership failures.

From 1929 they had made decisions to enrich themselves, using the Ford Motor Company as a seemingly endless supply of funds to support their actions. They paid themselves dividends even as they borrowed funds to support their failing banking group. We now know that from December 29, 1932, the Guardian Group was in thrall to the Ford Motor Company.[62] From that date, all the financial actions of the Guardian Group were subject to approval by the Ford Motor Company.

Whether Henry Ford knew of this arrangement at the time is unknown. But all of the principals in the Guardian Group were very much aware of the arrangement. In the meeting of February 13, Ballantine may have been the only one present who did not know of the actual memorandum obligating the Guardian Group to get Ford Motor Company approval for any attempt to borrow money, sell stock, or pay dividends. Edsel Ford, as president of the Ford Motor Company and largest stockholder in the Guardian, was responsible for these ties, and had to reveal the information to his father when the Ford Motor Company assumed his debts. Ernest Liebold knew of the memorandum and, with his involvement in the Guardian Group, most certainly so did Roy D. Chapin.

On the surface, Henry Ford was being asked to subordinate $7.5 million in the Union Trust subsidiary of the Guardian Group. In actual fact, Henry Ford, as he saw it, was being asked to put another $7.5 million into the Guardian Group. He had recently authorized a transfer of $7.5 million from the company to Edsel Ford to cover loans to the Guardian that Edsel had authorized. As Henry Ford said in his meeting with Ballantine and Chapin, "he had already done everything which he felt he ought to do to help the trust company."[63] There did not seem to be any end to the Guardian Group's need for Ford Motor Company money, and Henry Ford's sense of being put upon was aroused. After Ford had met with Ballantine and Chapin, the head of the Detroit Bankers Group came to meet with Ford. He left having heard that Ford intended to withdraw all of his deposits. Adding fuel to the fire, the revelation of the RFC loan to the so-called Dawes Bank had just taken place. This led Henry Ford to conclude that if the RFC could step in and act in Chicago in the summer of 1932, it could do so now.[64]

The last attempt to get Henry Ford to provide support for the Guardian was lost when Henry Ford turned down the offer from James Couzens. Acting as a messenger intermediary, Clifford Longley was able to share his knowledge of the circumstances with those still meeting in the Guardian building. When it became clear that the funds could not be raised to keep the Guardian open, both Chrysler and General Motors withdrew their previous offers of support. They were not about to put any money into a rescue effort for a bank with such strong Ford connections, especially when Henry Ford refused to do so.

Walter P. Chrysler and Alfred P. Sloan, Jr., had been good friends since 1910, when Chrysler was in GM but before Sloan had joined GM. Both men knew Henry Ford well. Sloan sold bearings to Ford before joining GM.[65] Unlike Ford, both Chrysler and Sloan were headquartered in New York City, and also unlike Ford, both Chrysler and Sloan headed corporations listed on the New York Stock Exchange. Also, in contrast to Ford, the Chrysler Corporation and General Motors had strong ties to the investment banking firms on Wall Street. While Henry Ford did not identify the names of the firms he thought were plotting against the Ford Motor Company, the only automobile corporations large enough to be rivals of Ford were GM and Chrysler.

Henry Ford had been the de facto leader of the auto industry, but he had reached the apex of his contributions. His fabled defeat of George Selden in the auto patent case and his championship of mass production put him into the leadership role. The introduction of the famed $5 a day wage that he espoused made him close to legendary. While he lost some luster as the Model T faltered, the successful introduction of the Model A gave him renewed credibility. When the Model A was soon outdated, the introduction of the first low-priced V8 regained him some of his former status. But his actions in February 1933 did not exhibit the daring vision he had once shown. Whether time had passed him by or he was showing evidence of being 70 years old, his refusal to subordinate his deposits resulted in the forfeiture of his status and leadership.

With knowledge of Henry Ford's intention to withdraw his deposits, the purpose of the meeting of auto executives and financiers shifted.[66] The role of Henry Ford had changed from being the possible savior of the Guardian Group to becoming an imminent threat. The foremost concern became keeping Ford from carrying out his threat to withdraw all of his funds on deposit in both banking groups. Various ideas were discussed to prevent a one-man run on the banks, but time was running out. The banks were scheduled to open for business on Tuesday, February 14.

The stopgap solution that came to be the consensus was for a temporary closure of all banks in Michigan, to provide time to find funds to save the Guardian. The banking system would have a time-out. The banks had to be closed to prevent Henry Ford from attempting to withdraw all Ford Motor Company deposits. A precedent had been set for state authorities to act. In October 1932, the Nevada state government closed banks so that reorganization could take place. This seems to be the first use of the term "bank holiday" for the purpose of closing banks and putting a moratorium on banking business.

Late in the evening of February 13, the group contacted William Comstock, governor of Michigan, and invited him to the meeting. He was in Lansing and had to drive to Detroit, delaying action until he arrived. Later testimony[67] noted that the opinion of the group was unanimous that the governor should declare a statewide banking holiday. The governor was uncertain of his authority to act as requested, and would not do so until he received a written request from local banking leaders. Among those supporting the request for the holiday were Ernest Kanzler, Arthur A. Ballantine, Alfred Leyburn, and Roy D. Chapin.[68]

About 550 national and state banks with nearly one million depositors were closed through Tuesday, February 21. The urgency of the situation led to the action taking place at 1:32 on Tuesday morning, February 14. The Lincoln Birthday national holiday and the preceding weekend prevented individuals and businesses from preparing for the situation. Shortages in the supply of cash on hand and the refusal to honor bank drafts soon led to panic buying of food by those who had cash. Within a short time, people began to hoard currency. The city that had once epitomized the growing industrial might of the United States was now in desperate straits, and along with it, the nation.

The idea of the banking holiday was to provide time to come up with solutions to resolve the crisis. Time was certainly needed, but it was running out. Now in the third year of the Depression, the country continued spiraling downward. The nation was in an economic and constitutional crisis as the defeated Herbert Hoover, who was not inclined to use presidential power, found that power continued to slip from his hands each day. One of Hoover's ploys in dealing with the worsening economy was to attempt to involve Franklin Roosevelt in approving his actions and statements. But Hoover readily admitted that Roosevelt supporting what Hoover intended to say or do would be a repudiation of the campaign promises Roosevelt had made.

Roosevelt, realizing that he was being asked to compromise his plans, not yet being president, chose repeatedly to respond that Hoover was still president and should take whatever action he thought was appropriate. When that did not stop Hoover from sending letters, memos, and messengers, Roosevelt simply did not respond.

The faith of the American people in the political and economic system had already weakened, affected by the continuing unemployment, strikes, hunger, and deprivation. Individuals and groups with political views ranging from Communist to proto–Fascist preached that the democratic political system had failed. Now, a banking crisis seemed imminent with effects and consequences nobody could predict. Another blow to the confidence of the American people came one day after the bank closure. While riding in a Miami motorcade, President-elect Franklin D. Roosevelt narrowly escaped an assassin's gunshots. Instead, the mayor of Chicago, sitting next to Roosevelt, was mortally wounded.

Suppose the assassins' shots had struck and killed Roosevelt? That would have precipitated an acute political and constitutional crisis. History often turns on the events of a second. In the Detroit banking crisis of 1933, however, the lead up to the disaster can be measured in years, with opportunity after opportunity to prevent the banking failure. Even after the closure of Michigan banks on February 14, the proclamation by Gov. Comstock provided one more week to resolve the problem.

The banking crisis in Detroit placed the automobile executives in a position to demonstrate significant national leadership. The nation had come to believe in the exceptional abilities of the individuals who were meeting in Detroit. Many were great achievers, but two are representative. Roy D. Chapin started at the very bottom of the auto industry and ascended to prominence and responsibility before becoming secretary of commerce. Walter Chrysler had risen from small-town Kansas, sweeping out railroad shops. He had climbed the ladder of success in the railroad industry before accomplishments at Buick and then Willys and then his own auto corporation.

It was reasonable to believe that the men of the auto industry would use their skills, abilities, connections and influence to resolve the situation in Michigan. Meeting in their home base, personally and collectively they stood to experience great financial losses if a solution was not found. Deliberating with the auto leaders were bankers and men from both the Michigan and United States governments. Leading the negotiations was Arthur

A. Ballantine representing the RFC, but the key decision makers were those who had invested in the Guardian and Detroit Bankers Group. It is not often that those responsible for a problem are given the opportunity to redress their mistakes.

To stem possible panics locally, as well as in the rest of the nation, finding some sort of solution to reopen Michigan banks became the goal. But closing the banks proved to be much easier than finding a way to reopen them.

6

"Your Friends Won't Hold It Against You"

Clifford Longley's associates and others who knew his work were surprised to read an announcement in February 1929 that the entire legal department of the Ford Motor Company would be discharged on the next payday. Longley had been an employee of Ford for ten years, eight of them as chief counsel.[1] As far as anyone knew, Longley had performed well. When questioned about the situation, Longley is reported to have smiled and pointed out that he and his partner, Wallace Middleton, had founded their own law firm and most of the former Ford legal department would join them in their new venture. Longley and Middleton would remain as counsel to the Ford Motor Company, without being employees.

We don't know the reason for this mass firing. Quite possibly Henry Ford didn't want anyone knowing his business. An alternative view is that Henry Ford did not like titles. Harry Bennett pointed out that when Ford employees were questioned about their duties and status, they carefully refrained from the use of titles. Instead, they "took care" of this or that subject or responsibility. Based on his own experience and observation of Henry Ford, Bennett thought Ford wanted people at his beck and call, ready to jump from one task to another.[2] Having Longley off the Ford payroll, presumably working on specific assignments or on work that was parceled out, he had less security and was more dependent on Ford's whims. Whatever the reasons for Longley's dismissal from Ford, he remained associated with Ford. In fact, his successor law firm, Bodman L.L.P., with offices at Ford Field in Detroit, represents the Ford family interests to this day.[3]

The Bodman name comes from Henry E. Bodman, who joined Longley, Middleton and others in 1931. Bodman, like most of the other principals of the Guardian Group, was well connected in Detroit. He was a director of the Packard Motor Car Company from at least 1918. In addition, he was vice president and also counsel for Packard. Bodman was involved with the group sponsoring the Lincoln Highway, serving as legal counsel for that group. In Guardian Group matters, Bodman was chairman of the board of the Union Guardian Trust, where his law firm partner Clifford Longley was president. Bodman had been involved in Guardian Trust from its formation, and was listed in a *New York Times* article about it on June 9, 1925.[4] Bodman is listed with other luminaries of the auto industry, no doubt based on his connection with Packard. Clifford Longley is not among those listed, possibly an omission on the part of the *Times* reporter. The assumption is that Longley did not yet have the name recognition of Bodman.

In a larger sense, the list of officers from Packard, Hudson, General Motors, and Ford who were involved with the Guardian beginning confirms the notion that economic interests were shared by individuals from firms who were commonly believed to be in rigorous competition. The partners in the Guardian may have shared other information, or may not have competed as diligently as expected. The opportunities for collaboration certainly existed. A more specific bit of information is to be found in the same news article: "Stockholders include a number of New Yorkers, among them W. A. Harriman." At the time, W. Averill Harriman was a partner with his brother in a Wall Street investment banking firm. They inherited the funds used to start the bank from their father, Edward H. Harriman. He had been one of the giants of American capitalism at the turn of the century, being one of a few men whose name could be mentioned in the same breath as that of J.P. Morgan. The reporter writing the article about the Guardian Trust thought it significant to mention the Harriman name. In effect, it was a reference to the significance of the new bank, giving it weight on Wall Street. It also reveals that W.A. Harriman, like the non–Ford auto men who were named, thought the Guardian was a means of sharing in the great success of the Ford Motor Company. Most importantly, the announcement suggested that Edsel Ford did not necessarily share his father's supposed anti–Wall Street bias. But as we have found out, when Edsel and Henry Ford held differing views, it was the view of the senior Ford that eventually was decisive.

Notwithstanding being involved as he was in Guardian and automotive matters, Henry Bodman gets little attention in accounts of the time. Yet Bodman was involved with the Lincoln Highway Association as early as 1913, when the route was announced. The organizational meeting of the Lincoln Highway group took place in the Detroit office of Henry B. Joy of Packard.[5] Joy moved Packard to Detroit from Warren, Ohio, and was responsible for the early success and achievements of Packard. He became the first president of the Lincoln Highway Association; no doubt Bodman was Joy's choice to be legal counsel. Others involved as officers or directors included John North Willys of Willys-Overland; F.A. Seiberling of the Goodyear Tire and Rubber Co.; Carl G. Fisher, automotive pioneer and promoter; and Roy D. Chapin of Hudson.[6]

There are at least three reasons for emphasizing Henry Bodman's involvement in the Guardian issues. First, he is representative of the interrelated and shared interests of men from the auto industry. Firms manufacturing automotive products might belong to organizations such as the National Automobile Chamber of Commerce. In the case of the Lincoln Highway Association, such firms belonged to improve the opportunities for cars to be used for inter-city or national transportation.

Secondly, of the leaders of Packard involved in Guardian matters, Bodman seems to have been more involved than either Alvan Macauley or Henry B. Joy. Macauley, who became general manager of Packard in 1910, was a member of the Guardian board of directors. He later succeeded Joy in the presidency in 1916, while maintaining the general manager position. In contrast, Henry Joy was only an investor in the Guardian. While Bodman stands out as compared with Macauley and Joy as chairman of the board of the Union Guardian Trust, all three of the top Packard leaders were involved in Guardian.

Third, Bodman is an example of what might have been an underlying, but informal, agreement about competitive practices in the auto industry. After all, one of Bodman's partners was Clifford Longley, counsel for the Ford Motor Company. As Bodman was counsel for the Packard Motor Car Company, you have to conclude that no one considered the notion of Ford and Packard being locked in legal issues. If there was a legal truce, what competition was there among the auto giants?

Beginning on February 10, 1933, Henry Bodman and others met with chief national bank examiner Alfred Leyburn to deal with the precarious position of the Guardian Group. Whom did Bodman represent? He was board chairman of the Union Guardian Trust, a director and chief counsel of Packard, and was partners with the chief counsel to the Ford Motor Company. In the first instance, keeping the Guardian Group solvent was a priority. But were the interests of the Packard Motor Car Company or the minority stockholders shortchanged by Bodman's personal interests? Unfortunately, Bodman's conflicting interests were representative for the time. Perhaps only Roy D. Chapin had a larger number of such conflicts.

After the Michigan Bank Holiday had been declared and the meetings in Detroit were stymied, Bodman went to the nation's capital. His purpose was to meet with the RFC and others in Washington in an attempt to open new and successor banks in Detroit.[7] Senator James Couzens accompanied Bodman when he went to see F.G. Awalt, the acting comptroller of the currency. Couzens is said to have been prepared to put up the capital to form a new bank in Detroit. Neither Bodman nor Couzens pursued the issue, as Awalt told them that Henry and Edsel Ford had offered a solution to the problem.[8] As we know, the Ford scheme was later considered to be much too self-serving. After the initial rush of excitement, the other interested parties would not support the Ford plan.

Couzens and Bodman's offer to open a new bank in Detroit was known by all of the interested parties in Detroit, including Bodman's partner, Clifford Longley. Longley's knowledge is important considering his later statements about Couzens's culpability in the Guardian Group failure. When Couzens was asked to mediate a plan to open the banks in Detroit, he met with leaders of both Detroit banking duopolies on March 1, 1933. Among those he met with were Clifford Longley and Henry Bodman.[9] Time and again Couzens is shown to have been in meetings held to resolve the banking problems in Detroit, often with Longley and Bodman present. In every instance, participants knew that Couzens was actively involved to limit the effect of the Detroit banking crisis following the banking holiday. It is misleading and probably self-serving for any of the men involved in the Detroit banking crisis to suggest that James Couzens did not have the best interests of his hometown as a high priority.

However, Couzens and others did not necessarily agree as to what was good for the Motor City. Couzens's history of bucking the powerful interests of Detroit led to a general distrust of him by powerful Detroit political interests. On one side were the regular Republicans of business and commercial interests. On the other side were what have become known as the Progressive Republicans, whose ideas Couzens favored. Antipathy toward Couzens on the part of the regular Republican leaders made it easy and convenient to later ascribe responsibility for the banking crisis to Couzens. His unwillingness to support the third RFC loan to the Guardian Group is one indictment. The second is his much-quoted statement about "screaming from the housetops."

As far back as the 1890s there was a significant dispute over municipal ownership of the streetcar lines in Detroit, an idea that Couzens favored. Couzens admired Hazen S. Pingree, the mayor who first brought up the issue. When Couzens successfully ran for mayor in 1918, he identified himself as a "second Pingree."[10] But the municipal rail issue was not limited to Detroit. Other large municipalities had the same conflicts. In nearly every city, the regular political establishment favored private ownership, usually obtained by a monopoly city franchise. In Detroit, the franchise was set at 30 years. Those favoring the status quo thought municipal ownership to be an example of "socialism."[11] At stake were all of the important social and political issues of the day. Those who favored municipal ownership generally also favored lower fares and improved working conditions, wages, and benefits for the rail employees. In some cases, as in Detroit, they also supported unionization of the trolley car workers.

Today, we can see how the use of the personally owned automobile has influenced the growth of suburbs, and the extensive construction of public roads. What may have been forgotten is the power that privately owned trolley car lines had before the advent of mass ownership of motorcars. In effect, the ownership of a municipal railway conferred on the owners the ability to determine how cities grew. Increasing fares by manipulating the availability of service was within the rights of the franchise holder. He could improve profits by causing the population density of a central city core to increase by denying or thwarting attempts to extend the trolley car lines. However, projects in which franchise holders had interests could be favored. Furthermore, rents were also affected by the availability of trolley lines to travel to work. Packard and Ford had contrasting production and marketing concepts, one for those who owned or invested in the streetcar lines, the other for the riders. To use a phrase of our time, the Model T empowered the average individual. Those who could afford a new or used Model T Ford could determine their own paths to work as well as their own personal boundaries. The inflexible schedules, fares, lack of prompt service, and routes of the urban trolley or streetcar lines did not circumscribe Model T owners. Today, there may be good reason to support mass transit in the form of light rail systems, but the time before the mass use of individually owned motorcars was not a golden age.

It may seem strange now to know that Alvan Macauley and Henry B. Joy of the Packard Motor Car Company were leaders of the opposition to the municipal railway ownership Pingree advocated, and Couzens later successfully implemented. It might have been thought that, as manufacturers of motorcars, their interests would have been in supplanting trolley cars with individually owned autos. But Packard was not a car for the masses, and both Joy and Macauley identified with the rights of private property and private ownership. An estimated half-million dollars was spent in the campaign in opposition to municipal ownership. But having lost one election, a second citywide referendum supported Couzens with a margin of 63 percent.[12] How Couzens fought for municipal ownership of the streetcars is a story quite illustrative of his personality, especially when he believed himself to be right.[13] The lawyers for the Detroit Union Railroad, the holders of the municipal franchise, characterized Couzens's actions as "an abominable, damnable outrage."[14]

One might assume that Henry Ford, with a car built for the masses, would have readily sided with his old partner James Couzens in the municipal rail issue. At first, Ford favored the idea but then he actively opposed the Couzens plan, partially due to some latent personal rivalry issues. But it happened that the railway issue came to a head as Henry Ford was intent on buying out the minority Ford stockholders, including Couzens. As the others sold their shares, including the Dodge brothers, Couzens waited to identify just who was buying up the Ford shares. Edsel Ford was dispatched to negotiate with Couzens, who received over $29 million in the sale. At the same time, Henry Ford had E.G. Liebold issue a release in which he corrected some "rumors," saying that Ford and Couzens were on good terms and both would cooperate with the other "for the best of the people."[15] With that, Henry Ford changed sides to support municipal ownership of the streetcar lines.

Ford and Couzens were thus again united against the apparent interests of other manufacturers in Detroit. They had been united in the early days, in the fight against the Selden Patent, with Henry Ford as visionary, mystic and practical mechanic while Couzens was successful in organizing the business operations of Ford Motor Company. When the famed $5 a day wage of the Ford Motor Company was announced by Couzens, both he and Ford were viewed by other industrialists as implementing a dangerous plan that would upset the social system and create significant problems for all other manufacturers. By the time of the Detroit banking crisis, the old partners had long been at odds with such pillars of the community as Alvan Macauley and Henry B. Joy. An additional set of circumstances involved Joy's brother-in-law and fellow Packard investor Truman Newberry. Newberry was a member of an established and wealthy family and had friends who had been investors in at least one of Henry Ford's earlier failures as an automobile manufacturer. Not everyone was pleased when the Ford Motor Company became a great success. The men who belonged to the social class of Newberry and Joy, who had lost money in Ford's earlier ventures, held negative views of Henry Ford.

To add to the rivalries, in the election of 1918, Newberry and Ford were pitted against each other in the race for United States senator. President Woodrow Wilson had convinced Ford that his election was necessary to support Wilson's idea of the League of Nations. The League appealed to Ford's notions of pacifism and as a means of preventing future wars. So, for the only time in his life, Henry Ford stood for election to a political office. It can't be said that he ran for office, as he put forth little effort and spent very little. The same could not be said for Newberry, whose campaign spent in excess of $500,000. Michigan law permitted cross-filing, so in the primary election Ford sought both the Republican and Democratic nominations. As a Republican he came in second to Newberry, but he was victorious as a Democrat. In the general election Ford lost by about 7,500 votes of a total of 433,000. Newberry's campaign picked up the costs of Ford's rival in the Democratic primary and brought Edsel Ford into the picture in the general election. The issue was that Edsel had received a deferment and did not serve in World War I. Much was

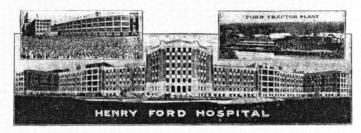

HENRY FORD HOSPITAL

100% WAR WORK

America Needs Henry Ford in the U. S. Senate
Help Make Him Senator

[OVER]

Six Great Principles of Henry Ford's Life

He has by his wonderful business ability and integrity established the largest industrial and philanthropic institutions in the world.

He has dedicated their vast production 100% to the Government to help win the war.

He has donated 100% of his individual profits to the Government to help win the war.

He has created a national public conscience for greater justice of capital toward labor.

He has humanized the attitude of employer toward employe, clothed the naked, fed the hungry and educated the ignorant into loyal Americans.

He has raised the standard of human living from five families in one room to one family in five rooms.

His dreams and ideals come true and become living things.

He is the greatest living American in civil life today.

Non-Partisan Ford-For-Senator Club.

When Henry Ford was a candidate for the U.S. Senate in 1918, he did not spend much money for his campaign. This actual sized card-stock, black and white card may be an indicator of the attitude of the Ford campaign. First, it is quite a modest item in size and appearance. But modesty is not evident on the reverse side, where the "Six Great Principles" are stated. Hyperbole is part of every political campaign, so Ford may not necessarily be faulted from that perspective. However, accuracy is a problem. One statement which has often been repeated but proven to be inaccurate is that Ford donated 100 percent of his "individual profits" to help win the war. Truman Newberry defeated Ford in 1918. Newberry later resigned, due to continued investigations regarding the election. James Couzens was appointed to complete Newberry's term, and was subsequently reelected (The Henry Ford).

made about this, with the jingoism of the time. Former President Theodore Roosevelt wrote in opposition to Ford's candidacy. In doing so, Roosevelt did not mince words, saying that Edsel sat home in "ignoble safety," leading to a clear-cut choice between patriotism and pacifism.[16] Newberry had served as an assistant secretary of the Navy in the McKinley administration and also had a naval title from an administrative position he had held at one point. Then, on the eve of the election, Ford was accused of employing a German national during the war. This turned out to be a false issue, but the contrast between Ford and Newberry had been simplified into evil versus glorious patriotism.

Henry Ford was indifferent in campaigning for office, but after the affront to Edsel, and the slurs on the unfortunate employee who was accused of being a German spy, Ford went into action. First, he filed for a recount, and when that was unsatisfactory he hired a private detective firm to dig up dirt about Newberry. It was rumored that the Newberry campaign had exceeded the legal restrictions on spending. Ford even brought his anti–Semitism into the conflict, accusing Newberry of being an instrument of a Jewish conspiracy. For four years Henry Ford pursued the feud, seeking some sort of victory. Eventually, Newberry despaired of the continued fight and resigned from the Senate of the United States.

In a surprise move, the governor of Michigan appointed James Couzens to fill the position vacated by Newberry. Couzens had been voted mayor of Detroit in the same election in which Newberry defeated Henry Ford. Couzens had done well as mayor, stepping on toes but pursuing policies that were popular with the general population, if not those who belonged to the social set of Henry Joy. In effect, Henry Ford had hounded Newberry out of office, resulting in his former compatriot becoming a senator. This set of circumstances was not lost on those who already disliked both Ford and Couzens. For the next ten years, Truman Newberry persevered in a grudge against Henry Ford.[17] Over the years, both Couzens and Ford were unpopular figures with the established families of Detroit. So when fault and responsibility for the banking crisis were to be assigned, they were readily available.

The Newberry family's involvement with the Guardian Group is an example of how Detroit insiders differentiated between Henry and Edsel Ford. Truman Newberry did not let his dislike of Henry Ford interfere with an investment opportunity, specifically one in which Edsel Ford was considered to be the major figure. The elder Newberry was among the investors identified in the *New York Times* article of 1925, while his son, Phelps Newberry, was noted as a director.[18] Phelps Newberry was a good friend of Edsel, who must have forgiven the Newberrys for the terrible things said about him in the Senatorial election. Obviously, Phelps Newberry's status in the Guardian Group was not affected. Like other directors he was among those who were provided with loans from the Guardian Group. Over a half-million dollars in indirect loans went to Phelps Newberry and were noted by the bank examiners in May 1932.[19] So it was that the major figures in the Packard Motor Car Company were involved with the Guardian Group. At the time, it was the only major banking group associated with the automobile industry. Edsel Ford's involvement with the Guardian meant to even casual observers that there was a Ford Motor Company relationship. But after the closure of the banks on the fateful Valentine's Day in 1933, two new auto-linked banks were subsequently formed. The dominance and power of the Ford Motor Company is consequently shown to have lessened. Instead of the very large Guardian group bank sharing a duopoly in banking with a non-automotive group, the two new successor banks were both connected with the auto industry, one with GM and Chrysler and the other with Ford. The list of the men involved in the two new banks is interesting and revealing. For example, the First National Bank listed as directors Alfred P. Sloan, Jr. of GM; Donaldson Brown, a GM vice president; Frank Couzens, son of James Couzens and an important local political figure; Walter P. Chrysler, of the Chrysler Corporation; and Henry E. Bodman, whose many roles have been detailed. In effect, the Packard Motor Car Company, through Bodman, chose the bank of GM and Chrysler.

Edsel Ford headed the newly formed Manufacturer's National Bank, founded by Henry and Edsel Ford. One of the directors was Clifford Longley. In fact, the telegram from the comptroller of the currency authorizing the start of Manufacturer's National was sent to Clifford Longley and dated July 25, July 1933.[20] One consequence of Bodman and Longley's involvement was that their law firm of Bodman, Longley, Bogle and Middleton had chairs in the inner offices of both successor Detroit banks.

It would seem that very little took place in Detroit in the arenas of auto manufacturing and banking that was unknown to Henry Bodman and Clifford Longley. An unanswered question is just how much information Longley shared with his clients Edsel and Henry Ford. The assumption seems to be that Henry Ford was not well informed about the financial status of the Guardian Group until shortly before he was asked to subordinate Ford Motor Company deposits within that organization. Yet he could have known if his son, Edsel, his general secretary Ernest Liebold, or his legal counsel, Clifford Longley, had chosen to inform him.

Edsel Ford did not do so, probably due to what one author calls the "humiliating and brutal" treatment by his father. Based on experience, Edsel would have expected his father to mock and criticize him for the financial situation in which he found himself.[21] On the other hand, as we have already learned, Edsel Ford did confide in Ernest Liebold about his financial situation during the banking crisis.[22] For Edsel Ford to confess to Ernest Liebold was interesting, for if we are to believe Harry Bennett, Edsel "never liked Liebold very much."[23] From most accounts, Liebold was not a very likable person. He has been described as "strict and impersonal"[24] as well as "stern, colorless, squat, and bull-necked."[25] Most accounts refer to his German heritage, as well as his efficiency and the thorough manner in which he carried out his responsibilities. It is widely believed that he had a significant role in the development of Henry Ford's anti–Semitic beliefs and actions.[26] Henry Ford was well aware of Liebold's personality, and is said to have stated, "When you hire a watchdog, you don't hire him to like everybody who comes to the gate."[27] It seems that Edsel may have unburdened himself to Liebold in hopes that the information would be passed to Henry Ford. This did take place, and by doing this Liebold partially fulfilled his watchdog role. But in alerting Henry Ford of Edsel's financial situation, stemming as it did from the problems of the Guardian Group, Liebold did not make the connection to the larger issue of Ford Motor Company deposits in Detroit banks. A lack of vigilance on this issue meant that Liebold had not fully carried out his duties as a watchdog.

When the Guardian Group was known to be in financial jeopardy, and meetings in Detroit took place to develop strategies to prevent failure, Liebold was assigned the task of representing the Fords and their company. When Arthur Ballantine and Roy D. Chapin met with Henry and

Edsel Ford, Liebold was present. Liebold had done his duty in keeping Henry Ford apprised of what was taking place in the meetings that continued even after the Michigan Bank Holiday had been declared. In advance of the meeting with Ballantine and Chapin, Henry Ford knew their talking points, and what they were going to request of him.

Of all of the individuals who were involved in the Guardian matters, the only person who seemed to be quite affected by what had taken place was Ernest G. Liebold. The man who was thought to be an accounting machine, who had carried out the task of personally confronting the Lelands, and giving them only hours to vacate the Lincoln Motor Company premises,[28] was found to have succumbed to the pressures of the time. On February 27, Liebold left work before midday, saying he was tired and was going home to take a nap. Instead, he had converted about $3,000 into traveler's checks and had sent letters of resignation to the Dearborn State Bank and the Guardian Bank of Dearborn. Because he was a man of regular habits, when he did not return home that evening, his wife reported him missing. She feared he had been kidnapped. Instead, he was found the following day in Traverse City, some distance north of the Detroit area, under an assumed name.[29] The Michigan State Police, who were responding to a request from Harry Bennett, had tracked him down.

The newspaper account says Liebold was "suffering from the strain of two weeks unremitting work on Detroit's complicated banking situation." The story went on to note Liebold's importance, saying he "had long been in charge of the Ford Motor Company's fiscal policies" and also was "charged with most of the details of a pending plan" to set up two new banks under Ford control.[30] Liebold's power within the Ford Motor Company came partially from the detail work he did for Henry Ford, but partly from what he knew. He knew what Ford did not want others to know. Just what pressures had affected Liebold? No doubt the newspaper article is true, as far as it goes. Something was clearly troubling Liebold. Did he feel he had failed in his duties to keep Henry Ford abreast of the Guardian issues? Had he given advice that proved to be unwise? Had he, like others, invested in the Guardian and now faced the potential expenses of double liability?

The general view is that from this time to his departure from the company in 1944, his influence declined and that of Harry Bennett increased. Despite this view, Liebold had sufficient influence with Henry Ford to convince him, in 1938, to accept a Nazi medal from the German consulates of Cleveland and Detroit, while Liebold received a slightly lesser award.[31] In 1940 Liebold accompanied Ford to lay the cornerstone for Ford Werke, a new plant in Cologne. However, Liebold's status after his disappearance must have been greatly lessened for Clifford Longley to feel free to tease him about his actions. Longley wrote on a margin of a newspaper article concerning Liebold's disappearance, "Dear Gus, In Chicago for the day and see where you are living a double life. Be of good cheer, your friends won't hold it against you."[32]

As the third person who could have warned Henry Ford about Guardian matters, Longley had the same problems that affected many of his associates in the Guardian Group: he had many conflicting interests. As counsel to both Henry and Edsel Ford, Longley had to make some interesting choices. Whom did he represent in the various matters in which he, or others, were involved? Whose interests did he favor in matters involving Henry or Edsel Ford? It was not true that the Fords had exactly the same interests. Some sort of prioritization needed to be determined, and in varying times and circumstances. To further complicate matters, Edsel Ford and Clifford Longley were partners in the Guardian Group and also in the Universal Credit Corporation while it existed. Even so, partners are not always equal in influence, interest, or investments. Edsel Ford had his name, wealth, and status invested in the Guardian Group. Those factors combined to make Edsel Ford a much superior partner. What might have been relatively inconsequential to Edsel Ford might have been a matter of great significance and importance to Longley.

It does not seem that Clifford Longley kept Henry Ford abreast of the critical state of Guardian Group matters before the crisis of early 1933. Yet Longley had been entrusted by the Fords with significant responsibilities and presumably had an obligation and duty to his very important client. The direct involvement of Clifford Longley in Ford Motor Company and the personal matters of the Fords is extensive. Even though Longley was in a law firm separate from the Ford Motor Company, his activities are those more akin to those of a Ford employee.

Longley's papers in the Benson Ford Research Library show his involvement in unrelated Ford Motor Company and Ford family activities, great and small.[33] In June of 1920, after the buyout of the minority shareholders of Ford Motor, Longley took charge of establishing Ford Motor Company as a recapitalized Delaware corporation.[34] He was involved in obtaining and running the Detroit and Ironton Railroad. He was a director of that Ford-owned line. He was also involved in the Ford railroad legal matters.[35] He handled purchases of iron ore, land, timber properties, and coal mines for Ford Motor. He even roughed it for Ford, as a 1924 photo shows him on horseback surveying land somewhere in Kentucky.[36] Another photo from 1924 shows Longley accompanying Henry Ford, Ernest Liebold and a Ford engineer on a visit to President Calvin Coolidge.[37] Their visit was meant to lay the groundwork for the Ford purchase of Muscle Shoals, a Tennessee power plant built by the federal government for World War I production purposes. The Ford plan was thwarted by the actions of the Progressive Republicans in the U.S. Senate, a group with which James Couzens was allied.

Longley was also involved in carrying out Ford's instructions in the purchase of the Lincoln Motor Company from the founding Leland family.[38] The Longley papers contain approximately thirteen newspaper clippings on the continuing legal battles with the Lelands from 1929 through 1933. Longley contended that Henry and Wilfred Leland were engaged in fraud as officers of Lincoln Motor Company.[39] He said that the Lelands improperly led their stockholders to believe that the Fords would reimburse them for their losses. The outcome of the legal battle was mixed, with Ford paying about $4 million to creditors and directors with endorsed notes.[40] However, a different lawsuit went to the Michigan Supreme Court, where the Fords were the winners. It may be that Longley gained an advantage through to the Leland papers, left behind when the Lelands were forced out of Lincoln. In one letter addressed to Henry Leland and saved by Longley, Longley describes Henry Ford as "the most unaccountable man he ever knew," jumping "at conclusions instinctively."[41] Longley's assessment, based on his extensive contact with Henry Ford in many unrelated matters, reinforces what many other Ford insiders have reported. It does not offer any unique insights, yet Longley lasted as legal counsel from 1919 to Ford's death in 1947. Perhaps only Charles Sorensen had a longer working relationship with Henry Ford; many others were forced out of the Ford Motor Company due to real or imagined transgressions. Harry

Bennett reported what seems to be the only issue on which Henry Ford evidenced a distrust of Longley. That was in regard to advice on avoiding inheritance taxes, with Longley advocating what Bennett characterized as Henry Ford being required to turn over "his money to Edsel immediately."[42] Bennett does not note the date when this was reported to have taken place, but Longley wasn't fired. As counsel, Longley collected his fees and or retainer regardless of whether Fords or their company won or lost high-stakes legal conflicts. But he was dependent on remaining on good terms, with confidence and trust at a high level, for his continuing relationship with the Fords and their company, and especially with Henry Ford. Unlike other large corporations whose management was divorced from their ownership, especially at rival General Motors, Ford Motor pursued the "one man tyranny in business"[43] style. This was an ownership style by which Henry Ford retained ultimate decision-making and power, despite Edsel Ford having the title of president. In practical terms, to the Ford officials whose livelihoods were dependent on the Ford Motor Company, it meant never challenging Henry Ford. Having some sort of useful relationship or connection with him was even better.

As trusted as Longley was with a wide variety of significant matters, he may have shared one prejudice with Henry Ford — anti-semitism. In addition to legal duties, Longley was the secretary for Ford's newspaper, *The Dearborn Independent*.[44] While serving in that capacity, he also was counsel to Ford in the Aaron Sapiro libel case. There is no need to go into details here, but the *Independent* was Ford's channel for spreading his anti–Semitic worldview. It was instrumental in publishing accusations about Sapiro, who responded by suing for libel. After considerable delay and the start of a trial which was followed by a mistrial, Henry Ford arranged to write a general letter of apology about the anti–Semitic views expressed in the *Independent*. In an exchange of letters with Missouri Senator James Reed, the lead lawyer for Ford in the Sapiro case, Longley responded to Reed's characterization of the Ford apology as a "miserable outcome." Longley seemed to agree, saying, "I understand thoroughly how you feel about the outcome." He went on to say, "No one connected with it [the trial] felt more disgust at what occurred than I did myself." He finished his response with, "I am trying to put that part of the episode of the recollection out of my mind."[45] Nevertheless, on behalf of Henry

Ford, he settled costs for Sapiro.[46] Longley loyally served Ford both at the newspaper and in the legal difficulty.

One hesitates to make too much of what Longley kept, things that are now among his papers at the Benson Ford Research Library. However, there are four documents of particular interest. One is a copy of *The Protocols and World Revolution* that contains *The Protocols of Meeting of the Zionist Men of Wisdom*. This is clearly another version of *The Protocols of the Wise Men of Zion*, the infamous anti–Semitic tract for which Henry Ford bears responsibility for worldwide distribution. A second set of items includes a letter from, and a pamphlet by, Major-General Count Sherep-Spiridovich, a refugee from Russia. The pamphlet, *The Hidden World Government or The Hidden Hand*, is another publication claiming to expose an alleged Jewish world conspiracy. Like variations of *The Protocols*, this publication is still available from conspiracy advocates.

The letter, seeking money and support from Ford via Longley, was dated October 1925, approximately when the Sapiro articles were appearing in the *Dearborn Independent*. It would seem that Ford, and others including Longley, might have received many other similar requests for financial support for many causes, but the fact is that two virulent anti–Semitic publications were retained in the Longley papers. The other two related articles are both on the other side of the controversy. One is *An Experience with American Justice* by Aaron Sapiro, which is a copy of an address by Sapiro suit against Henry Ford. The pamphlet contains hand-written notes in pencil that seem to be those of Mr. Sapiro. How Longley came to have this in his possession is unknown. The other item is *The Jews in Nazi Germany*, published and distributed by the American Jewish Committee, printed on June 19, 1933. Longley's apparent willingness to serve as an officer of the *Dearborn Independent*, these items and his comments to Senator Reed speak not only about the times but perhaps also about his relationship with Henry Ford. Even though he was not an employee of the Ford Motor Company, he certainly could be called a "Henry Ford man."

Longley was involved in day-to-day Ford matters, including contracts with dealers, patent matters, and many legal issues involving employees. The confidence and certainty confirmed in the scope of Longley's work make obvious the security of his relationship with the Ford Motor Company as well as with Henry Ford himself. For example, Longley was sent to take care of the expansion and reorganization of Ford interests in Great Britain as well as in Europe. Seven million dollars came to the Ford Motor Company as a consequence of Longley's work, along with new territorial concessions to Ford in Great Britain. In those days, before trans–Atlantic communication was easy or common, overseas corporate representative's were similar to diplomatic ambassadors. They had to know who they represented, speak with authority on behalf of those who sent them, and be trusted to make significant agreements. Over and over there is evidence that Longley was competent and important to Ford Motor Company. He was so trusted that in 1936, he played an important role in drafting the wills of both Ford men. This resulted in the formation of the Ford Foundation. Edsel Ford was the first president, and among the members of the board of directors was Clifford Longley. If his continued assignment to important matters is evidence of a positive evaluation by Henry and Edsel Ford, Clifford Longley had their full confidence.

Longley's relationship with the Fords is significant. He had many opportunities to warn Henry Ford about the precarious financial status of the Guardian Group. Being an insider in the Guardian Group, Longley was as well informed about the real situation as anyone. As Henry Ford's legal counsel, and with the trust that had many times been placed in him, Longley would seem to have had a legal and personal obligation to tell Ford about the possible financial consequences for the Ford Motor Company. Nothing indicates that Clifford Longley ever advised Henry Ford about the deteriorating condition of the Guardian Group. However, Longley was at a meeting in which Ford found out. The meeting, according to Harry Bennett, had been arranged after Bennett told Ford that had learned from a Detroit news reporter that the Guardian Group was in trouble. Meeting with Ford were Ernest Liebold, Clifford Longley and a state bank examiner. Ford emerged from the meeting with an understanding of the seriousness of the situation.[47] Yet nothing was done to safeguard the Ford deposits, or mitigate the potential losses, if that were in fact possible. Longley's relationship with the Ford family continued. There may have been ups-and-downs, but his performance in front of Judge Harry Keidan seems to have been an act of public loyalty to the Fords. That it was also self-serving may have eased Longley's mind.

For 69 working days, June 14 to September 18, 1933, Michigan District Judge Harry B. Keidan held what was called "a one man grand jury," with the purported goal being to examine the reasons for the banking crisis in Detroit. Representatives of the U.S. government, such as those from the various organizations that examined banks, refused to appear before Judge Keidan in the apparent belief that the hearing was inadequate for the seriousness of the Michigan events. Reports of the time written by four out-of-town reporters all concluded that the hearing was not a serious attempt to ferret out the facts.[48] *Time* magazine's October 2 issue characterized the testimony as "rattling salvos of highly personalized undocumented charge and countercharge."[49] It was in this irregular forum that Clifford Longley did some of his best lawyer talk on behalf of himself and Henry Ford.

Explaining why the RFC did not make a loan to the Guardian Group, Longley said there was considerable opposition. When asked to clarify, Longley singled out James Couzens. Harry Barnard, Couzens's biographer, emphasizes that Longley parsed his words. That is, Longley "gathered" Couzens was upset that he had not been contacted earlier. He also said he "gathered" that Couzens strongly opposed the loan and he "gathered" that Couzens's opposition stopped the loan.[50] The testimony was sufficient for the local Detroit papers to conclude that James Couzens was responsible. Longley made no direct accusations, and he offered no proof. Instead, he reported on information he had "gathered." He said nothing about the responsibility of the Guardian Group leadership. Of course, Longley was in that leadership. Most importantly for his legal firm and continued good relations with Henry Ford and the Ford Motor Company, he did not include the name of Henry Ford with that of James Couzens. But then, Longley was legal counsel to Henry Ford. In no way could Clifford Longley be considered to be an objective witness in front of Judge Keidan. In his testimony, Longley left much unsaid, but the indirect accusations seem to have had a considerable life span.

In his report, Judge Keidan concluded there was no evidence of criminal action on the part of the Detroit banking officials. He also found that there was no evidence of "smart money" withdrawals immediately preceding the bank closures. Lastly, he stated the banks of Detroit were solvent on February 11, their last day of operation before the closure. His conclusion was based on the notion that "the government would not permit an insolvent bank to operate."[51] In other words, the fact that they were open for business and not shut down by some regulatory agency was prima facie evidence of their solvency. Keidan said, "Criminations and recriminations are futile." Instead, "the actual aid of the government" was needed to "remedy the evil conditions which exist."[52] The Keidan-led hearing resulted in only one lasting conclusion: Longley's implication of James Couzens.

Had the Keidan hearing called Alfred P. Leyburn or John K. McKee to testify, and had they been permitted to do so by the agencies for which they worked, the story would have been much different. Leyburn was the chief national bank examiner of the Federal Reserve District headquartered in Chicago. McKee was chief of the investigating division of the RFC for bank reorganization. Both men, and others who worked with them, provided the same information. Neither Leyburn nor McKee disputed each other's findings. They had no jurisdictional rivalry or turf battle. What they found was a banking organization in very dire straits. As early as May 1932, Leyburn noted problems, which he called to the attention of the Guardian Group. He had found that the Guardian National Bank of Commerce, one branch of the Guardian Group, had almost $8 million in outstanding loans to its directors. Leyburn also found three other sets of figures were problematic: "excessive loans" to the Guardian Detroit Company of about $4.5 million, "slow assets" of $22.4 million, and doubtful assets of almost $12 million.[53] All of Leyburn's concerns just noted, and the payment of unearned dividends, were reported by him to a committee of the Guardian Group. In some cases, he informed the committee, he had found some branches of the Guardian actually going into the deposits of customers to obtain the funds needed to pay the dividends. Clifford Longley was among those warned by Leyburn.[54] In his report to the comptroller of the currency, Leyburn reported on the Guardian Group's loan practices to officers. It was the practice to provide loans to high-salaried officials, based on Guardian stock! Leyburn went on to recommend "the bank would be better off to dismiss the officers and charge off the loans."[55]

One Guardian Group problem that was not unique to Guardian was loans that had been made on real estate. In the one industry town of Detroit, bankers predicated all prosperity on sales successes of the auto industry. When Detroit workers lost their jobs or had severe cutbacks in work hours or wages, they could not meet their mortgage payments. It is estimated that by February 1933, almost three-fourths of the assets of the Guardian Trust Company were frozen due to unpaid mortgages.[56]

Leyburn met with officers of the Guardian Group on January 27, 1933, in Ernest Kanzler's office. Accompanying Leyburn was John McKee of the RFC. Kanzler, Longley and Bodman were among those representing the Guardian Group. McKee and Leyburn and the Guardian men worked out a plan that would permit an RFC loan. By the time the loan application was made on February 6, a dozen examiners had worked incessantly to identify sufficient collateral to obtain the loan. Or so they thought. Rumors of the impending failure of the Guardian Group had leaked out, leading to the need for a larger loan. They figured that the group would need to have 100 cents on the dollar to be able to pay off all the depositors who wished to cash out of their accounts. Furthermore, conditions were rapidly getting worse. On February 6, when McKee met with the RFC board of directors in Washington, he clearly reported that the Union Guardian Trust Company was insolvent. It became evident that the entire Guardian Detroit Union Group needed to be viewed as one entity. Leyburn and McKee agreed it was no longer possible to consider an RFC loan to only one branch. The sensitive relationships between and among the unit banks made apparent that failure would have statewide and possibly national consequences. The Guardian Group leaders, including Henry Bodman and Clifford Longley, despite what they later failed to report, knew all of the details and conclusions. After all Longley was president and Bodman was chairman of the board of the Union Guardian Trust. It was this branch of the Guardian Group that was the weakest link.

Of all the people involved in the banking crisis, the two most objective individuals were John McKee and Alfred Leyburn. Neither of them had any political axes to grind and no one has criticized their actions. Leyburn was involved in matters relating to the Guardian Group over a period of several years, in differing roles. At first, he was a bank examiner who reported potential problems of the Guardian. Next, he was a participant in attempting to prevent the bank crisis. That role led him to become a meeting facilitator in Detroit, both before and after the declaration of the Michigan bank holiday. When all the nation's banks were closed, Leyburn worked with others in evaluating the potential for reopening. Lastly, he was a key witness before the Senate investigating committee. His involvement led him to be in contact with every major participant in the banking crisis except Henry and Edsel Ford. The actions of Leyburn and McKee included attempts to resolve the problems, not simply to report on the critical situation that they had discovered. Despite their deep involvement in the entire banking crisis, their reports have not received the attention that they deserve.

However, some of Leyburn's statements, as reported in testimony before the Senate subcommittee, have often been quoted. For example, Leyburn said the consensus of the participants discussing an RFC loan to Guardian was, "Why should we bail out Mr. Ford?" This meeting was held in Washington on February 6, Leyburn having shuttled between Detroit and Washington. Among those present were undersecretary of the Treasury Arthur A. Ballantine; Secretary of the Treasury Odgen Mills; and Jesse Jones, who would later become RFC chairman.[57] It seems this group understood the association between the Guardian Group and the Ford Motor Company, even if the details had not yet been spelled out.

Another of Alfred Leyburn's statements that has often been quoted is one he used to describe the situation in Detroit about three days before the banks were closed. He had called the continued meeting, held in the Universal Credit Corporation offices, of all parties interested in seeking a solution to the banking problems in Detroit. This was the group to which Roy Chapin and Arthur Ballantine first reported when they arrived from Washington. Leyburn's evaluative statement was succinct and direct; he called the situation "a hell of a mess."[58]

Earlier, in a written report to the comptroller of the currency, Leyburn minced no words. In speaking of the Guardian Group president, Leyburn reported: "It is very apparent that Mr. Lord of the Guardian Group is not a banker and he never has been one and he never will be one. He is more of a glad-hand promotion type, and he always chooses the path of least resistance, which has now created the present problem with the group."[59]

But two of the most colorful Leyburn quotations came out in his testimony before the Senate subcommittee. In questioning Leyburn about the post-closure status of Guardian Group banks, Chief Committee Counsel Ferdinand Pecora inquired about the Union Guardian Trust Company that Longley and Bodman headed. Leyburn was asked if any attempt had been made to reopen the trust company. Leyburn said, "It would take Houdini to open that bank." "But Houdini is dead," said Pecora. "And so is that bank," Leyburn replied.[60] He also had a direct answer when asked by Pecora about the so-called "Wall Street plot" which prevented Guardian banks from reopening after the national bank holiday. His response was "I think it a wonderful fairy tale, if you ask my opinion."[61]

Too little attention has been paid to the objective and professional reports and evaluations of the various bank examiners, including Alfred Leyburn and John McKee. On the other hand, too much credence has been given to the opinions of those who appeared before Judge Keidan and in the conclusions of Judge Keidan. One of his conclusions was totally erroneous, specifically that the banks' being open for business on February 11 was proof of their solvency. As *Business Week* summarized, "National bank examiners found the banks in precarious condition in June, 1932, again in November, 1932, yet they were permitted to remain open."[62]

As to the reason the third RFC loan was not made to the Guardian, Leyburn told the Senate subcommittee, "The RFC did not make the loan. They figured the security was not adequate, and they told them so, and the consensus of the RFC board was that it was not adequate."[63] Ernest Kanzler, with Longley present, admitted to the February 6 meeting of the RFC that Guardian's assets were inadequate for a loan. He also doubted that Henry Ford would subordinate his deposits, believing it was an injustice to ask for further funds from those who had been very generous over the past three years.[64] It would seem that Kanzler was referencing Edsel Ford, whose own money, and that of the Ford Motor Company, had kept the Guardian Group afloat. Yet, according to Leyburn, asking Henry Ford to subordinate his deposits in the Guardian came from a meeting called by Kanzler, once again held in the offices of the Universal Credit Corporation.[65] This may have been an act of desperation on the part of Kanzler, as nobody had been able to raise sufficient collateral to satisfy the loan requirements of the RFC. It was not due to lack of trying on the part of both Leyburn and McKee. Leyburn had suggested that a recent but obscure amendment to the RFC law be used to shore up the loan request. This

Surrounding President Franklin Roosevelt are the men of the board of governors of the Federal Reserve System, the newly formed group replacing the Federal Reserve Board. Standing directly behind Roosevelt, in the middle of the seven men, is John McKee. McKee had played an important role in the matters relating to the Guardian Group and the banking crisis of 1933. Presumably, FDR appointed McKee for the experience and knowledge he had gained in his previous governmental positions. The photograph commemorates the passage of the Banking Act of August 23, 1935 (Herbert Hoover Presidential Library).

new provision permitted the creation of a special corporation to receive loans needed to support distressed banks. An attempt was made to use the special corporation, but McKee found that the actual loan value of the assets that had been scraped together was less than one-fifth of what was needed.[66] In what should have been an eye-opening statement, McKee concluded the previous RFC loans made to the Guardian in 1932 had maxed out the value of the accumulated collateral.[67] Despite all of the warning to the Guardian officers, no improvement in the actual value of the group had been achieved, even though dividends had continued to be paid and loans to officers were continuing to be approved.

McKee and Leyburn did not keep their findings secret. Their reports were made to the RFC, to the comptroller of the currency, and to the Federal Reserve. All of the data they accumulated and the conclusions they drew were shared with all appropriate governmental officials as well as with the leaders of the Guardian Group. The RFC rejected the third loan application by the Guardian, three days before James Couzens made his "housetops" statement. The participants in the events who pointed the finger at James Couzens knew better. When Clifford Longley said he "gathered" this or that, he was well aware of what he was doing.

7

The Banking System
Ceases to Function

In February and March of 1933, circumstances had combined to cause severe problems for the United States. Not since March 4, 1861, 72 years earlier, had the nation faced a greater crisis as one president succeeded another. Playing important roles in the events of the time were men with ties to the automobile industry. The most prominent were Henry and Edsel Ford, Ernest Kanzler James Couzens, and Roy D. Chapin.

The happenings of the time were played out on a stage set by the cumulative effects of the Depression as measured by unemployment, deprivation, farm and home foreclosures, and the vast numbers of people roaming the country looking for work. "Fifteen million people had no jobs; many others were working at reduced wages. At least three million crowded the relief rolls; and in countless places welfare facilities had broken down entirely."[1]

Immeasurable, but significant in effect, were the feelings of hopelessness and despair. Affluent Americans, whose wealth was based on the value of common stocks, watched as New York Stock Exchange values "had fallen from about ninety billion dollars to about fifteen billion."[2] Other Americans, who had considered themselves comfortable and protected, concluded their life's savings were in jeopardy as an increased number of banks became insolvent or closed down.

Secondly, from November 1932 into the beginning of 1933, an increasingly embittered, defeated president remained in office as conditions worsened. Seeing a potential problem with the time gap from election in November to inauguration in March, the country had provided a solution, with the ratification of the 20th Amendment to the Constitution. While it was needed immediately, the new amendment was not to become effective until October 15, 1933.

126

Hoover's response to the continuing crisis included his previous indirect policies combined with an almost fatal resignation in the worsening conditions. He also tried to co-opt Roosevelt into taking responsibility. Despite the fact that Roosevelt had been overwhelmingly elected in November, Hoover believed that Roosevelt was a cause of the worsening conditions, because of public fear of the policies of his incoming administration. Again and again Hoover attempted to get Roosevelt to accept Hoover's plans and renounce his own. For the most part, Hoover refused to take action unless he had Roosevelt's approval.

Roosevelt's position was that he was not yet president and had no constitutional status or power. In any case he was not going to subscribe to Hoover's plans, which generally were contrary to his own. Further, Roosevelt was not about to fritter away public confidence, which he would soon need, by backing or approving Hoover's plans. After all, the public had overwhelmingly rejected Hoover in the general election. Neither President Hoover nor President-elect Roosevelt distinguished himself in the interregnum from November 8 to March 4. But it is difficult to know what either man might have done to prevent what had become a serious economic and constitutional crisis. Both Roosevelt and Hoover found themselves in unique circumstances during the monstrous financial crisis, which was without precedent. Neither man could follow a script of how he should act for the good of the nation. National leadership was needed, but Hoover had been defeated and Roosevelt was not yet president.

A third factor that added to the growing crisis was an action of Hoover. In April 1932, Hoover requested that a Senate subcommittee investigate banking practices.[3] During his campaign for reelection, Hoover noted what he thought were suspect stock market practices. Many ideas for investigations had been put forth, but the one that materialized was the Senate Committee on Banking and Currency.

It was Hoover's view that an economic conspiracy was at work; in this belief he was not alone. Many people were of the same opinion, supported by commentators and politicians who were hard at work proclaiming that the economic circumstances were due to different conspiracies. But Hoover's view was more specific. He thought that prominent financiers who belonged to the Democratic Party were prolonging the Depression, dashing hopes for recovery, sowing additional fears about the economic system, and making his policies appear futile.

High on the list of those Hoover suspected of being complicit in an aggressive form of short selling then known as "bear raiding" was John J. Raskob. Raskob was chairman of the Democratic National Committee from 1928 to 1932. He had resigned as chairman of the General Motors finance committee and executive committee when he took on the Democratic committee duties. As a top executive of DuPont, Raskob was chiefly responsible for its investment of World War I profits into General Motors. Raskob and his friend Pierre DuPont also had large personal stakes in GM. Raskob's affiliation with DuPont and General Motors was well known and is one additional indicator of the importance of the automobile industry. Not only had the auto been the stimulus for economic growth and social change, the men who were associated with the industry could be found in widespread positions of power and responsibility.

No evidence was ever presented to show that Raskob was guilty, nor were any "bear raiders" found to have ties to the Democratic Party. It was a real gauge of his feelings of unease that President Hoover thought Raskob was pursuing economic advantage and causing further economic anxiety to Hoover's political detriment. At the time, in the worst years of the Great Depression, Raskob was the prime mover in the financing, construction, and then management of the Empire State Building. The newest skyscraper eclipsed the recently constructed Chrysler Building, also with ties to the automobile industry, as the world's tallest structure.

If the president of the United States could distrust a pillar of capitalism such as John J. Raskob and believe him to be enriching himself through aggressive stock market practices, one can imagine what ordinary Americans' suspicions about the economic system might have been

From their start in April 1932 until January 1933, the Senate hearings were highly publicized but inconclusive. Only with the January appointment of Ferdinand Pecora as chief counsel did the hearings take on substance to match public expectations. Pecora provided leadership, and his name, not that of previous Chairman Duncan Fletcher, is used to identify events, known as "the Pecora hearings." In the absence of a strong and decisive president, the Senate subcommittee hearings took on increased national importance.

As Ernest Kanzler and others were seeking a third loan from the RFC, Pecora was starting hearings that had a substantive effect on loan practices of the RFC and specifically on the Guardian Group application. What the hearings revealed caused great concern about apparent insider favoritism, and led to questioning of the judgment of the RFC. The concerns were based on an enormous and secret RFC loan that had been made to a bank headed by former U.S. Vice President Charles G. Dawes. Only three weeks before the loan was made, Dawes had been president of the RFC! That money from the RFC would be provided to shore up loans made by the Dawes bank, illegal under Illinois law, was bad enough. That the failure of the Dawes bank was due to the failed holding companies of Samuel Insull was an additional issue.

The wisdom, fairness, and appearance of hidden favoritism of the RFC was questioned to the point that the RFC, in effect, did not want to make another loan to a holding company. Furthermore, given the connection between the Guardian Group and the Ford Motor Company, the RFC most certainly did not want to look as if it were favoring Ford interests or succumbing to political influences.

And the subject of political influence was in the news. The RFC was still reacting to a charge published in December 1932. A national magazine alleged that Roy D. Chapin, secretary of commerce, auto industry pioneer and insider, and major shareholder in the Guardian Group, had previously used his political influence to obtain the earlier RFC loans made to the Guardian.[4]

Adding to the complexities of the time was that Henry Ford's old partner James Couzens, the senior senator from Michigan, served on the Senate Committee on Banking and Currency. Couzens was an active member of the subcommittee that carried out the investigation. He was described by one author as a "Michigan multimillionaire" who "contributed liberally to the poor," and "delighted in helping" the committee counsel "draw and quarter financial titans."[5]

Couzens had the lowest seniority of the three Republican senators on the Banking and Currency Subcommittee. Despite being the least senior senator of the minority party, Couzens played a decisive role in the hearings. Actual bipartisanship existed during the hearings, thanks to both Counsel Pecora and Chairman Fletcher. Both men were quite aware of their prominence on the national scene, as reflected in daily newspaper and radio reports. Pecora most likely arranged the committee schedule to meet deadlines for news to be included in the afternoon and evening newspapers. By his attention to detail, persistence, and use of staff members, Pecora set the standard for modern investigative hearings. The real bipartisan relationship and the excellent work by Counsel Pecora permitted the senators to question witnesses with authority and led them to draw moral conclusions. James Couzens found that his personality was well suited to these circumstances.

Like previous Senate hearings and those that have taken place since that time, the Pecora hearings tended to personalize issues. For example, Charles G. Dawes, who previously had a stellar national reputation, was personally disgraced. He had been a general in World War I, was the first director of the budget, revamped German reparations, and was ambassador to England, vice president, and president of the RFC. That a man who held such important positions of national trust was having his ethics publicly questioned set the tone for further committee hearings. What was termed the Dawes Bank broke Illinois law in lending funds to the holding companies of Samuel Insull. The subsequent RFC loan supported by President Hoover gave the appearance of insider favoritism. As the Pecora hearings continued it began to seem as if the bankers, brokers, and others involved in the national financial system were demonstrably incompetent, negligent, and irresponsible and showed evidence of significant avarice.

Some writers have concluded that the Senate investigation was ill timed. As one historian has written: "On the heels of the Michigan banking moratorium, precisely when they needed moral support, American's commercial bankers endured nine days of shatteringly bad publicity."[6] Criticizing the Senate committee for holding hearings as the bank crisis was unfolding is an interesting idea, and one that confuses cause and effect. If anything, the Senate hearings were belated and should have taken place one or two years earlier. Nevertheless, the hearings found that no support could possibly be provided to the bankers, as "the moral sense of the nation" was deeply shocked, with "the bankers guilty of most of the charges."[7]

The sense of moral outrage during the hearings gave James Couzens an opportunity to vent his feelings. When one of many witnesses was under questioning, Couzens is noted as having made "frequent bitter comments" denouncing the witness's banking practices as "reprehensible" and demonstrating "rotten ethics."[8] Couzens relished his reputation as hardworking, hard-nosed, extremely efficient, quick tempered, and defensive of what he believed to be his prerogatives while aggressive in maintaining them. He was ambitious and believed in keeping his word and maintaining his integrity. Most of all, as his biography states, he was an independent man.[9] He knew, but did not broadcast, the important role he had played in making the Ford Motor Company a great success. His achievements at Ford followed by his public roles as police commissioner and then mayor of Detroit enhanced his natural self-confidence. Couzens was not in awe of any of the witnesses who appeared at the hearings, least of all those who represented the Guardian Group. The men of the Guardian also knew Couzens and were aware of his views, notably expressed in an earlier hearing when he stated that a banker must not borrow from his own bank, nor must he permit associates in his bank to make loans to themselves.[10]

But James Couzens did not limit his activity to the Senate hearings. On February 20, he introduced a joint resolution designed to permit the national banks in Detroit to reopen, if the State of Michigan passed enabling legislation for state chartered banks. President Hoover, Secretary of the Treasury Mills, and the Federal Reserve Board approved the proposal. The idea was to freeze certain assets in the Detroit banks, thus reassuring depositors and preventing panic runs on the banks. Incredibly, considering the potential implications, conservative Democrats criticized the plan and no immediate action was taken.[11] The Couzens bill was finally passed on February 25. At Couzens's suggestion, and with Ernest Kanzler as the chief advocate, the Michigan legislature passed the necessary empowering legislation.[12] However the bankers, other businessmen, auto executives, and various governmental officials had to agree on a plan of implementation.

Unfortunately, no plan was found to be acceptable to the Michigan banking duopoly. Plans approved by the Guardian Group were turned down by the First National, and vice versa. Within each major group were smaller circles with specific interests they wished to protect. Finally, the largest depositor in both banking groups had to approve the plan of merger that was eventually suggested. That person was Henry Ford, who disdained involvement in the decision-making, and would not respond to requests for a resolution.[13]

The initiative seemed to be at a standstill when a new plan was announced. On Sunday, February 26, it was disclosed that Henry and Edsel Ford had agreed to invest capital in a merger of the Guardian and the First National groups. Considering Henry Ford's refusal to be involved in the discussions, the dire situation that had developed, and his previous public statements in regard to banking, this was a very significant declaration.[14] The immediate response was mixed relief and jubilation. In Dearborn, where Ford interests were paramount, a large contingent of people paraded bearing the banner "BANK WITH HANK."[15] The almost-universal acclaim that met the Ford announcement was almost immediately followed by individuals and groups who weighed their own best interests.

It appeared that the Fords were going to get a very good bargain, unlike all of the other interested parties. The bankers in Detroit read what Henry Ford had to say about how banks should be run, and realized they would not fit in. The New York banks, which were owed money based on loans made to the Guardian and First National, were not pleased. Neither were many Michigan banks outside of Detroit. Banking interests found that they would not be given preferred status in payoffs. The RFC, which had considered a loan to facilitate the merger of the Guardian and First National now wavered, negotiated with the various banking interests, and reversed course. Adding to the negativism over Ford's proposal was the displeasure of both General Motors and the Chrysler Corporation.[16]

The United States senators from Michigan took very differing positions in the attempt to gain a banking settlement in Detroit. Watching on the sidelines was the junior senator, Arthur Vandenberg. Despite his friendship with Roy D. Chapin, whose financial interests were very much involved, Vandenberg played no role in attempting to resolve the crisis. In contrast, James Couzens was very much involved. He had sponsored and supported national and state legislation to assist in solving the crisis. True to his character, he made public statements on the Ford proposal, like others initially favoring the Ford banking plan. Also like others, he changed his mind when the full import of the plan was understood. As the situation changed, he supported a smaller loan from the RFC, until on February 28 he was informed that non–Ford banking interests in Detroit asked that no RFC loan be made.[17]

With the Ford banking idea dead, the role of James Couzens changed dramatically. Politicians in Washington, his fellow senator, Vandenberg, bankers and civic leaders in Detroit, and even Henry Ford now urged Couzens to visit Detroit and broker a compromise solution.[18] Beginning when he arrived on March 1, for three days Couzens met with all of the interested parties. Among them were Ernest Kanzler, Clifford Longley, and Henry Bodman.[19] A well-known photo taken at the time shows Henry

Fathers and sons: (Left to right) Sen. James Couzens, Frank Couzens, Henry Ford, and Edsel Ford. This photograph was taken in the first days of March 1933, when James Couzens was in the Detroit area in an attempt to broker a solution to the Detroit banking crisis. The old partners, Henry Ford and James Couzens, had not posed together in a photograph for many years. A short time after this, Frank Couzens would become acting mayor of Detroit and later be elected to two terms as mayor. Almost a year later, in February 1934, Edsel Ford would be subjected to intense questioning by James Couzens in the U.S. Senate hearings into the Detroit banking crisis.

Ford and James Couzens posing together in apparent harmony. According to some captions, this was the first time in twenty years that both men had appeared in a joint photo.[20] In another photo, Henry and Edsel Ford pose with James Couzens and his son Frank, who in one month would become the mayor of Detroit.

While Couzens did meet with Henry Ford, nothing much was accomplished other than both men being cordial to one another. More success came in meetings with those who had previously been unable to agree on a plan. The agreement was not much different from previous plans, but it now appeared there was some promising give and take. Most everyone was complimentary to Couzens for his involvement, and it appeared that both the Guardian and the First National banks would avoid insolvency and soon be able to reopen.[21]

With the feeling of a job well done, Couzens left Detroit on March 3 so he could be in Washington for the inauguration of Franklin Roosevelt the following day. While the meetings continued in Detroit, the rest of the nation was not simply standing by. As the situation in Detroit remained unresolved, the financial situation was deteriorating throughout the nation. With the automobile industry having become a symbol of American economic vitality, the importance that Detroit had earned during the 1920s now became a problem. The symbolism of that city did not change when the banks closed in Detroit. Nor did the prominence of the automobile executives, who had been hailed as dynamic businessmen, alter. What did change was that the Detroit bank closures, and the subsequent failure to resolve the crisis in Detroit, caused a significant loss of confidence throughout the nation. It was not as if the banks of Minneapolis, Cincinnati or Los Angeles had failed. These were in Detroit, the symbol and center of the dynamic America of the 1920s.

The effect of the Michigan bank closures was almost immediate, as in the week ending February 16, the Federal Reserve recorded a new record high in the circulation of funds. This was the result of member banks drawing down on their reserves to the point of nearly reaching minimal legal requirements.[22]

International repercussions were also immediate as the dollar declined against foreign currencies. U.S. reserves of gold fell as foreign central banks demanded gold for the dollars that they held. Each successive day found the dollar continuing to decline while gold was set aside to meet continued demands from foreign banks. On February 16, U.S. gold reserves fell by nearly $11 million.[23]

As no resolution was found to localize the bank crisis to Detroit, the situation continued to deteriorate. Each day individuals demanded gold for their dollars, but the gold was not put into circulation. Instead, it was hoarded, or safeguarded, depending on one's perception. In one week, the national reserve of gold fell by $51 million. Banks, in turn, sold prime government bonds to obtain cash, thus causing securities to decline by almost 25 percent.[24]

In Michigan the first problem was a shortage of cash. This led to Michigan residents and businesses drawing on balances held in other states. As early as February 16, Alfred P. Sloan, Jr., president of General Motors, and Walter P. Chrysler, president of Chrysler Corporation, stressed to bankers the pressing need to come to some agreement so the normal operations of the motor industry might resume.[25]

In the rest of the nation time had run out. No longer could the banks in other communities and states withstand the failure of both the banks and the men in Detroit. "No one was sure what the next day would bring. The queues before the windows of tellers lengthened. Almost all Americans who could tried to get cash in hand to carry them over until rescue measures could be taken."[26]

On February 23 banks in Indiana were closed. Two days later those in Maryland succumbed to the pressures, and Arkansas banks closed on February 27. Ohio took the same action on the 28th. The Maryland closure had an immediate practical and psychological impact on Washington, D.C., as many government workers had their savings in Maryland banks.[27]

On March 1, Alabama, Kentucky, Nevada and Tennessee followed suit. On the next day the banks in Arizona, California, Louisiana, Mississippi, and Oregon were closed.[28] On the same day, March 2, the list expanded to include New Mexico, Washington, Utah, Texas, Georgia, Idaho, and Wisconsin.[29] Some states passed legislation enabling banks to close without a proclamation. On March 4, New York succumbed, as the pressures from the rest of the nation on banks in that state were overwhelming. Acting at almost the same time, the governor of Illinois closed banks there. "Governors of other States fell into line, and the suspension became general throughout the country."[30] A time of reckoning had come on inaugural day, March 4: "in the early morning before the inauguration, every bank in America had locked its doors. It was now not just a matter of staving off hunger. It was a matter of seeing whether a representative democracy could conquer the economic collapse. It was a matter of staving off violence, even (at least some thought) revolution."[31]

In retrospect, the banking crisis of 1933 did not occur without adequate warning. The system of American banking was widely recognized to be problematic, as the number of banking failures before 1933 attests. Periodic efforts were made to resolve the various problems, most notably on the national level by the creation of the Federal Reserve System in 1912. A combination of various interests, national history, economic theories and political differences led to neglect or compromise. The rise of a national economy based on manufacturing following the Civil War changed the nature of the problem. Boom times, followed by what were termed "panics," seemed to be part of the natural order of things. From 1923 to 1929 there were an average of almost two bank failures per day, for a total of nearly five thousand in seven years.[32] The difference was that most of the failed banks were small in size and located in rural areas.

Ranked next to the agricultural sector and railroads, the automobile industry was the biggest industrial enterprise in the United States.[33] "The Detroit Bank Holiday of 1933 was a chilling demonstration of the power that the Motor City had come to exercise in the American economy."[34] The psychological effect of the Detroit banking failure was profound. Detroit's contribution to the American belief in the highway of hope ceased. Instead, to most Americans, the falling domino of bank closures began with the problems in Detroit.

But the effect was not only psychological; there were financial consequences throughout the nation even before the banks in other states were closed. After the closure of the banks in Michigan, in the week following February 14, all motorcar sales were suspended throughout the nation. General Motors and Chrysler Corporation temporarily eliminated national advertising, while Ford Motor Company employment dropped to 27,000, from 42,000 the week before the holiday.[35]

The ripple effect of the bank holiday in suspending auto production was incalculable. Such effects obviously affected the national psyche while attacking business and personal income. The impact can be gauged to some degree by reckoning the impact of cancelled national advertising, a consideration that might not usually come to mind. Advertising agencies, publishers of magazines and newspapers, suppliers of newsprint and so on were directly affected. Employees faced layoffs, curtailed work hours, and possible salary reductions. During the Great Depression, nobody knew if the curtailment of auto production, or national advertising, was going to be temporary, or if there was any hope on the horizon. If an average citizen were to measure confidence in the executive offices of General Motors or Chrysler by their action in suspending advertising, the conclusion was not comforting.

The bank crisis struck a body blow to the national mood and economy. Already, 1932 had been a very bad year and the U.S. was extremely vulnerable to a total loss of national confidence. Automobile production, which had been the basis for an enormous change in American life, now reflected the dire situation. In 1932, production of Ford cars was 20 percent of 1929's level. Chevrolet production in 1932 dropped by 68 percent from 1929. In the luxury car category, Cadillac and LaSalle production in 1932 fell to one quarter of 1929's level, while Lincoln fell by two-thirds.[36] In 1933, auto volume was down by 75 percent from 1929.[37]

March 4, 1933, brought an end to the crucial time a discredited president remained in office during the worst financial crisis the nation had ever faced. Franklin Roosevelt had been overwhelmingly elected and was now president. It was time to act. Writing in 1935, when the results of the change in administration were not yet fully comprehended, Frederick Lewis Allen noted: "History does not often time its climaxes with precision. But in this instance the timing was diabolically perfect. No drama written to throw into bold relief the defeat of the financiers and the failure of Hoover's measures for recovery could have had a more effective curtain."[38]

The timing of the bank closures to coincide with Hoover's exit and FDR's entrance is more than dramatic history. The timing was a stroke of good luck for Franklin Roosevelt. The crisis provided Roosevelt an opportunity to demonstrate authentic leadership and create circumstances on which he could lay the foundation of success.

On Saturday, March 4, 1933, the newly inaugurated president gave the oft-quoted speech that set the tone for the new administration. Some phrases, such as "the only thing we have to fear, is fear itself," and "this nation asks for action and action now," have long become part of the national memory. With Biblical allusions, the new president also talked of "the unscrupulous money changers" having been driven from the temple and "indicted in the court of public opinion." The impact of the Senate hearings, well understood at the time, is the basis for this indirect but pointed reference. It is meaningful that Roosevelt chose to associate himself, in his most momentous first speech as president, with the disclosures of the Senate hearings. As William Leuchtenburg tells us,

> Now he had to back his vigorous words with action. He faced a fearful number of tasks. He had to restore the shattered economy. He had to give a new sense of purpose to the federal government and enlist it on behalf of the national interest more basic than that of business or any other single group. But most of all he had to restore the faith of a nation that seemed almost palsied with fear.[39]

On Tuesday, March 6, Franklin Roosevelt declared a national bank holiday. The basis of his action was an obscure law from World War I. The same law had been brought to the attention of Herbert Hoover, who thought it was not a basis on which he could act. The proclamation closing the banks gave official status to what had already happened and nationalized what had been the actions of various state governments. This was the first act of the new administration which demonstrated a transition of power, in this case from the individual states to the national government.

"No president or party ever came into power with a clearer popular mandate to break with past policies and inaugurate new ones, but just what the new program should be was still to be worked out."[40] Responding to Roosevelt's rhetoric and actions, Alfred P. Sloan, Jr., of General Motors sent a telegram off to the president. He said that his company "stood ready to accept whatever losses might result" from what FDR had termed "facing the facts."[41]

The first order of business, as everyone agreed, was to reopen the banks. Despite the change in administrations, Roosevelt requested that top officials of the Hoover Treasury Department remain to assist his newly appointed officials. With a realization of the serious nature of the crisis and a sense of uncommon patriotism, among those who remained to help were Secretary of the Treasury Ogden Mills and Undersecretary of the Treasury Arthur A. Ballantine. Ballantine knew Franklin Roosevelt from their days at Harvard, as did Mills. In addition, Mills's estate was only about five miles from the Roosevelt home at Hyde Park. Neither Ballantine nor Mills thought very highly of Roosevelt.[42] Nevertheless, the strange partnership worked well in the critical spring of 1933.

March 9 was a landmark day in American history, one not usually marked by any special celebrations or any other type of remembrance. The day began with the Congress responding to a special session called by President Roosevelt to deal with the banking crisis. To some, the day is remembered as the start of the New Deal, as Roosevelt termed his administration.

To others it is the first day of the New Deal period termed "the first hundred days," which lasted until June 16. Legislation affecting banking, industry, agriculture, labor, and unemployment relief resulted in a fundamental transformation in the way the national government relates to individual citizens, state governments, and important sectors of American life. In fact, to use a phrase associated with the automobile industry, a power shift had taken place. This was made possible by the actions and inaction of men in the banking and financial sector, notably those meeting in Detroit as well as those appearing before the Senate Committee on Banking and Currency. The failure of the banks in Detroit shifted public opinion about bankers from approbation to disgrace. With the passage of one bill on March 9, 1933, a shift was underway in which "the economic capital of the America moved from Wall Street to Washington."[43]

One observer has noted, "It would be extravagant to say that the closing of the banks was causal to the New Deal by which its crisis was met. It would be untrue, however, to insist that it did not have a dominant role in the creation of that program."[44] It would be difficult to find a better example of the incongruity between what the Detroit auto makers turned bankers wanted and what actually occurred. They had intended for the auto capital to become independent of the financial capital in Wall Street. Instead, due to the events in Detroit that triggered the nationwide banking crisis, with public opinion behind him, the economic initiative was now in the hands of Franklin Roosevelt.

Had they been able to choose, the auto industrialists would probably have preferred the power of Wall Street to the intervention of the national government. This would become more evident as various economic policies of the New Deal were found to be at cross-purposes with the interests of the auto manufacturers. After the passage of the National Labor Relations Act in 1935, this would become starkly apparent. Supported in principal by the New Deal, and after 1935 buttressed by law, auto industry unions were a consequence of the power shift.

All of the automakers had to live in the new landscape. But only Ford Motor Company had been heavily opposed to the interests of Wall Street. The other two dominant manufacturers, General Motors and Chrysler, were actually creations of the financial sector. While Ford was an international concern, the headquarters were in the Detroit area. Both Alfred P. Sloan, Jr., of GM and Walter Chrysler had their major offices in New York City. Neither Sloan nor Chrysler had taken leadership positions in the attempt to prevent the bank closures in Detroit. Both had been involved on the periphery, promising some support if Ford acted first and with the most substantial effort. They had purposefully refrained from leadership roles, no doubt due to their evaluation of the Ford involvement in the Guardian Group. We know that Henry Ford chose not to act to prevent the banking crisis, but, in effect, both Sloan and Chrysler made the same choice. Had they or Henry and Edsel Ford limited the banking problem to Detroit, their own best corporate interests would have been served.

But in the spring of 1933, the foremost need was to solve the banking crisis. The first bill introduced in the special session convened to deal with the banks was not available in print form for members of the House to read. That did not prevent legislative action. The Emergency Banking Relief Act was introduced, passed, and approved on the same day without referral to any committee. It confirmed every action the president and the secretary of the treasury had taken as emergency steps since March 4. Furthermore, the president was given broad discretionary powers over transactions in credit, currency, gold, silver, and foreign exchange. Domestic hoarding of gold and export of gold were forbidden, with penalties that included fines of up to $10,000 and 10 years in prison. Among other provisions, the secretary of the treasury was authorized to call in all gold and silver certificates.

The vote in the House of Representatives was unanimous in favor; in the Senate the vote was 73–7. Such was the mood of the time that the seven senators who voted against the bill said they thought it was much too moderate. At least two of those voting against the bill favored the more radical idea of nationalization of the banks.[45]

On Sunday, March 12, Franklin Roosevelt gave the first of his "fireside chats," addressing the American public using the national radio networks. In simple-to-understand language the president explained the nature of the banking crisis and the steps that were being taken to bring about a resolution of the problem.

Assisting in reviewing and editing the script used for the chat was Arthur A. Ballantine. The inability of Ballantine and Chapin to gain Henry Ford's acceptance of their plan for saving the Guardian did not negatively affect Ballantine's career. The prestigious Wall Street firm to which he had belonged headed by Elihu Root changed over the years to include former governor of New York and two-time Republican candidate for president Thomas E. Dewey. Ballantine stayed on to assist the Roosevelt administration during the bank crisis. He was among those responsible for making the plans to reopen the nation's banks, beginning on March 13.[46]

The Detroit banks were not among those slated to reopen on March 13, and after more data became available, they were never permitted to open their doors again. RFC investigators proved the banks were insolvent and conservators were appointed to receive payments and pay out available funds to depositors.

The meetings and negotiations that had begun in February 1933, originated to prevent a banking crisis in Detroit, had never been terminated. "Bitter wrangling as plan after plan for bank opening was proposed, dissected, [and] discarded" took place.[47] Couzens thought a solution had been brokered, only to have it fall apart when circumstances led to other states succumbing to inevitable financial pressures. The closure of banks in other states took place rapidly within a very short time period, creating a continuously changing reality, making all planning instantly irrelevant.

With banks in Detroit closed, the city needed normalcy in its financial sector. Almost $19 million in GM deposits were frozen, despite the company needing cash to pay workers and conduct business.[48] Alfred P. Sloan of GM later recounted that there were about one and half million people with all of their cash resources impounded. He recalled that "at Detroit's leading business club you had to pay cash in advance for your luncheon."[49] The situation had come close to being chaotic, and in conferences GM officials concluded action was needed. Alfred Sloan tells us:

> Finally it became obvious that the situation required that some strong organization, capable within itself of assuming the responsibility of affording the essential relief, should step forward. Otherwise exceedingly serious developments could be expected: people were suffering. It was not a problem of selection. General Motors was the only organization that had the resources to do the job and General Motors did it.[50]

The conferees, the RFC and other interested parties, decided to leave Henry Ford out of the formation of a new Detroit bank. Among those involved in the discussions were Alfred P. Sloan, Jr., Walter P. Chrysler, Alvan Macauley of Packard, Frederick and William A. Fisher of GM/Fisher Bodies, DuBois Young of Hupmobile and some old-line families including the Newberrys, who were long time Packard directors.[51]

Ford was left out after long and futile negotiations attempted to gain his support. He had been cooperative when it seemed he and Edsel would take over the failed banks in what was a very good deal for the Fords. When that scheme fell apart, he reverted to being unwilling to cooperate in any plan.

The new bank, the National Bank of Detroit, began operations on March 24. GM purchased all of the common stock for $12.5 million, while the RFC purchased the preferred stock for another $12.5 million. Among those on the board of directors were Henry E. Bodman (general counsel and director of Packard), Donaldson Brown (GM finance vice president), Walter P. Chrysler, Alfred P. Sloan, Jr., and Frank Couzens. Earlier attempts to form new banks in Detroit had foundered on the fear that Wall Street would be controlling the new banks. With GM behind the new bank and the Chrysler Corporation being one of the largest depositors, in effect the fears were realized. In taking charge to resurrect the financial system in Detroit, GM said it wanted to get out of the banking business as soon as possible. Due to the complications of the time and the advent of World War II, GM held onto the bank until April 1945.[52]

The $12.5 million invested in March 1933 had grown to a sales total of approximately $21.4 million in April 1945. The bank had become a success and helped GM to become the dominant automaker and the largest industrial organization in the world. By 1945, as measured by deposits, the First National was the 13th largest bank in the U.S.[53]

The Fords opened their rival bank in August. In charge until his death in 1943 was Edsel Ford. He and his farther spurned any assistance from the RFC for the Manufacturers National Bank. Directors who had been involved with the Guardian Group included Ford attorney Clifford Longley and George R. Fink, "maker of much automobile steel."[54]

By 1954 the deposits in the new Ford bank had grown to almost $600 million. In contrast, by 1954 the First National started by GM had deposits of approximately $1.7 billion,[55] yet another measure of the rise of GM and the decline of the Ford Motor Company.

The Great Depression, and specifically the bank failures in Detroit, spurred on the consolidation of the automobile industry. All of the auto firms had huge pressures, but how Roy D. Chapin had to hustle, negotiate, and use his extensive personal contacts to keep the Hudson Motor Company afloat is a prime example. Resuming leadership of Hudson, Chapin found the company in very bad shape. He needed approximately $6 million to pay off debts and move forward. His stake in the Guardian Group was now a significant liability. The plan of using the Guardian to free Hudson, as well as Packard, Reo, and Ford, from being dependent on Wall Street had failed. In fact, it was now necessary for Chapin to seek out Wall Street through contacts he had made as secretary of commerce. The convoluted negotiations took place from July 1934 to May 1935. A significant amount of assistance, however, did come from the Commercial Investment Trust (CIT) headed by Ernest Kanzler. CIT pledged to provide Hudson with $50 million each year for five years to finance the sale of Hudson autos.[56]

Equally significant was that neither of the two new Detroit banking firms took part in financing or supporting Chapin's actions to keep Hudson in business. Of course, one bank was under the control of the Ford Motor Company; the other was a GM and Chrysler creation. With the dominant sources of local funds under the control of the Big Three, additional pressures and competitive disadvantages became the reality for the smaller Detroit-based firms such as Hudson, Packard, Hupp and Graham-Paige. Even Chapin's friend Edsel Ford did not support the Hudson reinvigoration. Perhaps neither of the two new banks had sufficient capital.

Clearly, a lack of capital had not been the reason for Ford's reluctance to subordinate his deposits in the Guardian Group in February 1933. Neither was a lack of capital the reason for the automobile executives, the assembled bankers, or the civic leaders of Detroit failing to resolve the banking issues in February or early March. What had been lacking were leadership and a sense of responsibility. The vaunted belief that the auto men knew how to get things done was shown to be a fable. The most storied of the group, and the de facto leader of the automobile industry since about 1908, was Henry Ford. But in effect, he abdicated his position. His personal characteristics and beliefs had led to enormous success, but they were also problematic as the world changed around him.

The two other giants of the automobile industry, Walter Chrysler and Alfred P. Sloan, Jr., did not step up when they could have prevented a very chaotic situation. Perhaps their knowledge of the Ford relationship with the Guardian Group led them to promise support, but not leadership, in actions to prevent the Detroit banking debacle. Furthermore, both men were based in New York City. After the nationwide collapse of the banking system, but when their actions still counted, they did provide the leadership to help restart the financial system in Detroit. But by the time they acted, the legislation of the New Deal had begun lessening their economic independence.

The opening of the National Bank of Detroit, however, was not universally appreciated in Detroit. The GM and Chrysler plan was opposed as a Wall Street plot in which local control of the bank would be lost. The stockholders of the closed banks also objected, believing the new GM bank would result in the Guardian and First National groups being permanently closed. This would mean a total loss of the stockholders' investments. Just as worrisome as the permanent closure of the failed duopolies was that it would trigger a provision in the group charters assigning double liability to each shareholder.[57]

The legislation that permitted group banking in Michigan also assigned each shareholder double liability in the event of failure. When the per share levy for Guardian Group was announced on June 1, it came to $6.43. Edsel Ford, with approximately 50,000 shares, thus owed over

$640,000. The double liability provision and the requirement for payment by the stockholders brought about some interesting developments.[58] In addition to having lost their investment in the Guardian Group and being assessed double liability for their Guardian shares, the officers and directors had a lawsuit brought against them by Guardian depositors. The legal action was to have Guardian officers and directors account for their official conduct and to pay for property acquired for them or transferred to others as a consequence of their status. Among those listed in the legal action were Henry Bodman and his law firm partner Clifford Longley. Also included were Walter Briggs of Briggs Body, Roy D. Chapin, William A. Fisher, Carlton Higbie, Edsel Ford, Ernest Kanzler, Charles S. Mott, Ransom E. Olds, and Alvan Macauley.[59]

At least one shareholder attempted to avoid the assessment. In testimony before the Senate subcommittee, GM Vice President Charles S. Mott admitted that he had sold 20,000 shares of Detroit Guardian stock to an executive vice president of one of the Guardian subsidiaries. This sale took place in December 1932. The payment was in the form of a promissory note, for which no payment had been made. The purchaser, who by the time of the testimony was employed by Mott's sugar corporation, admitted he did not have sufficient income or means to purchase the stock. Despite being a member of the Guardian Group executive committee and of the advisory committee, Mott would not admit that he was attempting to rid himself of the stock, nor that he was aware of the perilous financial status of the Guardian Group.[60]

Part of Mott's defense against the implications of his sale of stock was his alleged belief that the provisions of the articles of association about double liability printed on the back of the stock certificates were not meaningful. In addition, Mott testified that in any case he had loaned the Guardian Group $2.5 million to cover an embezzlement, "which was more than three times any possible liability. So I dismissed the matter from my mind, feeling that I was not liable."[61] At the time of his testimony Mott still owned 120,000 Guardian shares.

James Couzens's response to the assessed liability contrasted to that of Mott and those who were suing to stop the assessments. It was an indicator of his personality and his fondness for tweaking his fellow Michigan investors. Couzens wrote two checks totaling over $30,000, one to the receivers of the National Bank Group and the other to the Guardian Group. The owner of record of the shares was his wife Margaret. After writing the checks, Couzens notified the press and stated, "The provisions of the law for double liability are plainly stated," and that he and Mrs. Couzens believed "the moral obligation is plain" and they would not "avail ourselves of any technical or other reasons for not paying the assessment."[62] In asserting his principled superiority in paying his assessments, Couzens further inflamed opinion about him among those who had been investors in the two failed banking groups.

The consequences of the bank closures in Detroit were real and serious. In addition to the bankruptcy of the city, the inability to pay salaries of public employees, the loss of individual bank deposits, the scarcity of cash, and the privations of individual citizens, the shareholders and officers of the Guardian Group and First National Group suffered significant financial losses. One result of the financial disaster was that finger pointing began immediately. The first person to do so was the Governor of Michigan, William Comstock, in a statement with his official proclamation closing Michigan banks on February 14. Comstock blamed the Ford Motor Company and Henry Ford for being unwilling to subordinate deposits and guarantee another loan from the RFC. Within a short time, the governor was pressured into retracting his statement, claiming he "misunderstood the facts."[63]

As the situation developed and it became clear that the closure of the Detroit banks had national and international implications and consequences, the attempt to fix blame became more intense. Herbert Hoover blamed both Governor Comstock, for unnecessarily declaring the bank holiday, and Franklin Roosevelt for undermining public confidence. Hoover also blamed James Couzens for failing to respond to Hoover's plan in the February 9 White House meeting. When Couzens publicly stated that the Hoover administration had purposely been lenient with the Detroit banks during the presidential campaign, Hoover increasingly faulted Couzens. Partisans of the former president soon took up his belief, turning it into the loyalist view. Republicans, who had not been fond of Hoover, took up Hoover's position so that it became Republican orthodoxy. This took root increasingly as the Democrats used Hoover as a personification of heartless Republican social and economic policies.

Many writers have summarily decided that the banking crisis in Detroit resulted from a long-standing feud between Henry Ford and James Couzens. The latter is assigned the role of having purposely stopped the RFC loan in February 1933, which presumably might have kept the Guardian Group solvent. Those views were given life in Detroit by local newspapers and by the last president of the Union Guardian Trust Company, Clifford Longley. He made his charge against Couzens in front of a so-called "one man grand jury" held by a Michigan judge. However, when the judge issued his report in October 1933, no blame was assigned to anyone, even Couzens.

Three national publications thought the report to have been what two termed a "whitewash." *Time* magazine, in an article titled "Whitewash in Detroit," reported, "It was a thorough whitewash of Detroit's banks and bankers."[64] Using the same terminology, John T. Flynn reported, "The one-man grand jury which was investigating the causes of the bank failures — the series of subtle depredations by which profit-crazed men wrecked the finance of a great city — ended abruptly with a whitewash."[65] Flynn brought an interesting perspective. Not only was he the economic columnist for *The New Republic* and a freelance writer for other publications, he was an investigator on the staff of Ferdinand Pecora, chief counsel for the Senate subcommittee holding the hearings on banking practices.

Occupying a place on the political spectrum to the right of *The New Republic*, *Business Week* concluded:

> Two months ago Detroiters were convinced that their banks had been the victims of Wall Street machinations, or a duel to the death between Henry Ford and the other motorcar giants, and a hard-boiled Washington attitude. Now after hearing the witnesses, they come back to their first impression — that a collapse was inevitable and, after all, the bank officials were responsible for it.[66]

Still, the view that Henry Ford and James Couzens brought about the Detroit bank failure has persisted. Couzens, in a revealing example of his combative personality, almost relished the accusations against him. "I did not stop the disputed loan," he said. "However, I'm glad to have the public think I stopped it, if the public wants to think that, because as it was presented to Washington, it was an illegal and wicked loan."[67] What did annoy him was that those who were responsible for the banking problems in Detroit were not held accountable. Since his testimony before the "one man grand jury" had been curtailed, he said, "I still have the forum of the Senate."[68]

Couzens's drive to expose the banking practices of the Guardian Group, and to a lesser extent the practices of the First National Group, was one stimulus for the hearings into the Detroit banking crisis that ran from December 19, 1933, to January 23, 1934. But Couzens alone was not enough. Part of the motivation was the desire of the public to know what brought about the national closure of all banks concurrent with the end of the Hoover administration, especially financial failure in Detroit, the formerly dynamic home of change and progress.

But the real reason to have the bankers and automobile executives testify was political. When the Senate committee heard from Samuel Insull, and then moved on to Charles Mitchell and the National City Bank of New York, the Democrats and their Progressive Republican allies realized the tactical value of the inquiries. This was made evident when the most astute politician of the period, FDR, voiced his support for the hearings in two separate instances, in addition to the oblique reference in his inaugural address.

In February, Franklin Roosevelt announced he intended to carry the investigation to the limit.[69] Then, on March 13, nine days after the inauguration and one week after the proclamation closing all banks, Franklin Roosevelt met with Committee Chairman Fletcher. In this meeting Roosevelt requested that Fletcher broaden the probe to include private banking operations and investment houses. The Senate concurred and increased the scope of the hearings and gave the subcommittee additional subpoena powers. "For the next two years this committee revealed practices which thoroughly discredited the American financial structure and laid the groundwork for New Deal reform."[70]

In the hearings that dealt with the Guardian Group, Couzens played an interesting role. He was an active member of the subcommittee, with bluntly stated views on the ethical behavior of the people who appeared as witnesses. Politically, while a registered Republican, he was fiercely independent, although associated with the Progressive wing of the Republicans. In the election of 1932 he had not supported either Hoover or Roosevelt, but made clear his preference for Roosevelt. Both he and his wife were investors in both of the Detroit banking groups. His investment and payment of the assessment, as well as his past business relationships with three key witnesses, would now be considered conflicts of interest. Counsels for the witnesses appearing before the subcommittee today would object to Couzens's involvement. Public watchdog groups and the press today would expect Couzens to voluntarily step aside and not take part in examining witnesses.

Considering Couzens's view of his own integrity, he probably never considered that he had real conflicts of interest in questioning Clifford Longley, Ernest Kanzler, and Edsel Ford. Both Kanzler and Longley had come to the Ford Motor Company after Couzens had resigned. However, they had ample opportunities for interaction with Couzens in the small circle of Detroit leadership. But James Couzens and Edsel Ford knew each other very well.

For approximately 13 years, from 1902 into 1915, Couzens was an integral part of in the Ford Motor Company, second only to Henry Ford in importance. When Couzens began work there, Edsel Ford was nine years old. When he left, Edsel was 22. In fact, James Couzens watched Edsel as he grew into a young man. It was not a casual relationship. Edsel started at Ford in 1912 or early 1913 and was assigned to work in the area that Couzens dominated. Charles Sorensen, who did not have good relations with either Couzens or Edsel Ford, reported that Couzens "resented Edsel's coming into the company, and at times [was] brutal about it." Then, when Henry Ford decided to avoid Ford Motor Company board meetings, he delegated the majority representative job to Edsel, who had to face the other investors, including the very blunt-speaking Dodge Brothers and an acerbic James Couzens. It did not help Edsel that he succeeded Couzens as secretary-treasurer.[71]

When Edsel Ford appeared before the Senate investigating committee, he had no reason to expect that Couzens would be kind or considerate, even though they had seen each other in a cordial meeting less than a year previously. In fact, based on Couzens's well-known personality and standards of probity, Edsel could only expect a grilling. When past history between the two men became part of the investigation, Edsel must have wished he were most any place else.

In reviewing the questioning of Edsel Ford, remember that Couzens and the other original shareholders of Ford Motor Company all accepted a buyout in 1919 from the Ford family. In fact the final negotiations, in which Couzens got special consideration for his shares, were between James Couzens and Edsel Ford.[72] Thus, knowing full well what the answers would be, Couzens asked, "Mr. Ford, may I ask how the stock of the Ford Motor Company is held?" Edsel replied, "Held by Mr. Henry Ford and Mrs. Ford and myself." Again with full knowledge, Couzens asked, "Not held by the public?" Edsel replied, "No sir."[73]

Perhaps Couzens got some type of enjoyment from asking Edsel Ford about ownership of the Ford Motor Company. However it did set on the record that when the Ford Motor Company took an action, Edsel and/or Henry Ford were the real decision makers. This meant that the memorandum of agreement, dated December 29, 1932, between the Ford Motor Company and the Guardian Group was made on behalf of Henry and Edsel Ford and could not have been made without the knowledge of at least one of them. The consequence of the memorandum was that the Ford Motor Company controlled the Guardian Group.

In his first day of testimony, Edsel identified himself as president of the Ford Motor Company as well as having various positions in Guardian Group subsidiaries and as a member of the Guardian Group advisory committee. The *New York Times* report of the January 11 testimony was titled, "Edsel Ford Hazy on Banking Detail." At least 18 times, Ford responded to questions with variations of "I cannot recall," or "I do not remember."[74] The following day the *Times* reported, "Edsel Ford ... was a much more satisfactory witness."[75] However, the damage had been done: Edsel Ford had been humiliated in a public forum.

Edsel Ford's testimony did not enhance his reputation and did not live up to the dynamic and bold leadership that had been ascribed to the leaders of the automobile industry. Since he was the most significant auto executive to testify, the negative perception extended to the entire industry. It was reinforced by the testimony of Charles Stewart Mott, Phillip Longley, and Ernest Kanzler. None were forthcoming about their involvement in the Guardian.

The achievements of the Guardian officers as pioneers in the automobile industry resulted in the accumulation of enormous wealth. Presumably, they were men who knew business matters very well. At the same time, the prevailing ethical standards, as reflected in the mentality of the 1920s, led them, as neophyte bankers, to follow the banking standards and practices of others. From our present perspective, banking ethics in the 1920s were reprehensible, but regrettably common. When Ferdinand Pecora of the Senate subcommittee asked one witness what had prompted him to act in such an irresponsible manner, the response was, "It was the times." Pecora, seeking clarification, asked, "I assume you mean the speculative atmosphere?" The banker agreed.[76] It seemed, at the time, as if the boom times would continue forever and business was conducted with that notion in mind.

Based on their successes, the leaders of the automobile industry had become accustomed to wielding power, and had developed into a class apart from most everyone else. The dual roles of industrialist and banker intensified their power and increased their isolation from ordinary stockholders. Their view of banks was quite different from the view citizens, who trusted banks as stable institutions into which funds could be safely deposited. In contrast, the insider shareholders, as both industrialists and bankers, viewed the Guardian Group as an organization created for their benefit. Their stakes in the Guardian provided a concentration of power far greater than their personal stakes. Despite the large sums of money involved, the Ford investment in the Guardian Group was very small relative to the Ford fortune and income. In actuality, the manner in which the Guardian Group was organized and funded was evidence of the type of banking that Henry Ford had long feared. That is, the decision makers of the Guardian Group controlled other people's money that they used for their own purposes.

If, when the Guardian was organized, the leaders had been held responsible for their decisions, perhaps its policies would not have been problematic. But several factors gave Ernest Kanzler, Clifford Longley, Charles S. Mott and the other officers and directors a false sense of security. Their fundamental error was in believing that the apparent backing of the Ford Motor Company provided safety. The erratic decision-making of Henry Ford was not taken into consideration. No doubt it was assumed that the deep involvement of Edsel Ford would provide protection for their investments and obligations.

Secondly, until the failure of the Guardian, bank closures throughout the nation, and the New Deal legislation that intensified banking oversight, regulation of banks was much less rigorous. Furthermore, the holding company structure exempted the Guardian from some of the standards that possibly could have encouraged more conservative behavior.

The Guardian Group had important political connections. One of the connections was Roy D. Chapin, who was very much involved in Guardian Group affairs. At the same time, Chapin had a special relationship with President Hoover in addition to being secretary of commerce in the last year of the Hoover administration. Charges were made that Chapin had arranged for two loans to the Guardian from the RFC.[77]

Alfred Leyburn, the chief national bank examiner, testified that he and other bank examiners were given written instructions to use "extraordinary discretion" and "leniency" in examining banks in 1931 and 1932.[78] In effect, the grave situation of the banking sector resulted in political calculations designed to avoid what now seems to have been inevitable.

An unforeseen consequence of the bank failures was that the problems in Detroit made clear that the automobile industry was not a powerful monolith. The Ford Motor Company's, worldwide leadership in the auto industry had previously obscured the differing interests of lesser companies. With the decline of Ford and the rise of General Motors and Chrysler, the differing interests came to the fore. The unwillingness of Henry Ford on one hand and Alfred P. Sloan, Jr., and Walter Chrysler on the other hand to unite in preventing the Detroit bank crisis was very revealing. When it came time for critical decision-making, differing interests trumped a collective unity.

The rise of the unions and the New Deal were two collaborative movements, one filling the power vacuum and the other taking advantage of the weakened power of the automobile industry. In effect, the auto industry was no longer in the driver's seat. Not only did new New Deal legislation support the union movement, there was also active intervention on its behalf. Neither the union leaders, the architects of the New Deal, or the auto leaders had any doubt of the significance of the shift in power.

The auto makers and their associates, who were affected by their lowered status, understood very quickly what had taken place. They knew power had slipped away; the evidence was to be found in the testimony before the Senate subcommittee, with James Couzens taking the dual role

July 28, 1933: The Auto Leaders Meet the New Deal: (From left to right) Robert Graham, vice president of Graham-Paige; Roy D. Chapin, president of Hudson; K.T. Keller, president of Dodge, vice president of Chrysler Corp.; Du Bois Young, president of Hupp Motor Company; Walter P. Chrysler, president and chairman of the board of the Chrysler Corp.; Fred J. Fisher, vice president of General Motors; Alvan Macauley, president of Packard and head of the National Automobile Chamber of Commerce; General Hugh S. Johnson, head of the National Recovery Administration; Alfred P. Sloan, Jr., president of General Motors; W.S. Knudsen, president of Chevrolet and Pontiac and vice president of General Motors; C.E. Wilson, vice president of General Motors; and Charles D. Hastings, chairman of the board of the Hupp Motor Car Co. The New Deal legislated the National Industrial Recovery Act in an attempt to regularize production and wages through codes written by each industry. Opponents of the act likened it to the idea of corporatism as introduced by Benito Mussolini. This photograph is taken at the initial meeting between representatives of the auto industry and the director of the N.R.A., General Hugh S. Johnson. Note that no representatives from Ford are present. The N.R.A. was the first New Deal attempt to intrude into business practices, angering Henry Ford, who avoided compliance with N.R.A. The other auto leaders attempted to write a code for the auto industry that would be self-serving. The Supreme Court declared the act unconstitutional in 1935. The N.R.A. is generally credited with furthering the automobile union movement. (The Henry Ford)

of interrogator and moralizer. On a personal level, Edsel Ford was publicly humiliated. Collectively, the revelations of how the Guardian Group and the First National operated tarnished the financial leadership in Detroit. The connection between the Guardian Group and the automobile industry, most specifically the Ford Motor Company, was made very clear.

It did not take long for the losers in the power shift to attempt to redress the imbalance. In August 1934, several months after Edsel Ford, Ernest Kanzler, Charles Stewart Moss, Clifford Longley, and others testified before the Senate subcommittee, the American Liberty League was announced. The goal of the Liberty League was to organize a coalition of Democrats and Republicans capable of defeating Roosevelt in the 1936 election. Among the leaders were John J. Raskob (presumably, by 1934, John J. Raskob was no longer persona non grata to Herbert Hoover) and others associated with General Motors, including the DuPonts, Alfred P. Sloan, Jr., Donaldson Brown, and William Knudsen. Mrs. Henry Joy, with connections to the Packard Motor Car Company, was also involved. In the election of 1936 the Liberty League dwarfed the Republican National Committee in staff and financing.

On the other, winning, side of the 1936 election battle was James Couzens. Even though he was a Republican, he supported Franklin Roosevelt for a second term. In the election of 1936, the automobile industry and other industrialists and financial leaders were overwhelmed. Only Maine and Vermont voted for the Republican candidate, Alfred P. Landon. The electoral vote was 523 for FDR, 8 for Landon, greater than the margin of victory against Hoover four years earlier. Clearly, the American Liberty League had not been a success. From the first, Couzens had generally supported Roosevelt and his policies. Of course, this made him a greater anathema to the leaders of the automobile industry.

No understanding of the bank failure is complete without considering the political positions of all of those who were involved. As has been suggested earlier, for years after 1932 the Democrats campaigned against Herbert Hoover and his policies. Their successful strategy was to associate any Republican candidate with Hoover and his allegedly heartless political philosophy that failed to alleviate the social and financial disasters of the Great Depression. In contrast, the Republican strategy became one of refocusing, restating, and revising the events of the time.

In assigning to James Couzens, or James Couzens and Henry Ford, the responsibility for closing the banks in Detroit, the collective automobile and financial leadership in Detroit was absolved. This seems to have worked, in the sense that the antagonism between Couzens and Henry Ford was a handy hook on which to hang the responsibility. They allegedly quarreled, but all references to that fact are usually stated generally, without any examples or proof.

Both Ford and Couzens had interesting personalities and did not much care if they were blamed. In fact, Couzens even welcomed the blame. Both Henry Ford and James Couzens had reached the apogee of their lives. Couzens was ill and died in October 1936. Henry Ford lived until April 1947, but slipped into apparent senility sometime before his death.

Putting the onus on Henry Ford and James Couzens does not change the fact that it was the collective automobile industry leadership that had gained great prominence and status in American life, which failed to live up to its reputation. First, these leaders demonstrated they were failures as bankers or bank owners. Then when the banking problems could have been limited to Detroit, they wasted away their opportunity to prove they knew how to solve problems and get things done. Putting the blame on Henry Ford and James Couzens for supposedly stymieing government rescue efforts, among other facts, disregards the time period from February 14 to March 3. During that time there were opportunities to localize the Detroit problems, to no avail.

The automobile industry and the men who ran it would not regain their status in American life until World War II intervened. Franklin Roosevelt signaled the opportunity for the auto industry on December 29, 1940. In his fireside chat of that date, President Roosevelt specifically made reference to his first fireside chat of March 12, 1933. He said it was a time "when the wheels of American industry were grinding to a halt, when the whole banking system of our country had ceased to function."[79] The reference was purposeful in this December 1940 talk. Roosevelt called upon management and labor to avoid both lockouts and strikes. In the almost eight years from the first fireside chat there had been an abundance of both strikes and lockouts, and considerable violence, with the New Deal favoring the labor movement.

It was in his December 1940 talk that Roosevelt called upon the

United States to become "the great arsenal of democracy." Within a short time period, the City of Detroit had adopted the phrase as a city slogan. Among other points that Roosevelt made, he announced a plan not used during the previous World War. Putting all industrialists on notice he said: "I am confident that if and when production of consumer or luxury goods in certain industries requires the use of machines and raw materials that are essential for defense purposes, then such production must yield, and will gladly yield, to our primary and compelling purpose."[80]

Roosevelt was operating from strength in his request, as in November he had been reelected to an unprecedented third term. Perhaps coincidentally, as part of the "blitz" the night of December 29, 1940, the Luftwaffe staged its largest incendiary bomb raid on London. The happenings across the Atlantic were well known to the American public through both newspaper and radio accounts. The combination of current events and the timing of the fireside chat influenced public opinion in favor of Roosevelt's policies. The auto leaders were wise to accept the opening Roosevelt offered. As in 1933 and 1936, the auto industry did not stand a chance against FDR.

Earlier, in June 1940, President Roosevelt recruited William S. Knudsen, once of the Ford Motor Company but then president of General Motors, to be in charge of revamping industry to produce armaments and other material needed for national defense. Both Alfred P. Sloan, Jr. and Henry Ford thought he should not have taken the task. They did have differing motives: Sloan intensely disliked Franklin Roosevelt, and while Henry Ford had the same view, he really did not want anyone else being the hero of productivity. Furthermore, Ford's old prejudices still colored his worldview.

At first Knudsen had a largely symbolic role while Roosevelt sorted out the issues and waited to see what the political fallout would be. What he found was that neither Sloan nor Ford had taken Knudsen's appointment as an opportunity for the auto manufacturers to step forward.

It was more than coincidental that at the same time Roosevelt announced the arsenal of democracy concept, Knudsen's role became more explicit, as he became director of the Office of Production Management. Eventually, he was commissioned as a lieutenant general to give him appropriate status in dealing with the various government bureaucracies. Along with his earlier Ford Motor Company experience and his GM success, Knudsen had considerable clout and public exposure. He became the symbol of the auto industry working under the leadership of Franklin D. Roosevelt, an idea not appreciated by either Sloan or Henry Ford.

Despite the initial resistance of both Sloan and Ford, the mobilization of the productive powers, and organizational acumen of the auto industry were critical in the victory of the United States and its allies. For the automobile industry this resulted in a resurgence of status, with one postwar consequence being an era of triumphalism, which came to an end sometime in the late 1960s.

But from March 1933 until the productive power of Detroit had been harnessed for the national military, the auto manufacturers found themselves playing defense against the rise of the industrial union movement. In their relative state of powerlessness they had been matched against the New Deal, the unions, and public opinion. And it all stemmed from the events that began in Detroit in February 1933.

In May 1941, the Ford Motor Company, the last auto firm that had held out against the labor union movement, gave in and signed a very favorable union contract. Surely this was not an outcome that Henry Ford had expected when he rejected the proposal to use his funds to prevent the Guardian failure. Ford had even thought the failure of the bank might be beneficial to the nation. In his meeting with Arthur Ballantine and Roy D. Chapin on February 13, 1933, he had said that "the country had to have a general cleaning up process, and that he did not care how soon it came about."[81]

Rather than the United States having a "general cleaning up process," the nation experienced a significant economic and political crisis in February and March 1933. Perhaps Henry Ford really thought that as he said, "The general effect would be that everybody would have to get to work a little sooner; that it might be a very good thing; and that in any event it had to come."[82] The unintended consequences completely overwhelmed what he had projected.

The actions of the principals of the Guardian Group which led to their request for a third loan from the Reconstruction Finance Corporation, and of the others who met in Detroit and vainly attempted to limit the consequent banking failure, are also illustrative of some of the causes of unintended or unanticipated consequences. That is, the Guardian chiefs could not foresee everything that did result from the banking crisis becoming nationwide. Their evident ignorance belied their prowess as captains of industry. Furthermore, their concern over their varied immediate interests during the failed negotiations to check or control the banking crisis, trumped their long-term interests.

Many unintended consequences have resulted from the pervasive use of the personal automobile. Some have been geographic as, for example, city centers gave way to shopping centers on the edge of town. The new shopping areas could be situated where large parking lots could be constructed. Other unforeseen results have been improved roads, greater mobility, and an increase in death and injury from traffic accidents. In recent years other health issues have surfaced, such as air quality. This has been mixed with environmental considerations about ozone depletion.

That the automobile and the automobile industry have had significant effects is common knowledge. But few people understand the role the leaders of the automobile industry had in creating a fundamental change in American political and economic history. The leaders of that industry did not set out to do so, but they were responsible for circumstances in which the power over economic decision-making became a political prize. The consequence was that a power shift that took place in the United States on March 4, 1933, with the closure of banks throughout the nation. This action taken by President Franklin Roosevelt was the first in a series of actions by which the federal government acquired power formerly held by the individual states as well as private industrial and financial interests. The precipitating critical event which led to this shift was the Detroit banking crisis of February 1933, itself the result of failed decision making by the leaders of the automobile industry.

Epilogue

It is common knowledge that historic events do not simply take place sequentially, or in a vacuum. History evolves in real time and has varying consequences. However, in focusing on some events to develop a theme and tell a story, it is easy to forget the surrounding reality. As certain events are spotlighted and a particular perception is advanced, in the shadows, life is going on. The glare of the spotlight on certain events or human interactions generally does not tell the full story of a particular period. A narrow focus permits one to comprehend fine details. But tangential questions arise that are unanswered because they stray from the subject.

This chapter is an attempt to answer a number of such questions. In actions of the Guardian Group leadership, were any of the Guardian Group's leaders indicted and tried? What were the legal issues? There are many questions about Sen. James Couzens, foremost, what happened to him after the banking crisis? After all, he did remain in office through 1936.

Legal Consequences

What were the legal ramifications after the Senate committee hearings ended? We might start with Herbert R. Wilkin, unknown so far in this book. Wilkin is the only person sentenced in connection with the Detroit banking crisis.[1] The record regarding his penalty and how long he served is confused and cannot be reported here accurately. According to a newspaper report, Wilkin held various positions in the Guardian Group, once as vice president of the Union Guardian Trust Company.[2] Henry Bodman was the chairman of the board of the Union Guardian Trust, while Clifford Longley was president. In testimony before the Senate committee,

Wilkin admitted that he had falsely reported bills payable of the Union Industrial Bank and Trust Company of Flint by $600,000. He did this at least twice, once in a signed statement and again in a similar statement in the annual report to the stockholders in 1931.[3] The Union Industrial Bank and Trust Company of Flint was under the leadership of Charles S. Mott.

Wilkin was not the only executive of the Guardian Group to be indicted. Robert O. Lord, former president of the Guardian Group; Wilkin as a former general manager and executive vice president; and James Walsh, who was also a former executive vice president, were all indicted in August 1934 on a charge of making false entries in a report to the Federal Reserve Board. The report was about the condition of the Union Industrial Trust and Savings Bank of Flint on December 31, 1931.[4] Thus when the Guardian Group applied for an RFC loan, the data used in applying for loans understated the real financial circumstances.

A total of 28 men were indicted at the same time, including E.D. Stair, who was the former president of the other part of the duopoly, the Detroit Bankers Company. Most of those indicted were from the Detroit Bankers Company. Stair was also the publisher and owner of the *Detroit Free Press*, which needs to be kept in mind when that paper is cited for news accounts of any matters relating to banking in Detroit. Stair's newspaper and his columnist Malcolm Bingay certainly used the power of the press when culpability for the banking crisis was a hot topic.

Even afterward, in his book published in 1946, *Detroit Is My Own Home Town*, Bingay defended almost everyone in Detroit. The two most evident exceptions were Father Charles Coughlin and James Couzens.[5] Couzens was directly assailed in two chapters, which seem to be a source for others who have written about the Detroit banking crisis and Couzens's role in it. Bingay does agree that the banking problems in Detroit were responsible for the collapse of banks throughout the nation. But he stated, "The Detroit banks could have been saved — nothing that the directors or officers had done had wrecked them."[6] In fact, Bingay claimed the "bank holiday was illegally declared."[7] Couzens is identified as the sole reason the RFC did not provide an emergency loan to the Guardian Group, and is thus responsible for the banking crisis. However, Bingay issued a clear disclaimer. "I am not a historian. I lack the patience to worry too much about minute exactitudes."[8] Nevertheless, he used direct quotes from individuals in recording what he stated were "the things I have seen and heard, the life and legends of my old home town."[9]

The views expressed by Bingay in his book are similar to those that had appeared in the *Detroit Free Press* in the 1930s, some under his byline. In Detroit there was an unwillingness to accept responsibility for the financial situation. In addition there was a defensiveness that led to delays in sorting out the various legal issues. As *Time* reported in 1936, it took "two years of fiddling" to get "the judicial machinery into satisfactory operating condition" to move forward in legal action on the banking mess in Detroit.[10] Part of the "fiddling" was due to the nature of our political system. Federalism had some effect. With some banks chartered by the United States (national banks) and others chartered by the State of Michigan (state banks), jurisdictional disputes arose. Who should file charges? Should it be a United States district attorney or a Michigan attorney? In which court system, federal or state, should the charges be brought and tried? However, as events were to show, the State of Michigan, which had the power to take action, lacked the desire to do so. Aside from a gathering together of Michigan folk against the world, the evidence was to demonstrate that some of the leaders of Michigan were compromised. The boom of the 1920s affected everyone, and residents of Michigan, including those in various branches of state and local government, wanted to benefit financially from the great automotive expansion. Some had debts payable to the closed banks; others had purchased shares in the banks. If the banks were to be permanently closed they would lose two ways: as investors and in having to pay assessments for settlement with depositors of the banks.

The first legal issue that arose was when a group of stockholders in both of the duopoly banking companies went to court to contest the assessments levied against them. Michigan law for holding companies such as the Guardian Group and the Detroit Bankers Company provided for double assessment of each stockholder to make good the losses to depositors. The initial amounts would have paid $25 million to the Detroit Bankers depositors and $10 million to the depositors of the Guardian.[11] The per share levy for Guardian stockholders was fixed at $6.43. With about one-and-a-half million shares, that would total almost $10 million. June 23 was the date by which stockholders were to have paid the receivers, the lawsuit contesting the assessment notwithstanding.[12] Edsel Ford is reported to have owned 50,000 shares, or about one-third of the total number of Guardian shares. If $6.43 was the single share assessment, then at twice that amount Edsel Ford was due to pay over $640,000. Even for Edsel Ford this was a substantial amount of money. If $6.43 included the double penalty, then Edsel Ford would have had to pay in excess of $300,000, still a very significant quantity.

In March 1934, a federal judge in North Carolina ruled that the levies imposed in May were lawful, and stockholders should begin to make payment.[13] The case had purposely been filed in North Carolina as a means of avoiding local sympathies for the stockholders in Michigan. The local feelings were such that the attorney general of the United States appointed a special assistant attorney general, Guy T. Bard, who had been handling bank cases in California. He was to head a federal grand jury, because the workload for the resident U.S. attorney for Michigan would have been overwhelming.[14] Nobody was fooled; the issue really was keeping local Michigan interests from trumping all other considerations. Delays and other tactics were used to keep legal matters against the banking leaders from moving forward. However, evidence was not a problem, as representatives of the U.S. Department of Justice had sat in on all of the hearings of the Senate investigating committee. But time was a challenge, as the statute of limitations became an issue. That brought about relatively fast action, as Special Attorney Bard empanelled a grand jury and issued the indictments against Robert O. Lord, James L. Walsh and Herbert L. Wilkin. Along the way a decision was made that directors of the banking groups would be exempt from indictment. Only charges that could be quite readily proven were filed, such as making false entries. It appears that authorities wanted to change the individuals whose actions were on record, through carrying out their duties in making reports to regulatory agencies. This approach apparently eliminated the possibility of Edsel Ford, Charles S. Mott, Roy D. Chapin, Ernest Kanzler and others having to respond to indictments and appear in a court of law. But at the time, they were not sure they would be free from indictment or having to appear in court. The former leaders of the Guardian Group were thus subject to tension and stress as the legal issues dragged on.

By January 1935 it the Department of Justice was ready to bring the indicted individuals to trial. It looked as though all was ready to move forward when questions came up about the impartiality of the judge who was assigned to the case.[15] However the judge would not step aside despite evidence that he and his wife together had outstanding debts of about $30,000 to the National Bank of Detroit.[16] A new circuit court was established to avoid the judge in question, and a new judge was brought in from Chicago. This judge responded with an indictment of E.D. Stair, who was publisher and owner of the *Detroit Free Press*. Stair's newspaper took up the cause of the previous judge, whose appeal eventually went to the Supreme Court of the United States. The Supreme Court declined to hear the case, whereupon Chief Justice Charles Evans Hughes assigned yet another judge to the newly created district, as the first replacement judge had announced he would not try the bankers.[17] Altogether four federal judges were involved, the first three being members of the Republican Party. Wilkin was the only person who was imprisoned. He did avoid another trial, in a Michigan state court, when that judge dismissed the case, saying that a state court lacked jurisdiction over the Guardian Group because it belonged to the Federal Reserve System, even though it was chartered by the State of Michigan.[18] This was a new legal interpretation, with the local implication that no state court in Michigan could try matters relating to either of the two major banking groups. At the time, there was little likelihood of a Michigan court actually going to trial against the two banking groups, their officers, or employees. But the ruling that Michigan courts lacked jurisdiction due to Federal Reserve membership gave a legal reason for inaction.

In the course of the trials, some other individuals were fined token amounts. However, it seems that most of those decisions were later reversed upon appeal. So in legal terms, there finally were no consequences for the leadership of the Guardian Group. The real effects of the almost daily coverage of the legal action from 1933 through 1936 were another matter. It is unlikely that the public read the details of each article, but they could scan the leads to the articles and draw conclusions. Furthermore, radio newscasts at the time picked up the same stories that appeared in the national newspapers, condensed them, and passed them on as news. The public was left with an impression of improper behavior. The real change resulting from the bank crisis was the federal government's assumption of powers previously exercised by state governments and the leaders of the industrial and financial sectors.

Epilogue

In Michigan, a number of conditions combined to limit individual legal penalties. One factor was the pervasive power of the auto-manufacturing firms. Second was the local pride associated with the importance of Michigan in the national economy. Third was the considerable self-interest of Michigan residents in the banking crisis. While there was more drama associated with the economic problems in Detroit, nationwide hardly anyone went to jail as a consequence of decisions that led to bank failures, corporate bankruptcies, or the like. There were no enforceable laws against bad judgment, speculation, or involvement in the boom times preceding the stock market crash or in the subsequent decisions made in a time of unparalleled economic difficulty.

James Couzens

Before he died on October 22, 1936, James Couzens was involved in yet another critical event. Concurrent with the consequences of the Detroit banking crisis, an economic conference was held in London, in June 1933. Like most other Americans, Couzens was caught up in the confusion and uncertainty of New Deal policies as they evolved. Unlike others, Couzens was involved, and his participation was on an international stage.

On March 6, while the banks were still closed, FDR issued a proclamation prohibiting the export or hoarding of gold. By taking this action, but without officially saying so, the U.S. went off the gold standard. Roosevelt's intention was, as he put it, to "reflate" the economy. This was an attempt to put a positive spin on the inflationary policies toward which he was leaning. It was FDR's response to the enormous deflationary period in which the U.S. had found itself. Unfortunately, the closing of the banks in February and March along with the new regulatory acts had the effect of intensifying the deflationary pressure on the economy. The seriousness of the banking crisis had almost monopolized everyone's attention, but among many other critical problems was the monetary problem. To get the economy moving, the New Deal belief was that prices had to increase. With wholesale commodity prices at 59.6 percent of what they had been in the basis year of 1926 and farm commodity prices down to 40.6 percent, proponents of the New Deal thought action needed to be taken.[19]

Farmers were especially distressed, as they had borrowed money to expand food production during World War I. Many businesses had expanded at the same time. All debtor groups favored inflationary policies so they could, in effect, repay their debts with cheaper money than they had borrowed.

Old battle lines of Democrat and Republican were no longer useful for defining who was in favor of "sound money" based on the gold standard and who supported the policy of inflation. James Couzens, who was identified with the Progressive Republicans, was for inflation. When President Roosevelt replaced Arthur A. Ballantine as undersecretary of the treasury, Couzens opposed the new nominee, Dean Acheson. It was as if he and Henry Ford were still partners. He objected to Acheson because Acheson was too closely associated with the Wall Street firm of J.P. Morgan. Differences existed between James Couzens and Henry Ford, but on some issues they had a fundamental agreement.

However, Henry Ford's ideas no longer represented the views of the motor industry. Ford no longer united the policies of the auto executives. Couzens opposed lowering tariffs and giving up the gold standard as the basis of U.S. currency. In contrast, Alfred P. Sloan, Jr., who was replacing Henry Ford as the most powerful of the auto executives, was in favor of free trade and low tariffs. Sloan believed that high tariffs would hurt competitive American industries, reduce world trade, and exacerbate the contemporary situation. Sloan also favored a return to the gold standard.

Alfred Sloan's support for low tariffs and free trade was consistent with his position as chief executive of General Motors, a corporation that had achieved great success in international trade. In the period leading up to World War II, the U.S. auto manufacturers had no competition. The mass manufacturing capabilities of General Motors, Ford, and Chrysler, along with significant leads in engineering reliable products at relatively low prices, placed the U.S. auto industry in a very advantageous position. The American automakers were dominant; they could ship their products anywhere in the world and be competitive in every way. Even the smaller auto companies found that they could profitably sell their vehicles throughout the world as long as tariffs were low. However, during the Hoover administration the passage of high-tariff legislation led to retaliatory tariffs by other nations. Switzerland responded to increased U.S. tariff rates on Swiss watches by increasing duties on American automobiles and other manufactured products. Swiss imports from the United States fell by almost 30 percent, compared with a drop of about 5 percent in imports from all other nations.[20] Other nations developed their own retaliatory responses to the high U.S. tariff.

One might think that a senator from Michigan would advocate policies beneficial to the auto industry, these advocated by the auto executives. One senator from Michigan, Arthur Vandenberg, did in fact adhere to policies supporting the auto industry. But that was not the case with James Couzens. His views, expressed as early as 1929, put him in opposition to the manufacturers. He advocated public works as a means of providing employment, from the local to the national level. Industrialists believed that such action would distort the labor market, causing wages to artificially increase. He also supported an old age pension system, which was opposed by business interests for many reasons. Couzens even spoke out in opposition to the use of installment plans for the purchase of automobiles,[21] a view similar to that held by his old partner Henry Ford, but contrary to those of the other auto leaders. When the New Deal created public works programs, Couzens supported them as a means of solving employment issues and because the wages paid would put more money into circulation. In 1935, during what was termed "the second New Deal," Couzens supported and spoke out for the Social Security Act, the National Labor Relations Act (Wagner-Connery Act), and the Revenue Act of 1935. The latter piece of legislation put a surtax on individual incomes of $50,000 or more and greatly increased taxes for those making over $1 million, with incomes of $5 million being taxed at a rate of 75 percent. Executives of most corporations, including those of the automobile industry, opposed all three acts. The National Labor Relations Act created a National Labor Relations Board and included provisions that upheld the right of employees to join labor unions and bargain collectively through representatives they had selected. This law became the basis for the labor strife that eventually led to the unionization of all auto firms. Soon after passage of the Wagner-Connery Act, a group of lawyers representing the American Liberty League published an opinion that the act was unconstitutional.[22] Among those who had supported the organization of the Liberty League were Alfred P. Sloan, Jr., and William Knudsen, both of General Motors.[23] At a conference of over three hundred bankers and industrialists, Alfred

P. Sloan led a session griping about New Deal policies of taxation, excessive government regulation, and elimination of freedom.[24]

Couzens publicly supported the New Deal and defended it against charges that it was "communistic." Animosity toward Couzens, especially from those with whom he had been associated in the automobile industry, had long been based on his liberal views. But now he was termed either a "New Deal Republican," or even worse, a "Roosevelt New Dealer."

While the banking crisis and related domestic economic issues was the focus of the newly installed administration of Franklin Roosevelt, international matters were significant and could not be ignored. An international conference that the Hoover administration had supported demanded immediate attention. Other nations had waited for the American presidency to change, and now wanted to hold the conference, referred to under various names. The two most common are the World Economic & Monetary Conference and the London Economic Conference. James Couzens was a delegate to the conference, having been selected and appointed by President Franklin Roosevelt. He landed the assignment for a number of reasons. His party affiliation as a Republican was one factor. Traditionally the U.S. sent a bipartisan delegation to international conferences. Secondly, he was considered to be a "suitable Republican."[25] His open support for the New Deal was full qualification. Furthermore, Roosevelt and Couzens had an amiable relationship and shared basic ideas about monetary policy.

The problem that could not be remedied was that the conference had been planned during the Hoover administration, based on premises not shared by Roosevelt. By 1932, Hoover had begun to believe that domestic policies that attempted to resolve the Depression were futile. Everything had been tried. In his view the problems were international and could only be resolved through a resumption of significant international trade. The prevailing view was that "economic warfare" was being waged through the use of high protective tariffs. But Hoover thought steadying the currencies of the industrialized nations would stabilize the world. For currency constancy, Hoover thought the gold standard was a basic requirement. This was in contrast to the New Deal idea, shared by Couzens, of inflationary policies and economic nationalism.

In actuality, the London conference was doomed from the start due to the conflicting policies of the various nations in attendance. Even so, the actions of Franklin Roosevelt are said to have torpedoed the conference. It was clear that the U.S. delegation was ill-disciplined and working at cross-purposes. The nominal head of the American group was Secretary of State Cordell Hull. His political life had been spent in attempting to lower tariffs and provide a good export market for the rural South, meaning his agenda was contrary to that of President Roosevelt and some of the other delegates. In clear, blunt language, FDR stated that U.S. policy was to be economic nationalism. One observer says that this statement was the "most momentous" decision of all his years as president, from 1933 to 1945.[26] This conclusion is based on the belief that the U.S. position, as enunciated by Roosevelt, greatly contributed to the international and economic deterioration that led to World War II.[27] At the London conference, the United States purposely stated an unwillingness to become the preponderant or dominant economic force in the world. American isolationism can be marked from this conference,[28] and James Couzens was involved and on the international stage. He did not find the experience to be satisfactory, and aside from being consistent in his loyal support of Roosevelt, it was not a highlight of his political career.

While he was more of an internationalist than many other Senators from the West or Midwest, Couzens supported protective tariffs and inflation. He agreed with the Roosevelt policy of increasing commodity prices at home while ignoring international instability in exchanges or prices. Couzens spoke out in favor of increased employment, higher wages, and increased consumption, all of which could only be achieved by public works projects. He had early noted that U.S. policy was in direct conflict with the goals of the London conference. His record of representation of U.S. policy at the conference was spotty. As usual his personality was the basis for negative evaluations. One member of the delegation characterized Couzens as "a self-made and pernickety [sic] millionaire who had no cohesive view of the policies to be discussed in London, and little liking for international associations."[29] In keeping with his reputation, Couzens got into a quarrel with former Democratic presidential candidate James Cox over a newspaper story Cox thought Couzens was behind. He also had disagreements with Secretary of State Hull, and was indifferent about arriving at any agreement or arrangement at the conference. It is said that when he arrived, he "looked forward to returning home quickly."[30] Despite the importance the U.S. gave to the World War I indebtedness of the European nations, Couzens ceased attending any of the monetary committee meetings.[31] His agreement with the monetary policies of Roosevelt were such that an observer believed that Couzens would rather have seen the conference fail, as it did, than to have the value of the dollar stabilized.[32] Couzens had long been at odds with his former auto industrialist associates, and his views and positions taken at the London conference further reduced his status. When he was attacked and blame was placed at his door for the failure of the Detroit banks, there was no one who was willing to speak on his behalf; most everyone in the auto industry had been alienated.

On the international scene, the London conference and the start of the New Deal were both contemporaneous with the Nazi rise to power in Germany. While they had wasted no time in establishing their reactionary domestic policy, in their first two years they were more circumspect in international matters. As the U.S. turned toward greater isolationism, the leadership of the Nazi party calculated it could safely ignore American protestations about the treatment of German Jews. Furthermore, the Nazis believed they could pursue their policies of geographic expansion without U.S. action. In the auto world, Ford's investments in Germany and the GM ownership of Opel would come under increasing pressure. The Nazi plan was to develop as much self-sufficiency as possible, toward a conscious policy of autarky. Obviously, this was contrary to the international trade aspirations of both Ford and GM. At the same time, the Nazi government demanded that more corporate executives be German nationals. As time went on, the Nazis developed a segmented market, assigning differing price markets to each auto manufacturer. Perhaps a strong U.S. presence in international affairs might not have been able to modify Nazi policies, but the U.S. also had very little standing or influence in economic policy.

Couzens had never developed a political organization of his own. He had purposely refrained from using patronage to develop people who owed their jobs to him and whose self-interest would be served by being his supporters. As he became thoroughly associated with the Roosevelt administration, his status with the Republican Party was insufficient to gain re-nomination to the Senate. It had been suggested that he change political parties, and was given assurances that the Democrats were willing to name him as their candidate. He gave some thought to running as an independent, and also to being a candidate in both the Republican and Democratic primaries. Practical matters and his sense of honesty prevented Couzens from changing parties. Those who actively opposed him over the years, including friends of E.D. Stair, sought out a Democrat to run against Couzens if he chose to register as a Democrat.[33] In the primary election he was defeated for re-nomination as the candidate of the Republican Party. Even at the time, it was evident that he did not really care to be re-elected and did no campaigning.

As it became evident he would not be re-elected he was sounded-out by emissaries from President Roosevelt for a number of appointed positions. Among those were secretary of the interior, postmaster general and secretary of the treasury. It is doubtful that Roosevelt seriously considered him for the two cabinet posts. The only formal tender from FDR came in September 1936, to be head of the planned Maritime Commission. Couzens turned it down, saying he had no expertise, but the real fact was that he was tired and worn out. He had undergone many surgeries and he knew his health was not good. The zest he had always exhibited in making judgments and forcibly stating opinions and positions on issues was gone. On September 18 he was hospitalized. He left for a short time and then was re-admitted about a month later. In the meantime, he had become honorary chairman of the committee in charge of the Detroit reception for Roosevelt. He met FDR at the rail station, spent a day being a host, and returned to his bed. He underwent yet another surgery, from which he did not recover, and died on October 22, 1936. Many tributes followed his death, most on the common theme of his individualism and courage of convictions.[34] He was the first man from the auto industry to enter government at the national level, but was followed most immediately by John North Willys and Roy D. Chapin. In more recent times, auto executive George Romney, as governor of Michigan, secretary of commerce, and a candidate for the presidency, soared even higher than Couzens. However, Couzens remains the only U.S. senator who was once an executive of an automobile company.

Chronology

1925

May

19 Intent to start Guardian Trust Co. of Detroit announced in New York City

June

9 Directors and investors named for Guardian branch in New York City

1926

July

27 Kanzler's departure from Ford is announced

1927

May

26 End of Model T production

December

2 Model A Ford introduced

1928

May

3 Edsel Ford announces Universal Credit Corp. as Ford financing arm

July

• Plymouth brand introduced by Chrysler

July

13 Dodge cars and Graham trucks become part of Chrysler

August

• DeSoto brand introduced by Chrysler

November

6 Herbert Hoover elected president

December

17 Senator James Couzens receives over $900,000 in a tax refund for overpayment of income taxes paid in 1919 when he sold his Ford Motor Co. stock.

1929

September

• Guardian Detroit and Union Commerce Corp. merge to form Guardian Detroit Union Group

October

14 Celebration of 50th anniversary of Edison's light bulb at opening of Edison Institute at Greenfield Village and Henry Ford Museum

24 New York Stock Exchange experiences "wild panic" of selling

29 Worst sell off of stocks on NYSE

1930

1931

January

25 Kanzler becomes chairman of the board of the entire Guardian Group

April

• Arthur A. Ballantine becomes undersecretary of the treasury

June

25 Kanzler decides to report consolidated Guardian statement in "standard form"

August

• All Ford plants close in changeover from Model A to V-8.

1932

January

22 Reconstruction Finance Corporation (RFC) authorized

March

7 Four killed at Ford plant in riot over work

31 Ford V-8 Models introduced to public

April

11–12 Senate committee hearings begin

May

23 First RFC loan of $4.25 million to Guardian Group

June

14 Alfred Leyburn reports Guardian condition is "very unsatisfactory"

• RFC makes loan to "Dawes Bank"

July

• Second RFC loan to Guardian, of $8.7 million

21 Essex-Terraplane introduced by Hudson

28–29 Bonus Expeditionary Force violence in Washington, D.C.

August

3 Roy D. Chapin visits President Hoover to discuss cabinet position

12 Roy D. Chapin named secretary of commerce in recess appointment

December

• Hudson Motor Car Co. stock hits low of 4¼.

• National magazine article accuses Roy D. Chapin of political influence to secure RFC loans for Guardian

14 Roy D. Chapin confirmed by U.S. Senate as secretary of commerce

29 Ford Motor Co. lends $3.5 million to Guardian and requires "memorandum of agreement" with the loan.

1933

January

• Kanzler reports on 1932 Guardian status, calling it one of "notable improvement"

11 Strike at Briggs manufacturing plant in Detroit

15 Alfred Leyburn meets with Kanzler and others. "We have to get more money."

22–24 Ferdinand Pecora becomes counsel of Senate committee

27 Alfred Leyburn meets with Guardian officers to prepare application for RFC loan

30 Strike starts at Hudson Motor Car Co.

February

6 20th (Lame Duck) Amendment to Constitution declared ratified, effective October 15

6 Guardian Group applies for an additional RFC loan; Kanzler admits collateral is insufficient but predicts banking collapse if not approved

6 John McKee reports to RFC that Union Guardian Trust is insolvent

7 Jesse Jones of RFC informs Couzens of Guardian loan application

8 John McKee informs RFC that Union Guardian Trust is insolvent

8 Edsel Ford meets with RFC and Ogden Mills to facilitate Guardian loan

• RFC tells Edsel it is the Fords' duty to resolve the Guardian problems

9 White House meeting, Couzens's statement of "Shouting," etc.

10 Alfred Leyburn calls meeting in Detroit to develop plans to forestall bank crisis

11 Walter Chrysler and Alfred P. Sloan, Jr., meet with Hoover to back loan for Guardian

11 Hoover meets with RFC chairman and requests loan for Guardian; no action taken

12 Detroit Bankers Group, other

Michigan banking duopoly, requests RFC loan

13 Roy D. Chapin and Arthur A. Ballantine meet with Henry and Edsel Ford

13 Strike ends at Hudson Motor Car Co.

14 Michigan governor declares bank holiday

15 Meeting called by Alfred Leyburn, held in UCC building, continues

16 Couzens gets Senate resolution passed to facilitate reopening of Detroit banks

21–22 Charles Mitchell of National City Bank begins revealing testimony

24 Governor of Maryland proclaims bank holiday

24 Henry Bodman in Washington to meet with RFC to start successor banks

25 Couzens bill passed and signed by President Hoover, plan to resolve Detroit problem

26 "Bank with Hank" idea announced

28 Legislatures of West Virginia and Nevada pass bank holiday enabling legislation

March

• Charles Mitchell testifies again.

1 Kentucky and Tennessee declare bank holidays

1 "Bank with Hank" plan is turned down by other bankers

2 Bank holidays proclaimed in Oregon, New Mexico, Washington, Utah, Texas, Idaho, Wisconsin and Georgia

1–2 Senator James Couzens in Detroit to facilitate reopening of Detroit banks

4 Inauguration Day. Hoover leaves, FDR becomes president

4 FDR's oft-quoted inaugural speech with allusions to Senate committee hearings

4 Bank holidays proclaimed in New York, Illinois and most other remaining states

5 President Roosevelt declares nationwide bank holiday and calls Congress into special session to meet on March 9

9 Special session of Congress passes emergency legislation in one day, starts "Hundred Days" of New Deal

12 First "fireside chat" by FDR, subject is banking situation

20 Approximate date that conservators were appointed for Detroit bank groups. New GM and Chrysler backed bank, the National Bank of Detroit, opens

22 Controversy envelopes Edsel Ford regarding Diego Rivera mural

26 Suit against directors of Guardian Group is filed

May

13 Universal Credit Corporation is sold to rival Commercial Investment Trust

• Dean Acheson replaces Arthur Ballantine as undersecretary of the Treasury

June

15 Special session of Congress

ends, 16 major laws enacted from March 9

July

1 Albert Erskine of Studebaker takes his own life

August

7 approximate date Senator James Couzens sends assessment payments to receivers of closed Detroit banks

21 approximate date Senator James Couzens appears before Keidan "one man grand jury."

December

19 Robert O. Lord, president of Guardian Group testifies

21 Prohibition repealed

1934

January

4 Ernest Kanzler testifies before Senate committee

12 John McKee testifies before Senate committee

12–13 Alfred Leyburn testifies before Senate committee about directives given bank examiners

12–13 Edsel Ford testifies before Senate committee

12–13 Ernest Kanzler testifies before Senate committee

June

6 Securities Exchange Act passed by Congress, establishes Securities and Exchange Commission to regulate the securities markets

19 National Labor Relations Board established by Congressional action

August

- American Liberty League organization announced
- 22 Rumor about possible merger of Reo, Hudson, Cord, Pierce Arrow, and possible other independent auto makers is published

1935

July

- 5 National Labor Relations Act passes, creating a new National Labor Relations Board

August

- 14 Social Security Act passes

1936

February

- 16 Roy D. Chapin dies

April

- After much delay, new federal judgeship created to try Detroit bankers

October

- 22 James Couzens dies
- 27 Henry Ford serves as honorary pall bearer in James Couzens's funeral

November

- 3 Roosevelt re-elected

Notes

Chapter 1

1. U.S. Congress, Senate Subcommittee on Stock Exchange Practices of the Committee on Banking and Currency, 73rd Congress, 2nd Session, 1934, 4626.

2. Ibid., 4619.

3. Ibid., 4036–4039.

4. C.C. Colt and N.S. Klein, *28 Days: A History of the Banking Crises* (New York: Greenberg, 1933), 2.

5. Edward M. Lamont, *The Ambassador from Wall Street: The Story of Thomas W. Lamont, J.P. Morgan's Chief Executive* (Latham, Md.: Madison Books, 1964), 329.

6. Susan Estabrook Kennedy, *The Banking Crisis of 1933* (Lexington: University Press of Kentucky, 1973), 19.

7. Harry Barnard, *Independent Man: The Life of Senator James Couzens* (Detroit: Wayne State University Press, 2002), 81.

8. Colt and Klein, 2.

9. Reinhold Niebuhr, *Leaves from the Notebook of a Tamed Cynic* (San Francisco: Harper & Row, 1929), 123.

10. Peter Collier and David Horowitz, *The Fords: An American Epic* (New York: Summit Books, 1987), 130.

11. Robert Conot, *American Odyssey: A Unique History of America Told Through the Life of a Great City* (New York: William Morrow & Co., 1974), 275.

12. Barnard, 203.

13. G. Walter Woodworth, *The Detroit Money Market, 1934–1955* (Ann Arbor: University of Michigan, 1956), 14.

14. Ibid., 15.

15. Alfred P. Sloan, Jr., *Adventures of a White Collar Man* (New York: Doubleday, Doran, 1941), 199.

16. Frederick Lewis Allen, *The Big Change: 1900–1950* (New York: Harper and Row Bantam Edition, 1965), 130–131.

17. J.C. Long, *Roy D. Chapin: The Man Behind the Hudson Motor Car Company* (Detroit: Wayne Sate University Press, 2004), 219.

18. *New York Times,* 10 December 1932.

19. Bascom Nolly Timmons, *Jesse H. Jones: The Man and The Statesman* (New York: Henry Holt, 1956), 179–180.

20. Howard Ralph Neville, *The Detroit Banking Collapse of 1933* (East Lansing: Bureau of Business and Economic Research, College of Business and Public Service, Michigan State University, 1960), 9–10.

21. "Detroit Industrialists to Confer Here Today on Michigan City's Finances," *New York Times*, 23 December 1932, 27.

22. David Burner, *Herbert Hoover: A Public Life* (New York: Alfred A. Knopf, 1979), x.

23. Arthur M. Schlesinger, Jr., *The Age of Roosevelt: The Crisis of the Old Order, 1919–1933* (Boston: Houghton Mifflin Co., 1957), 432.

24. Ibid., 238.

25. Kennedy, 77.

26. C. David Tompkins, *Senator Arthur H. Vandenberg: The Evolution of a Modern Republican, 1884–1945* (East Lansing: Michigan State University Press, 1970), 76.

27. Ford R. Bryan, *Henry's Lieutenants* (Detroit: Wayne State University Press, 1993), 177.

28. Subcommittee, 4627.

29. Barnard, 219–222.

30. Timmons, 180–181.

31. Kennedy, 84.

32. Barnard, 219.

33. Subcommittee, 4627.

34. Barnard, 221.

35. Kennedy, 88.

36. Tompkins, 77.

37. Timmons, 180–181.

38. Barnard, 225.

39. Tompkins, 77.

40. Barnard, 226.

41. Tompkins, 77.
42. Barnard, 123.
43. Ibid., 131.
44. Ibid.,185–192.
45. Ibid., 205.
46. Ibid., 208.
47. Ibid., 123.
48. Ibid., 199.
49. Tompkins, 77.
50. Arthur Vandenberg to Herbert Hoover, 3 September 1932, RFC Correspondence 1932, Herbert Hoover Presidential Library, West Branch, Iowa.
51. Tompkins, 104.
52. Barnard, 227.
53. Keith Sward, *The Legend of Henry Ford* (New York: Rinehart and Company, 1948), 251.

Chapter 2

1. Nick Georgano, ed., *The Beaulieu Encyclopedia of the Automobile* (London: The Stationery Office, 2000), 1:561.
2. Alfred P. Sloan, Jr., *My Years with General Motors* (New York: MacFadden, 1965), 62.
3. Peter Collier and David Horowitz, *The Fords: An American Epic* (New York: Summit Books, 1987), 120.
4. William C. Richards, *The Last Billionaire: Henry Ford* (New York: Charles Scribner's Sons, 1948), 196.
5. David Lewis, *The Public Image of Henry Ford: An American Folk Hero and His Company* (Detroit, Mich.: Wayne State University Press, 1987), 367.
6. Ibid., 365.
7. Ferdinand Pecora, *Wall Street Under Oath* (Clifton, N.J.: Augustus M. Kelly, 1973), 237–238.
8. Henry Dominguez, *Edsel: The Story of Henry Ford's Forgotten Son* (Warrendale, Penn.: Society of Automotive Engineers, 2002), 77.
9. "Wall Street Sees Ford as a Banker," *New York Times,* 20 May 1925, 33.
10. "New Trust Company Here Backed by Ford," *New York Times,* 19 May 1925, 1.
11. Robert Lacey, *Ford: The Man and the Machine* (Boston: Little, Brown, 1986), 328.
12. "Auto Men Join Ford in Guardian Trust," *New York Times,* 9 June 1925, 34; "Guardian Trust to Open," *New York Times,* 8 July 1925, 28.
13. "Auto Men Join Ford in Guardian Trust," 34.

14. Clarence H. Young and William A. Quinn, *Foundation for Living: The Story of Charles Stewart Mott and Flint* (New York: McGraw Hill, 1963), 87.
15. Charles Sorensen with Samuel T. Williamson, *My Forty Years with Ford* (New York: W.W. Norton, 1956), 67–68.
16. "Who Holds GM," *Time* , 31 August 1931, <http://time.com/time/archives/print out,0,23657,929790,00 hmtl >21 June 2005.
17. Sorensen, 226.
18. J.C. Long, *Roy D. Chapin: The Man Behind the Hudson Motor Car Company* (Detroit: Wayne State University Press, 2004), 105.
19. Susan Estabrook Kennedy, *The Banking Crisis of 1933* (Lexington: University Press of Kentucky, 1973), 77–78.
20. Ibid., 77–79.
21. Ibid.
22. Young and Quinn, 61.
23. U.S. Congress, Senate Subcommittee on Stock Exchange Practices of the Committee on Banking and Currency, 73rd Congress, 2nd Session, 1934, 4212.
24. Young and Quinn, 110–111.
25. Lacey, 330–331.
26. Keith Sward, *The Legend of Henry Ford* (New York: Rinehart and Company, 1948), 244.
27. Harry Bennett and Paul Marcus, *We Never Called Him Henry* (New York: Fawcett Publications Gold Medal Books, 1951), 23–24.
28. Ibid., 5.
29. Kennedy, 79–80.
30. "Senate Revelations,7:2," *Time,* 1 January 1934, <*http://time.com/time/archives/ printout/023657,746898,99 hmtl*>21 June 2005.
31. Dominguez, 120.
32. Ibid., 125.
33. Frederick Lewis Allen, *The Lords of Creation* (New York: Harper & Brothers, 1935), 243.
34. Robert Conot, *American Odyssey* (New York: William Morrow, 1974), 302.
35. Frederick Lewis Allen, *The Big Change: 1900–1950* (New York: Bantam Books, 1952), 128–129.
36. Allen, *The Lords of Creation*, 397.
37. Maurice Hendry, "Studebaker: One Can Do a Lot of Remembering in South Bend," *Automobile Quarterly* 10, no. 1 (1972), 244.
38. Robert S. McElvaine, *The Great Depression: America, 1929–1941* (New York:

Times Books, 1984); and Ernest R. May, *Boom and Bust: Volume 10: 1917–1932* (New York: Time-Life Books, 1974) 43.

39. Maury Klein, *Rainbow's End: The Crash of 1929* (New York: Oxford University Press, 2001), 255–256.

40. Daniel Aaron, ed., *America in Crisis: Fourteen Crucial Episodes in American History* (New York: Alfred P. Knopf, 1952), 271.

41. Samuel Eliot Morison and Henry Steele Commager, *The Growth of the American Republic,* vol. 2 (New York: Oxford University Press, 1962), 636.

42. McElvaine, 18.

43. Klein, 255–256.

44. Frederick Lewis Allen, *Only Yesterday* (New York: Bantam Books, 1931), 118.

45. Morison and Commager, 656.

46. *Time,* 27 July 1925, 5.

47. *Time,* 7 January 1929, 37.

48. Allen, *Only Yesterday,* 114.

49. Pecora, 241.

50. Ibid.

51. Richard Bak, *Henry and Edsel: The Creation of the Ford Empire* (Hoboken, N.J.: John Wiley and Sons, 2003), 211.

52. "Senate Revelations," Ibid.

53. Ibid.

54. Subcommittee, 4664.

55. "Pecora Turns Fire on Detroit Bank," *New York Times,* 20 December 1933, 33.

56. Subcommittee, 4685–4686.

57. Ibid.

58. "Edsel Ford Hazy on Banking Detail," *New York Times,* 12 January 1934, 42.

Chapter 3

1. "Tsar Kanzler," *Time,* 2 February 1942, <http://wwwtimecom/time/archive/printout/23657,849772.00 hmtl> 21 June 2005.

2. "Guardian Detroit Elects," *New York Times,* 27 January 1932, 34.

3. "Ernest Kanzler, Ford's Aide, Dies," *New York Times* 12 December 1987, 47.

4. "Auto Men Join Ford in Guardian Trust," *New York Times,* 9 June 1925, 34.

5. Robert Lacey, *Ford: The Men and the Machine* (Boston: Little, Brown & Co., 1986), 255–267.

6. Peter Collier and David Horowitz, *The Fords: An American Epic* (New York: Summit Books, 1987), 121; "Ernest Kanzler, Ford's Aide, Dies," 47; and "Kanzeler [sic] Leaves Ford Co.," *New York Times,* 27 July 1926, 30.

7. "Ernest Kanzler , Ford's Aide, Dies," 47.

8. Carol Gelderman, *Henry Ford: The Wayward Capitalist* (New York: The Dial Press, 1981), 365.

9. "Fords Plan to Sell Their Car on Credit," *New York Times,* 28 April 1928, 21.

10. Ford R. Bryan, *Henry's Lieutenants* (Detroit: Wayne State University Press, 1983), 129.

11. "Listing Gives Plan of Finance Merger," *New York Times,* 16 December 1938, 43.

12. "Ernest Kanzler, Ford's Aide, Dies," 47.

13. Lacey, 155–167.

14. Collier and Horowitz, 21.

15. Charles Sorensen with Samuel T. Williamson, *My Forty Years with Ford* (New York: W.W. Norton, 1956), 310.

16. Collier and Horowitz, 116.

17. Lacey, 264.

18. Collier and Horowitz, 117–118.

19. "Ernest Kanzler, Ford's Aide, Dies," 47.

20. Sorensen, 307.

21. Ibid., 308.

22. Collier and Horowitz, 117–118.

23. Sorensen, 308.

24. Collier and Horowitz, 117, and Bryan, 2670.

25. Sorensen, 310.

26. Bryan, 140.

27. Collier and Horowitz, 121.

28. Ibid., 121.

29. "Kanzeler [sic] Leaves Ford Co.," 30.

30. Harry Bennett and Paul Marcus, *We Never Called Him Henry* (New York: Fawcett Publications Gold Medal Books, 1951), 25–26.

31. Bryan, 147.

32. "Edsel Ford Hazy on Banking Detail," *New York Times,* 12 January 1934, 35.

33. Clarence H. Young and William A. Quinn, *Foundation for Living: The Story of Charles Stewart Mott and Flint* (New York: McGraw Hill, 1963), 100.

34. Harry Barnard, *Independent Man: The Life of Senator James Couzens* (Detroit: Wayne State University Press, 1992), 215.

35. Letter from Alvan Macauley, Jr. to Roy D. Chapin, 10 September 1929, Roy D. Chapin Papers, Box 19, August 19 to March 27, 1930, Bentley Historical Library, University of Michigan.

36. Bryan, 139–144 and Barnard, 70.

37. Chapin papers, ibid.

38. "New Detroit Bank," *New York Times,* 26 March 1933, N7 and 12.

39. Chapin papers, ibid.

40. Frederick Lewis Allen, *The Big Change: 1900–1950* (New York: Bantam Books, 1952), 73.

41. Susan Estabrook Kennedy, *The Banking Crisis of 1933* (Lexington: University Press of Kentucky, 1973), 103.

42. Barnard, 216.

43. Kennedy, 22–24.

44. Jesse Jones and Edward Angly, *Fifty Billion Dollars* (New York: Macmillan, 1951), 417–418.

45. Kennedy, 39.

46. Frederick Lewis Allen, *The Lords of Creation* (New York: Harper & Bros., 1935), 417–418.

47. Kennedy, 108.

48. Herbert Hoover, *The Memoirs of Herbert Hoover: The Great Depression, 1929–1941* (New York: Macmillan, 1952), 170.

49. Merlo J. Pusey, *Eugene Meyer* (New York: Alfred A. Knopf, 1974), 224.

50. Kennedy, 39–43.

51. "Michigan Magic," *Harpers Magazine*, December 1932, 168, quoted in *The Banking Crisis of 1933*, 85.

52. U.S. Congress, Senate, Subcommittee on Stock Exchange Practices of the Committee on Banking and Currency, 73rd Congress, 2nd Session, 1934, 4038.

53. Young and Quinn, 100.

54. "Senate Revelations 7:1," *Time*, 1 January 1934, <http://www.timecom/time/archives/printout/0.23657,746688.hmtl>21 June 2005.

55. Ibid.

56. John T. Flynn, "Other People's Money," *The New Republic*, 10 January 1934, 211–212.

57. Ferdinand Pecora, *Wall Street Under Oath* (Clifton, N.J.: Augustus M. Kelly, 1973), 247–248.

58. Ibid., 245–246.

59. "Directors of Bank Got $7,755,382 Loan," *New York Times*, 22 December 1933, 33 and 37.

60. Howard Ralph Neville, *The Detroit Banking Collapse of 1933* (East Lansing: Bureau of Business and Economic Research, College of Business and Public Service, Michigan State University, 1960), 37–39.

61. Robert Conot, *American Odyssey* (New York: William Morrow, 1974), 303.

62. "Pecora Turns Fire on Detroit Bank," *New York Times*, 20 December 1933, 39.

63. Neville, 31.

64. "Reports Differed on Detroit Banks," *New York Times*, 5 January 1934, 31.

65. Subcommittee, 4601.

66. "Directors of Bank Got $7,755,362 Loan," 31 and 37.

67. "Reports Differed on Detroit Banks," 31.

68. Ibid.

69. Ibid.

70. Ibid.

71. Neville, 37.

72. Subcommittee, 4619.

73. "Says RFC Gave All Possible Aid," *New York Times*, 13 January 1934, 14.

74. Neville, 34–35.

75. "Directors of Bank Got $7,755,362 Loan," 31 and 370.

76. Keith Sward, *The Legend of Henry Ford* (New York: Rinehart and Company, 1948), 248.

77. "Pecora Turns Fire on Detroit Banks," 33.

78. "Treasury Asked Ford to Aid Banks, But He Refused," *New York Times*, 13 January 1934, 1.

79. Pecora, 247–248.

80. Subcommittee, 4608–4609.

81. Pecora, 242–243.

82. Barnard, 175 and 215.

83. "22 in Nation Hold $3,000,000 Policies," *New York Times*, 12 September 1931, 2.

84. Pecora, 241.

85. Kennedy, 80.

Chapter 4

1. "Auto Men Join Ford in Guardian Trust," *New York Times*, 9 June 1925, 34, and "Guardian Trust to Open," *New York Times*, 8 July 1925, 28.

2. Receipt from Roy D. Chapin to Ernest Kanzler, 7 January 1933, Roy D. Chapin papers, Box 25, Bentley Historical Library, University of Michigan, Ann Arbor.

3. Telegram, Roy D. Chapin to Charles Stewart Mott, 12 January 1933, Roy D. Chapin papers, Box 25, Bentley Historical Library, University of Michigan, Ann Arbor.

4. J.C. Long, *Roy D. Chapin: The Man Behind the Hudson Motor Car Company*. (Detroit: Wayne State University Press, 2002), 27.

5. Jerry Heasley, *The Production Figure Book for U.S. Cars* (Osceola, Wis.: Motorbooks International, 1977), 126.

6. Long 36.

7. Ibid., 36.

8. E.R. Thomas to President Herbert Hoover, 4 August 1932, Cabinet File, Herbert Hoover Presidential Library, West Branch, Iowa.

9. Long, 105.

10. Ibid., 104.

11. Ibid., 103.

12. Ibid., 36.

13. Ibid., 5.

14. Ibid., 147 ff.

15. Ibid., 184.

16. Ibid., 216.

17. George S. May, *R.E. Olds: Auto Industry Pioneer* (Grand Rapids, Mich.: William B. Eerdmans, 1977), 179.

18. Ibid., 219.

19. Charles Sorensen with Samuel T. Williamson, *My Forty Years with Ford* (New York: W.W. Norton, 1956), 67–68.

20. Long, 109–113.

21. May, 219.

22. Roy D. Chapin to head of W.R. Grace and Co., 7 February 1933, Roy D. Chapin papers, Box 25, Bentley Historical Library, University of Michigan, Ann Arbor.

23. R.M. Dill to Roy D. Chapin, 12 January 1933, Chapin papers, Box 25; and Roy D. Chapin to Charles S. Mott, 12 January 1933, Chapin papers, Box 25.

24. Long, 110.

25. Alan Nevins and Frank Hill, *Ford: The Times, The Man, The Company* (New York: Charles Scribner's Sons, 1954), 339–340.

26. Roy D. Chapin to Henry Ford, 4 November 1929, Chapin papers Box 19.

27. Arthur Ballantine to J.C. Long, 16 March 1944, Cabinet Box, Hoover Library.

28. Long, 3 and 212.

29. Ibid., 212.

30. Ibid., 204.

31. U.S. Congress, Senate, Subcommittee on Stock Exchange Practices of the Committee on Banking and Currency, 73rd Congress, 2nd Session, 1934, 4600.

32. "Auto Men Join Ford in Guardian Trust," 34 and "Guardian Trust to Open," 28.

33. "Fords Plan to Sell Their Car on Credit," *New York Times*, 28 April 1928, 21, and "Universal Finance Co.," *Time,* 7 May 1928, <http://www. time.com/time/archive/printout/0,23657,785934.00hmtl>21 June 2005.

34. "Ford Dickers," *Time,* 1 May 1933, <*http://www.time.com/time/archive/printout/0.23657,847262.00.hmtl*> 31 June 2005.

35. "Ford Credit Plan $10,000,000 Venture," *New York Times,* 4 May 1928, 39.

36. "Ford Dickers," ibid.

37. Harold Katz, *The Decline of Competition in the Automobile Industry, 1920–1940* (New York: Arno Press, 1977), 38–45.

38. Robert S. McElvaine, *The Great Depression: America, 1929–1941* (New York: Times Books, 1993), p18.

39. Daniel Boorstin, *The Americans: The Democratic Experience* (New York: Random House, 1973), 422.

40. Alvan Macauley, Jr. to Roy D. Chapin, 10 September 1929, Box 19 Chapin papers.

41. Roy D. Chapin to J.S. Lawrence, 10 January 1933, Box 25 Chapin papers.

42. REO Motor Car Company to Roy D. Chapin, 29 October 1929, Box 19, Chapin papers.

43. Alfred P. Sloan, Jr., *My Years with General Motors* (New York: MacFadden, 1965), 11.

44. "Ford Dickers," ibid.

45. Long, 186–187.

46. Sloan, 159.

47. Ibid.

48. Long, 189.

49. Harry Bennett and Paul Marcus, *We Never Called Him Henry* (New York: Fawcett Publications Gold Medal Books, 1951), 108–109.

50. John A. Conde, *The Cars That Hudson Built* (Keego Harbor, Mich.: Arnold-Porter Publishing, 1980), 89.

51. Arthur Vandenberg to Herbert Hoover, 27 July 1932, Senate Box, Hoover Library.

52. For an overview of this event see Arthur M. Schlesinger, Jr., *The Crisis of the Old Order, 1919–1933*,(Boston: Houghton Mifflin, 1957), 356–365.

53. "Communists in the Automobile Industry in Detroit Before 1935," *Michigan History* 57, no. 3 (1973), 187.

54. G. Walter Woodworth, *The Detroit Money Market, 1934–1955* (Ann Arbor: University of Michigan School of Business Research, 1956), 15.

55. Peter Collier and David Horowitz, *The Fords: An American Epic* (New York: Summit Books, 1987), 130.

56. For an overview of this event see *The Crisis of the Old Order,* 356–365.

57. Long, 230.

58. "Hoover Tries Automobile Man in His Old Job," *Business Week,* 17 August 1932, 4.

59. David Burner, *Herbert Hoover: A Pub-*

lic Life (New York: Alfred A. Knopf, 1979), 209–210.

60. "Chapin for Lamont," *Time,* 15 August 1932, <*http://www.time/archive/printout/0,236 57.744159,000hmtl*> 21 June 2005.

61. Ibid.

62. Long, 222.

63. "Chapin for Lamont."

64. Long, 239.

65. "Only Chapin Wins Senate Approval," *New York Times,* 15 December 1932, 10.

66. "Chapin Takes Oath: Hopeful of Upturn," *New York Times,* 9 August 1932, 21.

67. "Chapin Tells Gains in Some Industries," *New York Times,* 22 September 1932, 12.

68. "Gains in Many Lines Reported by Chapin," *New York Times,* 6 October 1932, 31.

69. "140 Trade Groups See Real Recovery," *New York Times,* 13 October 1932, 1.

70. "Chapin Scans the Wide Trade Horizon," *New York Times,* 16 October 1932, Section IV, 6.

71. Ibid.

72. "Winning the War on Hard Times," *Sunday New York Herald Tribune,* 6 November 1932, 1–2.

73. Long, 241.

74. Burner, 209–210.

75. Conde, 75–93.

76. Long, 253.

77. Ibid. 254.

Chapter 5

1. Bascom Nolly Timmons, *Jesse H. Jones: The Man and the Statesman* (New York: Henry Holt, 1956), 104.

2. Susan Estabrook Kennedy, *The Banking Crisis of 1933* (Lexington: University Press of Kentucky, 1973), 90.

3. Lawrence Sullivan, *Prelude to Panic* (Washington, D.C.: Statesman Press, 1936), 86.

4. Harry Barnard, *Independent Man; The Life of Senator James Couzens* (Detroit: Wayne State University Press, 2002), 225.

5. C. David Tompkins, *Senator Arthur Vandenberg: The Evolution of a Modern Republican, 1884–1945* (East Lansing: Michigan State University Press, 1970), 77–78.

6. Keith Sward, *The Legend of Henry Ford* (New York: Rinehart and Company, 1948), 251.

7. Kennedy, 88.

8. "Congress Aid Asked in Michigan Tie-up," *New York Times,* 16 February 1944, 6.

9. Kennedy, 80.

10. Timmons, 180–183.

11. Arthur M. Schlesinger, Jr., *The Age of Roosevelt: The Politics of Upheaval* (Boston: Houghton Mifflin Co., 1960), 20.

12. "Coughlin on Detroit et al," *Time,* 4 September 1933, <http://www.time.com/timearchive/printout/0,23657.746000.00 hmtl> 21 June 2005.

13. Kennedy, 85.

14. "The Week," *The New Republic,* 7 October 1931, 191–192.

15. "The Week," *The New Republic,* 9 February 1933, 335–336.

16. Robert L. Cruden, "The Great Ford Myth," *The New Republic,* 16 March 1932, 116.

17. James R. Prickett, "Communists and the Automobile Industry in Detroit before 1935," *Michigan History* 57, no. 3 (1973), 185–208.

18. "The Week," *The New Republic,* 9 February 1933, 335–336.

19. J.C. Long, *Roy D. Chapin: The Man Behind the Hudson Motor Car Company* (Detroit: Wayne State University Press, 2004), 235.

20. "Arthur Ballantine, Lawyer, Dies," *New York Times,* 12 October 1960, 39.

21. "Full Sub-Cabinet," *Time,* 2 March 1931, <*http://time/archive/printout/0.23657, 741112,00 hmtl*> 21 June 2005.

22. Harry Bennett and Paul Marcus, *We Never Called Him Henry* (New York: Fawcett Publications Gold Medal Books, 1951), 97–98.

23. Sward, 251.

24. Ford R. Bryan, *Henry's Lieutenants* (Detroit: Wayne State University Press, 1993), 1701.

25. Robert Conot, *American Odyssey* (New York: William Morrow, 1974), 211.

26. Bryan, 170.

27. "A.A. Ballantine Is Named Aide to Mellon," *New York Times,* 22 February 1931, 13.

28. Vincent Curcio, *Chrysler: The Life and Times of an Automotive Genius* (New York: Oxford University Press, 2000), 384.

29. Jerry Heasley, *The Production Figure Book for U.S. Cars* (Osceola, Wis.: Motorbooks International, 1977), 87–149.

30. John A. Conde, *The Cars That Hudson Built* (Keego Harbor, Mich.: Arnold-Porter Publishing, 1980), 84–86.

31. Sullivan, 86.

32. Kennedy, 90.

33. Ernest Liebold, *Reminiscences,* 1029–1030, as quoted in Henry Dominguez, *Edsel: The Story of Henry Ford's Forgotten Son* (Warrendale, Penn.: Society of Automotive Engineers, 2002), 126.

34. "Pecora Turns Fire on Detroit Banks," *New York Times,* 20 December 1933, 33.

35. "Senate Revelations, 7:2," *Time,* 21 January 1934, <*http://time.com/time/archive/printout/0,23657,746898.00hmtl*> 22 June 2005.

36. Richard Bak, *Henry and Edsel: The Creation of the Ford Empire* (Hoboken, N.J.: John Wiley and Sons, 2003), 212.

37. "Treasury Asked Ford to Aid Banks, But He Refused," *Time,* 13 January 1934, <*http://time.com/time/archive/printout/0,23657,746898.00hmtl*> 22 June 2005.

38. Arthur A. Ballantine and Roy D. Chapin, "Statement of interview with Mr. Henry Ford in Detroit, February 13, 1933," Presidential file, Herbert Hoover Presidential Library, West Branch, Iowa.

39. Ibid.

40. Ibid, 1.

41. Ibid.

42. Ibid., 2–6.

43. Ibid., 5–6.

44. Ibid., 6.

45. Ibid., 7.

46. Ibid.

47. Ibid., 8.

48. Ibid.

49. Ibid., 9.

50. Ibid., 10.

51. Ibid., 11.

52. Ibid.

53. Tompkins, 78.

54. Kennedy, 93.

55. Charles A. Miller, "Memorandum to Harry Barnard," quoted in Harry Barnard, *Independent Man,* 232.

56. Tompkins, ibid.

57. Miller, ibid.

58. Barnard, 233.

59. Barnard, 233 and Tompkins, 78.

60. Barnard, ibid.

61. Barnard, 233 and Tompkins, 78.

62. U.S. Congress, Senate, Subcommittee on Stock Exchange Practices of the Committee on Banking and Currency, 73rd Congress, 2nd Session, 1934, 4685.

63. Ballantine and Chapin, "Statement of Interview," 10.

64. Ferdinand Pecora, *Wall Street Under Oath* (Clifton, N.J.: Augustus M. Kelly, 1973), 256.

65. Alfred P. Sloan, Jr., *My Years with General Motors* (New York: MacFadden, 1965), 21–22.

66. Barnard, 235.

67. Howard Ralph Neville, *The Detroit Banking Collapse of 1933* (East Lansing: Bureau of Business and Economic Research, College of Business and Public Service, Michigan State University, 1960), 54.

68. Kennedy, 93–94.

Chapter 6

1. "Ford's Lawyer," *Time,* 11 February 1929, <*http://time.com/time/archives/printout/023657,737374,00 hmtl*> 21 June 2005.

2. Harry Bennett and Paul Marcus, *We Never Called Him Henry* (New York: Fawcett Publications Gold Medal Books, 1951), 15.

3. "Crain's Interactive Web List," <*http://www.crainsdetroit.com/List/lawfirm/7hmtl*> 5 June 2008.

4. "Auto Men Join Ford in Guardian Trust," *New York Times,* 9 June 1925, 34.

5. Jerry M. Fisher, *The Pacesetter: The Untold Story of Carl G. Fisher* (Fort Bragg, Calif.: Lost Coast Press, 1998), 95.

6. Lincoln Highway Association Web Archives, <http://www.lincolnnet.net/users/lxpkfrst/http/lhhist81.htm>.

7. "New Detroit Banks Formed," *New York Times,* 25 February 1933, 21.

8. Harry Barnard, *Independent Man: The Life of Senator James Couzens* (Detroit: Wayne State University Press, 2002), 241.

9. "Couzens in Detroit to Aid State Banks," *New York Times,* 2 March 1933, 8.

10. Melvin G. Holli, *Reform in Detroit: Hazen S. Pingree and Urban Politics* (New York: Oxford University Press, 1969), 123.

11. Barnard, 129.

12. Ibid., 130.

13. Ibid., 113 ff.

14. Ibid., 131.

15. Ibid., 130.

16. Richard Bak, *Henry and Edsel: The Creation of the Ford Empire* (Hoboken, N.J.: John Wiley and Sons, 2003), 99.

17. Keith Sward, *The Legend of Henry Ford* (New York: Rinehart and Company, 1948), 123.

18. "New Detroit Banks Formed," *New York Times,* 25 February, 1933, 21.

19. "Directors of Bank Got $7,755,362

Loan," *New York Times,* 22 December 1933, 33 and 37.

20. Clifford B. Longley papers, Accession 1740, Benson Ford Research Library Archives, The Henry Ford, Dearborn, Mich.

21. Bak, 160.

22. Henry Dominguez, *Edsel: The Story of Henry Ford's Forgotten Son* (Warrendale, Penn.: Society of Automotive Engineers, 2002), 126.

23. Bennett, 100.

24. Ford R. Bryan, *Henry's Lieutenants* (Detroit: Wayne State University Press, 1993), 173.

25. Bak, 144.

26. Max Wallace, *The American Axis: Henry Ford, Charles Lindbergh and the Rise of the Third Reich* (New York: St. Martin's Press, 2003), 24 and 131.

27. Bryan, 173.

28. Robert Conot, *American Odyssey* (New York: William Morrow, 1974), 207.

29. "Ford Secretary, Missing, Is Found," *New York Times,* 1 March 1933, 4.

30. Ibid.

31. Wallace, 148.

32. Longley papers.

33. Ibid.

34. Bryan, 178.

35. Longley papers.

36. Ibid.

37. Ibid.

38. Ibid.

39. Ibid.

40. David L. Lewis, *The Public Image of Henry Ford* (Detroit: Wayne State University Press, 1976), 184.

41. Longley, op cit.

42. Bennett, 86.

43. Gilbert Seldes, *The Years of the Locust* (Boston: Little, Brown, 1933), 24.

44. Longley, op cit.

45. Ibid.

46. "Ford's Lawyer," op cit.

47. Harry Bennett and Paul Marcus, *We Never Called Him Henry* (New York: Fawcett Publications Gold Medal Books, 1951), 97–98.

48. "Inquiry Absolves Bank in Detroit," *New York Times,* 19 September 1933, 3; "Detroit's Dirty Linen," *Business Week,* 12 September 1933; and John T. Flynn, "Other People's Money," *The New Republic,* 18 October 1933, 2.

49. "Whitewash in Detroit," *Time,* 2 August 1933, <http://time.com/timearchive/printout,0,23657,746141,00 hmtl> 21 June 2005.

50. Barnard, 275.

51. "Inquiry Absolves Banks in Detroit."

52. Ibid.

53. "Directors of Bank Got $7,755,362 loan."

54. U.S. Congress, Senate Subcommittee on Stock Exchange Practices of the Committee on Banking and Currency, 73rd Congress, 2nd Session, 1934, 4619.

55. Ibid., 4039.

56 Susan Estabrook Kennedy, *The Banking Crisis of 1933* (Lexington: University Press of Kentucky, 1973), 80.

57. Ferdinand Pecora, *Wall Street Under Oath* (Clifton, N.J.: Augustus M. Kelly, 1973), 253.

58. Kennedy, 88.

59. Pecora, 251.

60. "Treasury Asked Ford to Aid Banks, But He Refused," *New York Times,* 13 January 1934, 1.

61. Ibid.

62. "Detroit's Dirty Linen," *Business Week,* 12 September 1933, 5.

63. Senate committee, 4627.

64. Kennedy, 84.

65. Senate committee, 4626.

66. Kennedy, 83–84.

67. Ibid.

Chapter 7

1. Susan Estabrook Kennedy, *The Banking Crisis of 1933* (Lexington: University Press of Kentucky, 1973), 68.

2. Herbert Feis, *1933: Characters in Crisis* (Boston: Little, Brown & Co., 1966), 10.

3. Gilbert Courtland Fite, *Peter Norbeck: Prairie Statesman* (Columbia: The University of Missouri, 1948), 153–176.

4. "Michigan Magic," *Harpers Magazine,* December 1932, 168, quoted in Susan Estabrook Kennedy, *The Banking Crisis of 1933* (Lexington: University Press of Kentucky, 1973), 85.

5. Wayne Flynt, *Duncan Upshaw Fletcher: Dixie's Reluctant Progressive* (Tallahassee: Florida State University Press, 1971), 171–172.

6. Kennedy, 103.

7. Ibid.

8. Thomas L. Stokes, *Chip Off My Shoulder* (Princeton, N.J.: Princeton University Press, 1940), 358.

9. Harry Barnard, *Independent Man: The Life of Senator James Couzens* (New York: Scribners, 1958), 311–314.

10. Ibid., 149.

11. C.C. Colt and N.S. Keith, *28 Days: A History of the Banking Crisis* (New York: Greenberg Publishers, 1933), 18.

12. Barnard, 240.

13. Ibid.

14. Colt and Keith, 30–31.

15. Barnard, 241.

16. Ibid., 242.

17. Ibid., 242–244.

18. Ibid., 244.

19. Harold N. Denny, "Couzens in Detroit to Aid State Banks," *New York Times*, 2 March 1933, 8.

20. Colt and Keith, 161.

21. Barnard, 246–247.

22. Colt and Keith, 14.

23. Ibid., 14–15.

24. Ibid., 27.

25. Ibid., 14.

26. Feis, 12.

27. Ibid.

28. Robert Lacey, *Ford, The Men and the Machine* (Boston: Little, Brown & Co., 1986), 340.

29. Colt and Keith, 41.

30. Ibid., 47.

31. Arthur M. Schlesinger, Jr. *The Age of Roosevelt: The Crisis in the Old Order, 1919–1933*, (Boston: Houghton Mifflin Co., 1957), 3.

32. Frederick Lewis Allen, *The Lords of Creation* (New York: Harper & Brothers, 1935), 308.

33. "Business," *Time*, 18 January 1932, 39.

34. Lacey, 140.

35. "Shut Michigan," *Time*, 27 March 1933, <*http://time.com/time/archive/printout/0.23657.745428.00*.hmtl> 21 June 2005.

36. Jerry Heasley, *The Production Figure Book for U.S. Cars* (Osceola, Wis.: Motorbooks International, 1977), 33–117.

37. Alfred P. Sloan, Jr., *Adventures of a White Collar Man* (New York: Doubleday, Doran, 1941), 176.

38. Allen, 425–426.

39. William E. Leuchtenburg, *New Deal and Global War* (New York: Time, Inc. 1964), 9.

40. Samuel Eliot Morison and Henry Steele Commager, *The Growth of the American Republic*, vol. 2 (New York: Oxford University Press, 1962), 699.

41. Kennedy, 160.

42. Feis, 34.

43. Allen, 433.

44. Daniel Aaron, ed., *America in Crisis: Fourteen Crucial Episodes in American History* (New York: Alfred P. Knopf, 1952), 280.

45. Arthur M. Schlesinger, Jr., *The Age of Roosevelt: The Coming of the New Deal* (Boston: Houghton Mifflin Co., 1959), 5.

46. "Arthur Ballantine, Lawyer, Dies," *New York Times,* 12 October 1960, 39.

47. "Open Detroit," *Time,* 3 April 1933, <htttp://time.com/time/archive/printout/0,23657.7536429.00hmtl>.

48. Sloan, 172–173.

49. Ibid., 173.

50. Ibid., 174.

51. "Shut Michigan."

52. "Emergency's End," *Time,* 16 April 1945, <*http://time.com/time/archive/printout/0.23657.775599.00.hmtl*> 21 June 2005.

53. Ibid.

54. "Ford Bank," *Time,* 7 August 1933, <*http://time.com/time/archive/printout/0.23657.745870.00hmtl*> 21 June 2005.

55. Bascom Nolly Timmons, *Jesse H. Jones: The Man and The Statesman* (New York: Henry Holt, 1956), 192–193.

56. J.C. Long, *Roy D. Chapin: The Man Behind the Hudson Motor Car Company* (Detroit: Wayne Sate University Press, 2004), 259.

57. "Open Detroit."

58. "Assessed Senator," *Time,* 14 August 1933, <htttp://time.com/time/archive/printout/0,23657.745897.00hmtl> 21 June 2005.

59. "New Detroit Bank Gains in Deposits," *New York Times,* 26 March 1933, N7 and 12.

60. U.S. Congress, Senate Subcommittee on Stock Exchange Practices of the Committee on Banking and Currency, 73rd Congress, 2nd Session, 1934, 4891.

61. Ibid.

62. "Assessed Senator."

63. Colt and Keith, 8–9.

64. "Whitewash in Detroit," *Time,* 2 October 1933, <htttp://time.com/time/archive/printout/0,23657.746151.00hmtl> 21 June 2005.

65. John T. Flynn, "Other People's Money," *The New Republic,* 11 October 1933, 240.

66. "Detroit's Dirty Linen," *Business Week,* 12 September 1933, 12.

67. Barnard, 238.

68. "Whitewash."

69. Fite, 182.

70. Flynt, 169.

71. Charles Sorensen with Samuel T.

Williamson, *My Forty Years with Ford* (New York: W.W. Norton, 1956), 303–304.

72. Barnard, 130.

73. Subcommittee, 4685.

74. "Edsel Ford Hazy on Banking Detail," *New York Times*, 12 January 1934, 35.

75. "Treasury Asked Ford to Aid Banks, But He Refused," *New York Times*, 13 January 1934, 1.

76. Allen, 335.

77. "Michigan Magic," *Harpers Magazine*, December 1932, 168, quoted in Susan Estabrook Kennedy, *The Banking Crisis of 1933* (Lexington: University Press of Kentucky, 1973), 85.

78. "Edsel Ford Hazy on Banking Detail," *New York Times*, 12 January 1934, 421.

79. Franklin D. Roosevelt, Russel D. Buhite and David W. Levy, *FDR's Fireside Chats* (Norman: University of Oklahoma Press, 1992), 153–173.

80. Ibid., 172.

81. Arthur A. Ballantine and Roy D. Chapin, "Statement of interview with Mr. Henry Ford in Detroit, February 13, 1933," presidential file, Herbert Hoover Presidential Library, West Branch, Iowa.

82. Ibid.

Epilogue

1. Harry Barnard, *Independent Man: The Life of Senator James Couzens* (Detroit: Wayne State University Press, 2002), 290.

2. *Chicago Herald Tribune*, 27 June 1933.

3. "Detroit Banker Defends Dividends," *New York Times*, 24 January 1933, 33.

4. "Indict 28 Bankers in Detroit Crashes," *New York Times*, 2 August 1934, 8.

5. Malcolm Bingay, *Detroit Is My Own Home Town*, (New York: Bobbs-Merrill, 1946).

6. Ibid, 130.

7. Ibid., 129.

8. Ibid., 19.

9. Ibid.

10. "Judge for Bankers," *Time*, 20 August 1931, <http://time.com/timearchive/printout, 0,23657,848540,00 hmtl > 21 June 2005.

11. "Bank Share Levies Fought in Detroit," *New York Times*, 27 May 1933, 19.

12. "Assessed on Bank Shares," *New York Times*, 1 June 1933, 31.

13. "Shareholders Levy Upheld in Detroit," *New York Times*, 8 March 1934, 29.

14. "Federal Grand Jury Gets Detroit Bank Case," *New York Times*, 4 May 1934, 3.

15. "To Press Detroit Cases," *New York Times*, 27 January 1935, N 16.

16. "Won't Disqualify Himself as Judge," *New York Times*, 7 February 1935, 28.

17. Ibid.

18. "Puts Reserve Bank Outside State Law," *New York Times*, 26 April 1935, 15.

19. Arthur M. Schlesinger, Jr., *The Age of Roosevelt: The Coming of the New Deal* (Boston: Houghton Mifflin Co., 1959), 195.

20. Julius W. Pratt, *A History of United States Foreign Policy* (Englewood Cliffs, N.J.: Prentice-Hall, 1959), 568.

21. Barnard, 196.

22. Schlesinger, 406.

23. Ibid., 486.

24. Ibid., 501.

25. Barnard, 268.

26. Broadus Mitchell, *Depression Decade: From New Era Through New Deal, 1929–1941* (New York: Harper & Row, 1969), 140.

27. Ibid.

28. Schlesinger, 213–242.

29. Herbert Feis, *1933: Characters in Crisis* (Boston: Little, Brown & Co., 1966), 173.

30. Ibid., 193.

31. Ibid., 237.

32. Ibid., 208.

33. Barnard, 306.

34. Ibid., 322–326.

Bibliography

Books

Aaron, Daniel, ed. *America in Crisis: Fourteen Crucial Episodes in American History*. New York: Alfred P. Knopf, 1952.

Allen, Frederick Lewis. *The Big Change*. New York: Bantam, 1965.

_____. *Lords of Creation*. New York: Bantam, 1935.

_____. *Only Yesterday*. New York: Bantam, 1931.

_____. *Since Yesterday*. New York: Bantam, 1940.

Bak, Richard. *Henry and Edsel: The Creation of the Ford Empire*. Hoboken, N.J.: John Wiley, 2003.

Baldwin, Neil. *Henry Ford and the Jews*. New York: Public Affairs, 2003.

Bardoux, Jean-Pierre, Jean-Jacques Chanaron, Patrick Fridenson, and James M. Laux. *The Automobile Revolution: The Impact of an Industry*. Chapel Hill: University of North Carolina, 1982.

Barnard, Harry. *Independent Man: The Life of Senator James Couzens*. Detroit: Wayne State University Press, 2002.

Baruch, Bernard. *The Public Years: My Own Story*. New York: Holt, Rinehart & Winston, 1960.

Bennett, Harry, *We Never Called Him Henry*. New York: Gold Medal Books, 1951.

Bingay, Malcolm. *Detroit Is My Own Home Town*. Indianapolis, IN: Bobbs-Merrill, 1946.

Boorstin, Daniel. *The Americans: The Democratic Experience*. New York: Random House, 1973.

_____. *The Americans: The National Experience*. New York: Random House, 1965.

Bryan, Ford R. *Beyond the Model T*. Detroit: Wayne State University Press, 1997.

_____. *Henry's Lieutenants*. Detroit: Wayne State University Press, 1993.

Burner, David. *Herbert Hoover: A Public Life*. New York: Alfred A. Knopf, 1979.

Burns, James MacGregor. *Roosevelt: The Lion and the Fox*. New York: Harcourt Brace, 1956.

Collier, Peter, and David Horowitz. *The Fords: An American Epic*. New York: Summit Books, 1957.

Colt, C.C., and N.S. Keith. *28 Days: A History of the Banking Crisis*. New York: Greenberg, 1933.

Conde, John. *The Cars That Hudson Built*. Keego Harbor, MI: Arnold-Porter, 1980.

Conot, Robert. *American Odyssey*. New York: William Morrow, 1974.

Curcio, Vincent. *Chrysler: The Life and Times of an Automotive Genius*. New York: Oxford University Press, 2000.

Dominguez, Henry. *Edsel: The Story of Henry Ford's Forgotten Son*. Warrendale, PA: Society of Automotive Engineers, 2002.

Farber, David. *Sloan Rules: Alfred P. Sloan and the Triumph of General Motors*. Chicago: University of Chicago Press, 2002.

Bibliography

Feis, Herbert. *1933: Characters in Crisis.* Boston: Little, Brown, 1966.

Fisher, Jerry. *Pacesetter: The Untold Story of Carl G. Fisher.* Fort Bragg, CA: Lost Coast Press, 1998.

Fite, Gilbert Courtland. *Peter Norbeck: Prairie Statesman.* Columbia: University of Missouri, 1948.

Flynt, Wayne. *Duncan Upshaw Fletcher: Dixie's Reluctant Progressive.* Tallahassee: Florida State University Press, 1971.

Gelderman, Carol. *Henry Ford: The Wayward Capitalist.* New York: The Dial Press, 1981.

Georgano, Nick, ed. *The Beaulieu Encyclopedia of the Automobile.* Vol. 1. London: The Stationery Office, 2000.

Heasley, Jerry. *The Production Figure Book for U.S. Cars.* Osceola, Wisc.: Motorbooks International, 1977.

Herndon, Booton. *Ford.* New York: Avon Books, 1971.

Holli, Melvin. *Reform in Detroit: Hazen S. Pingree and Urban Politics.* New York: Oxford University Press, 1969.

Hoover, Herbert. *The Memoirs of Herbert Hoover.* New York: Macmillan, 1952.

Jackson, Robert H. *That Man: An Insider's Portrait of Franklin D. Roosevelt.* New York: Oxford University Press, 2003.

Jones, Jesse, and Edward Angly. *Fifty Billion Dollars.* New York: Macmillan, 1951.

Katz, Harold. *The Decline of Competition in the Automobile Industry, 1920–1940.* New York: Arno Press, 1977.

Kennedy, David M. *Freedom from Fear.* New York: Oxford University Press, 2005.

Kennedy, Susan Estabrook. *The Banking Crisis of 1933.* Lexington: University Press of Kentucky, 1973.

Klein, Maury. *Rainbow's End: The Crash of 1929.* New York: Oxford University Press, 2001.

Lacey, Robert. *Ford: The Men and the Machine.* Boston: Little, Brown, 1956.

Lamont, Edward M. *Ambassador from Wall Street.* Latham, MI: Madison, 1964.

Leuchtenburg, William E. *New Deal and Global War.* New York: Time, 1954.

Lerner, Max. *America as a Civilization: Culture and Personality.* New York: Simon & Schuster, 1957.

_____. *America as a Civilization: The Basic Frame.* New York: Simon & Schuster, 1957.

Lewis, David L. *The Public Image of Henry Ford.* Detroit: Wayne State University Press, 1976.

Long, J.C. *Roy D. Chapin: The Man behind the Hudson Motor Car Company.* Detroit: Wayne State University Press, 2004.

May, George S. *R.E. Olds: Auto Industry Pioneer.* Grand Rapids, MI: William B. Eerdmans, 1977.

McElvaine, Robert S. *The Great Depression: 1929–1941.* New York: Times Books, 1995.

Mitchell, Broadus. *Depression Decade: From New Era through New Deal, 1929–1941.* New York: Harper & Row, 1947.

Morison, Samuel Eliot, and Henry Steele Commager. *The Growth of the American Republic.* Vol. 2. New York: Oxford University Press, 1962.

Myers, Gustavus. *History of Bigotry in the United States.* New York: Capricorn Books, 1960.

Neville, Howard Ralph. *The Detroit Banking Collapse of 1933.* East Lansing: Michigan State University Press, 1960.

Nevins, Allan, with Frank Ernest Hill. *Ford: Expansion and Challenge.* New York: Scribner's, 1954.

_____. *Ford: The Times, the Man, the Company.* New York: Scribner's, 1954.

Niebuhr, Reinhold. *Leaves from the Notebook of a Tamed Cynic.* San Francisco: Harper & Row, 1929.

_____. *Moral Man & Immoral Society.* Louisville, KY: Westminster John Knox Press, 1960.

Pecora, Ferdinand. *Wall Street under Oath.* Clifton, NJ: Augustus M. Kelly, 1973.

Pelfrey, William. *Billy, Alfred and General Motors.* New York: American Management Association, 2006.

Pratt, Julius W. *A History of United States Foreign Policy.* Englewood Cliffs, NJ: Prentice Hall, 1959.

Pusey, Merlin J. *Eugene Meyer.* New York: Alfred A. Knopf, 1974.

Rae, John B. *The American Automobile: A Brief History.* Chicago: University of Chicago Press, 1965.

Richards, William C. *The Last Billionaire: Henry Ford.* New York: Scribner's, 1948.

Roosevelt, Franklin D., Russel D. Buhite and David W. Levy. *FDR's Fireside Chats.* Norman: University of Oklahoma Press, 1992.

Seldes, Gilbert. *The Years of the Locust.* Boston: Little, Brown, 1933.

Schlesinger, Arthur, Jr. *The Coming of the New Deal.* New York: Houghton Mifflin, 1959.

_____. *The Crisis of the Old Order.* New York: Houghton Mifflin, 1956.

Sloan, Alfred P., Jr. *Adventures of a White Collar Man.* New York: Doubleday Doran, 1941.

_____. *My Years with General Motors.* New York: MacFadden, 1979.

Sorensen, Charles E. *My Forty Years with Ford.* New York: W.W. Norton, 1956.

Stokes, Thomas L. *Chip Off My Shoulder.* Princeton, NJ: Princeton University Press, 1940.

Sullivan, Lawrence. *Prelude to Panic.* Washington, D.C.: Statesman Press, 1936.

Sward, Keith. *The Legend of Henry Ford.* New York: Rinehart, 1948.

Timmons, Bascom Nolly. *Jesse H. Jones, The Man and the Statesman.* New York: Henry Holt, 1956.

Tompkins, C. David. *Senator Arthur Vandenberg: The Evolution of a Modern Republican, 1884–1945.* East Lansing: Michigan State University Press, 1970.

Wallace, Max. *The American Axis: Henry Ford, Charles Lindbergh and the Rise of the Third Reich.* New York: St. Martin's Press, 2003.

Weiss, H. Eugene. *Chrysler, Ford, Durant and Sloan.* Jefferson, NC: McFarland, 2003.

Woodworth, George Walker. *The Detroit Money Market.* Ann Arbor: University of Michigan, 1956.

Yarnell, Duane. *Auto Pioneering: A Remarkable Story of Ransom E. Olds.* Lansing, MI: Duane Yarnell, 1949.

Young, Clarence H., and William A. Quinn. *Foundation for Living: The Story of Charles Stewart Mott and Flint.* New York: McGraw Hill, 1963.

Periodicals

"Assessed Senator." *Time,* August 14, 1933, <*htttp://time.com/time/archive/printout/0,23657.745897.00hmtl*>.

"Business." *Time,* January 18, 1932, 39.

"Chapin for Lamont." *Time,* August 15, 1932, <*http://www.time/archive/printout/0,23657.744159,000hmtl*>.

"Coughlin on Detroit et al." *Time,* September 4, 1933, <*http://www.time.com/timearchive/printout/0,23657.746000.00hmtl* >.

"Crain's Interactive Web List," <*http://www.crainsdetroit,com/List/lawfirm/7hmtl*>.

Cruden, Robert L. "The Great Ford Myth." *The New Republic,* March 16, 1932, 116.

"Detroit's Dirty Linen." *Business Week,* September 12, 1933, 3.

"Emergency's End." *Time,* April 16, 1945, <*http://time.com/time/archive/printout/0.23657.775599.00.hmtl*>.

Flynn, John T. "Other People's Money." *The New Republic,* October 11, 1933, 240–241.

_____. "Other People's Money." *The New Republic,* October 18, 1933, 278–279.

_____. "Other People's Money." *The New Republic,* January 10, 1934, 211–212.

"Ford Bank." *Time,* August 7, 1933, <*http://time.com/time/archive/print out/0.23657.745870.00hmtl*>.

"Ford Dickers." *Time,* May 31, 1933, <*http://www.time.com/time/archive/printout/0.23657,847262.00.hmtl*>.

"Ford's Lawyer." *Time,* February 11, 1929, <*http://time.com/time/archives/printout 023657,737374,00 hmtl*>.

"Full Sub-Cabinet." *Time,* March 2, (1931), <*http://time/archive/printout/ 0.23657,741112,00 hmtl*>.

Hendry, Maurice. "Studebaker: One Can Do a Lot of Remembering in South Bend," *Automobile Quarterly* 10:1(1972), 244.

"Judge for Bankers." *Time,* August 20, 1936, <*htttp://time.com/time/archive/printout/0,23657.746151.00hmtl*>.

Lincoln Highway Association Web Archives, <*http://www.lincolnnet.net/users/lxpkfrst/http/lhhist81.htm*>.

"Open Detroit." *Time,* April 3, 1933, <*htttp://time.com/time/archive/print out/0,23657.7536429.00hmtl*>.

Prickett, James R. "Communists and the Automobile Industry in Detroit before 1935." *Michigan History* 57 (1973): 185–208.

"Senate Revelations, 7:2." *Time,* January 1, 1934, <*http://time.com/time/archives/printout 023657,746898,99 hmtl*>.

"Shut Michigan." *Time,* March 27, 1933, <*http://time.com/time/archive/printout/0.23657.745428.00.hmtl*>.

Time 13:1 (1929) 37.

Time 6:4 (1925) 5.

"Treasury Asked Ford to Aid Banks, But He Refused." *Time,* January 13, 1934, <*http://time.com/time/archive/printout/0,23657,746898.00hmtl*>.

"Tsar Kanzler." *Time,* February 2, 1942, <*http://wwwtimecom/time/archive/print out/23657,849772.00 hmtl*>.

"Universal Finance Co." *Time,* May 7, 1928, <*http://www. time.com/time/archive/printout/0,23657,785934.00 hmtl*>.

"The Week." *The New Republic,* October 7, 1931, 191–192.

"The Week." *The New Republic,* February 8, 1933, 335–336.

"Whitewash in Detroit." *Time,* October 2, 1933, <*htttp://time.com/time/archive/printout/0,23657.746151.00hmtl*>.

"Who Holds GM." *Time,* August 31, 1931, <*http://time.com/time archive/printout,0,23657,929790,00 hmtl* >

Newspapers

The New York Herald-Tribune
The New York Times

Unpublished Source Materials

Chapin, Roy D. Papers. Bentley Historical Library, University of Michigan, Ann Arbor, MI.

Longley, Clifford. Papers. Accession 1740. Benson Ford Research Library Archives, The Henry Ford, Dearborn, MI.

Hoover, Herbert. Presidential Papers. Herbert Hoover Presidential Library, West Branch, IA.

Government Documents

U.S. Congress, Senate Subcommittee on Stock Exchange Practices of the Committee on Banking and Currency, 73rd Congress, 2nd Session (1934), 4036–4039, 4212, 4600–4601, 4608–4609, 4619, 4626–4627, 4664, 4685–4686, 4891.

Index

Numbers in **bold italics** indicate pages with photographs.

Acheson, Dean 165
Addams, Jane 19
American Liberty League 154, 166
anti-semitism 96, 110, 112, 116
Arkansas 13
arsenal of democracy 156
athletic group 80
"Auto Leaders Meet the New Deal" *153*
Auto Workers Union 85
automobile executive 7, 38, 41, 51, 61, 77, 79
Automobile Manufacturer's Association 32
automobile market revolution 73
automobile production 3, 15, 27, 41, 65, 71, 73, 89, 137
automobile revolution 6
Awalt, F.Gloyd 105

Bak, Richard 90
Ballantine, Arthur A. 21, 23, 26, 64, 69–70, 82 85, *86*
bank examiners 59
bank failures 10, 84, 158
Bank of America 35, 53
Bank of Detroit 50
bank run 113
banking chains 36
banking holiday 1, 99, 105, 113, 135, 138
Bard, Guy T. 162
Barnard, Harry 68, 119
bear raiders 128
Bennett, Harry 36, 49, 87, 102, 112–113, 116, 118
Benson Ford Research Center 114, 116
Big Three *28*, 38
Bingay, Malcolm 160–161
blitz 156
Bloomfield Hills Country Club 34
Bodman, Henry E. 32, 45, 83, 102, 104–105, 111, 121, 123, 133, 142, 145, 151
Bodman L.L.P. 102
Bolsheviks 18
Bonbright, Howard 51

Bonus Expeditionary Force (BEF) 2, 24
Bonus Marchers 2, 76
Briggs, Walter 145
Briggs Manufacturing Company 51, 85, 145
Brown, Donaldson 111, 142, 154
Buchanan, James 4
Buick Motor Division 100; *see also* General Motors Corporation
Business Week 123, 147

Chalmers, Hugh 66
Chalmers-Detroit automobile 66
Chandler auto firm 3
Chapin, Roy D. 7, 19, 25–27, 32–34, 42, 45, 53–54, 60–61, *68*, 63–80, 85, 49, 91–94, 96–97, 100, 104–105, 112–113, 122, 126, 129, 132, 141, 143, 152–153, *153*, 157, 170
Chevrolet Motor Company 153; *see also* General Motors Corporation
Chicago 30, 85
Chicago Democratic National Convention 53
chief national bank examiner 21; *see also* Leyburn, Alfred
Children's Fund of Michigan 24; *see also* Couzens, James
Chrysler, Walter P. 22, *28*, 33–34, 41, 83, 100, 111, 140, 142, 144, *153*
Chrysler Building 128
Chrysler Corporation 16, 22, 27, 38, 77, 83, 88–90, 97–98, 111, 132, 135–137, 140, 142, 144, 152–153, 159: *see also* DeSoto; Dodge; Plymouth
Cleveland: production losses 3
Coffin, Howard 32
Commercial Investment Trust (CIT) 46, 71, 80, 143
Commission for the Relief of Belgium 17; *see also* Hoover, Herbert
Communist 2, 76, 85
Comstock, William 99, 146
consolidation of auto firms 3

Index

Continental Bank 43, 90
Coolidge, Calvin 18
Coughlin, Rev. Charles 84, 160
Couzens, Frank 32, 111, *133*, 134, 162
Couzens, James 7–9, 13, 15–16, 21–24, 32,
   50–51, 54, 60, 68–69, 82, 84–85, 92,
   94–95, 105, 107–111, 119, 125–126, 129–
   134, *133*, 141, 144–145, 152, 155, 159–160,
   164–170
Couzens, Margaret 146
Cox, James 168
Craig, B.J. *95*
Crimson, Harvard 86; *see also* Ballantine,
   Arthur
Crosley, Powel, Jr. 61
Curie, Marie 19
Curved Dash Olds 65; *see also* Chapin, Roy
   D.

Dahlinger, Raymond 49
Davis, Jefferson 4
Dawes, Charles G. 53, 129–130; loan 54
Dawes Bank 130
Dearborn, MI 2
Dearborn Independent 116
Dearborn State Bank 113
deficits 55
Democratic National Committee 128
deposits, subordination of 22, 23, 91, 93,
   97, 146
DeSoto automobile 3; *see also* Chrysler Cor-
   poration
Detroit 6; employment statistics 15, 76
Detroit Athletic Club (DAC) 34, 66
Detroit Bankers Group 38, 51–52, 84, 89,
   97, 160
Detroit Free Press 84, 160, 163
Detroit Institute of the Arts 29
Detroit Is My Own Home Town 160; *see also*
   Bingay, Malcolm
Dewey, Thomas 86, 141
Dillon Reed 88
dividends 55
Dodge brothers 107
Dodge Brothers Company 88
Dodge division 3, 153; *see also* Chrysler
   Corporation
double assessment/liability/penalty 144–145,
   161–162
duopoly in banking 52, 160–161
DuPont, Pierre 128
Durant, William C. (Billy) 7, 35

Earhart, Amelia 14
Eastern banking/money interests 12, 31; *see
   also* Wall Street

Edison, Charles 69
Edison, Charles A. 8, *19*
Edison Institute 8, 67
Edsel automobile 27
Einstein, Albert 69
Eisenhower, Lt. Col. Dwight 76
Emergency Banking Relief Act 140
Empire State Building 128
Erskine, Albert Russell 39, 55
Essex automobile 72, *73*, 89; *see also* Hud-
   son Motor Car Company
Essex coach *73*, 74
Essex-Terraplane automobile 3
Experience With American Justice 116

Federal Reserve 30, 82, 92, 120, 124, 131,
   135, 163
Ferry, Hugh 16
Fink, George R. 113
fireside chats 141, 155–156
Firestone, Harvey *95*
Firestone Tire and Rubber Company 60
First National Bank 111, 131–132 143, 154
Fisher, Carl 66, 104
Fisher, Fred J. 32, 45, 60, 142, *153*
Fisher, William A. 51, 142, 145
Fisher Body Corporation 32, 45, 51
Fletcher, Duncan 129, 148
Flint, MI 35, 38, 80
Flynn, John T. 147
food production in America 18
"Food Will Win the War" 17; *see also*
   Hoover, Herbert
Ford, Ballantine 91–94
Ford, Edsel 7, 9, 11, 16, 21–23, 26–32, *28*,
   34, 36–37, 42, *47*, 54, 58–59, 61, 63–64,
   68, 70, 73, 85, 89, 91, 96–97, 103, 105,
   108, 110–111, 116, 118, 122–123, 126, 132,
   133, 134, 140, 143, 145, 149–151, 161–162
Ford, Mrs. Edsel (Eleanor Clay) 34, *47*
Ford, Henry 7–9, 12–13, *19*, 21–24, 26–33,
   36–37, 41, 46–50, 53, 63–65, 67–68, 70,
   81, 84–85 87–89, 91–97, 102–103, 114–
   115, 107–110, 112, 114, 116, 118–119, 122,
   126–129, 132–134, *133*, 140141, 144, 146–
   147, 150, 153, 155, 155–157, 165–166
Ford, Mrs. Henry (Clara) 30, 150
Ford, Henry, II 45
Ford Motor Company 7–8, 13, 16, 21–22,
   24, 27, 29–33, 37–38, 43–44, 46, 48–51,
   62–63, 65, 70, 77, 83, 85, 87, 102–103,
   105–106, 108, 113, 115–116, 118, 123, 129,
   131, 135, 143, 146, 150, 152–153, 157, 165
Ford V8 automobile 14, 98
Ford Werke 114
Foster, William Z. 2

General Motors (GM) 3, 5, 22–24, 27, 32–33, 35, 37–38, 45, 50–51, 77, 85, 90, 92, 97–98, 103, 116
General Motors Acceptance Corporation (GMAC) 72
General Motors of Canada 51
German Army 17
Giannini, A.P. 35
gold standard 164–165, 167
good roads movement 66–67
Goodyear Tire and Rubber Company 66, 104
Graham, Robert *153*
Graham-Paige Motors 143, 153
Great Engineer 17; *see also* Hoover, Herbert
Great Humanitarian 17; *see also* Hoover, Herbert
Greenfield Village 19, 69
Grosse Pointe 31, 48
group banking 35–38, 144

Hamilton, Alexander 12
Harding, Warren G. 18
Harriman, Edward H. 103
Harriman, W. Averill 103
Harvard 87
Hastings, Charles *153*
Hayes Body Plant 85
Hearst, William Randolph 66
Henry and Edsel 90
Henry Ford and Son 46
Henry Ford Museum 69
Henry's Lieutenants 7
Hidden World Government 116
Higbie, Carlton 31–32, 60, 145
Highland Park State Bank 50
Highway Transport Committee 67; *see also* Chapin, Roy D.
holding companies 34–36
Hoover, Herbert 1–2, 9, 15–17, *19*, 20, 22–25, 39–40, 63–65, 67, 75, 77–82, 85–86, 96, 99, 127–128, 131, 146, 148, 152, 154, 165, 167
Hoover flags 20
Hoover hogs 20
Hoover leather 20
Hoover shoes 20
Hooverball 80
Hoovering 20
Hudson, J.L. 34
Hudson Motor Car Company 3, 26, 32–34, 37, 45, 54, 66, 68–73, 77, 80, 85, 89–90, 93, 103, 143, 153: *see also* Essex
Hughes, Charles Evans 163
Hull, Cordell 168
Hupmobile 142
Hupp, Robert 6–7, 142

Hupp Motor Company 143
Hutchison, B.E. 16, 83
Hyatt Roller Bearing Company 33
Hyde Park 139

Illinois 13
inauguration day 1933 4–5, 9, 17, 24, 135, 137, 140
Indiana 13
Indianapolis 40
Indianapolis Speedway 61
installment buying 71, 74
Insull, Samuel 3, 5, 129–130, 148
Iowa 13; farm unrest 3
Iran 40
Iraq 40

Jackson, R.B. 61
Jefferson, Thomas 12
Jews In Nazi Germany 117
Johnson, Gen. Hugh S. *153*
Jolson, Al 61
Jones, Jesse 21, 83, 94, 122; *see also* Reconstruction Finance Corporation
Jordan Motors Corporation 3
Joy, Henry B. 104, 107–108, 110
Joy, Mrs. Henry B. 154

Kahn, Albert 51, 60
Kaiser's Army 18
Kanzler, Ernest 7, 11–12, 22, 26, 31–32, 34, 37, 45–49, *47*, 53, 55–58, 60–61, 63, 70, 83, 96, 99, 121, 123, 126, 129, 131–133, 143, 145, 149–151, 154, 162, 166
Kanzler, Mrs. Ernest (Josephine Clay) 34, *47*
Keidan, Harry 118–119, 123
Keller, Kaufman T. *153*
Kennedy, Susan Estabrook 53
Kettering, Charles 13
Knudsen, William S. *153*, 154, 156–157

Landon, Alfred 154
Lansing, MI 38
League of Nations 108
Leland, Henry 115
Leland, Wilfred 115
Lewis, David 29
Leyburn, Alfred 11–12, 16, 21–22, 26, 58, 83, 87, 89, 99, 105, 120–123, 125, 152; *see also* chief national bank examiner
Leibold, Ernest G. 26, 83,84, 87–88, 90–91, 94, 97, 107, 112–115, 118
Light's Golden Jubilee 19
Lincoln, Abraham 4, 26
Lincoln Highway Association 66, 103–104

Index

Lincoln motorcar 29
Lincoln Motorcar Company 115
London 156
Long, J.C. 68–69
Longley and Middleton 102
Longley, Clifford 21–22, 51, 58, 83, 87, 94–97, *95*, 102, 104–105, 11, 112, 114–116, 118–123, 125
Lord, Robert O. 60, 122, 160, 162

MacArthur, Gen. Douglas 76
Macauley, Alvan 32, 37, 45, 51, 70, 72, 104, 107–108, 142, 145, *153*
Manufacturer's National Bank 111, 143
Maxwell, Jonathan 67
Maxwell Motors Corporation 52
McAneeny, John 32
McKee, John 21, 120–121, 123–125, *124*; see also Reconstruction Finance Corporation
McKinley, William 86, 110
memorandum of agreement 43–44
Mendelsohn 32, 45
Michigan bank closures 1, 24, 44
Middleton, Wallace 102
Miller, Charles 21–23, 94
Mills, Ogden 21–23, 122, 131, 134
Mississippi River flood 18
Missouri 13
Mitchell, Charles 148
Mitchell, W. Ledyard 51 70
Model A Ford 14, 98
Model T Ford 14, 27, 31, 46, 48, 71, 98, 107
Morgan, J.P. 52–53, 103, 165
Mott, Charles Stewart 33, 35, 37, 42, 50, 54, 58, 60, 64, 69–70, 72, 145, 150–151, 160, 162
Murphy, Frank 84
Murray, James R. 32
Murray Manufacturing Company 32
Muscle Shoals 9, 115
Mussolini, Benito 153

Nash Motor Car Company 72
National Automobile Chamber of Commerce 32, 70, 104, 153
National Bank Group 146
National Bank of Commerce 55
National Bank of Detroit 4, 142, 163
national food administrator 19; see also Hoover, Herbert
National Industrial Recovery Act 153, 166
National Labor Relations Act 140
National Labor Relations Board 166
National Recovery Administration (NRA) 153
Nazi Germany 96, 114, 169

New Deal 140, 148, 152–153, 155, 157, 164, 167
New Republic 147
New York City 30, 98
New York Stock Exchange 98
New York Times 30, 79, 103, 150
Newberry, Phelps 32, 111
Newberry, Truman 32, 51, 108–111
North Carolina 13, 162

Office of Production Management 156
Olds, Ransom E. 33, 37, 51, 64–65, 68–70, 145
Olds Motor Works 65, 67
Opel auto firm 167

Packard Motor Car Company 16, 32, 45, 51, 66, 72, 83, 103–107, 111, 142–143, 153
Pecora, Ferdinand 56–58, 123, 128–130, 147, 151
Peerless automobile 3
Pickford, Mary 61
Pingree, Hazen 106–107
Plymouth Division of Chrysler Corporation 3
Pomerene, Atlee 23, 25–26, 82, 91; see also Reconstruction Finance Corporation
Pontiac Motor Car Company 66
Prest-O-Lite Company 66
Protocols and World Revolution 116
Protocols of Meeting of the Zionest Men of Wisdom 116
Protocols of the Elders of Zion 96
Protocols of the Wise Men of Zion 116

Raskob, John J. 128, 154
Reconstruction Finance Corporation (RFC) 11, 13, 23, 25, 53–54, 57–58, 63, 75, 82, 84–85, 88–89, 94, 101, 105–106, 121–123, 129, 141–143, 146, 152, 160; chief appraiser 21; see also McKee, John
Reed, James 116
REO Motor Car Company 32–33, 37, 51, 72, 90
replacement sales 71
Revenue Act of 1935 166
Rickenbacker, Eddie 61
River Rouge riot 75
Rivera, Diego 29
Rogers, Will 19, 61
Romney, George 170
Roosevelt, Franklin Delano (FDR) 2, 16, 40, 53, 75, 78–79, *124*, 127, 134, 137, 139, 148, 155–156, 164–165, 167–168, 170; attempted assassination 100; first hundred days 139

Roosevelt, Theodore 78, 86, 88, 99–100, 110
Root, Elihu 88, 111
Root and Clark law firm 88

Sapiro, Aaron 116
Saturday Evening Post 67, 69
Securities and Exchange Commission 34
Seiberling, F.A. 104
Sherep-Spiridovich, Count 116
Sloan, Alfred P., Jr. 7, 15, 22, 26, *28*, 33, 72, 83, 111, 138, 140–142, 144, *153*–154, 156–157, 165–166
Smith family 65, 68
Social Security Act 166
Socialist 2
Sorensen, Charles 33–34, 48, 67, 115
Soviet Union 18
Stair, E.D. 160, 163, 170
Stimson, Henry L. 88
stock pools 23, 42–43, 56, 60
stock prices, banks 42, 62
Studebaker Corporation 39

Taft, William Howard 86, 88
Tennessee 13
Terraplane motor car 74; *see also* Hudson Motor Car Company
Thomas, E.R. 66
Thomas, Norman 2
Thomas-Detroit Auto Company 66; *see also* Chapin, Roy D.
Tiedeman, Carsten 72
Time 77,114, 147,161
TransAmerica 35

Traverse City, MI 113; *see also* Liebold, Ernest G.
Truman, Harry S. 88
20th Amendment to the Constitution 5

U.S. banking system 12
U.S. Congress: Senate Subcommittee on Stock Exchange Practices 23, 44, 56, 127, 129; *see also* Pecora, Ferdinand
U.S. Department of Justice 162
U.S. Rubber Corporation 66
U.S. Steel Corporation 54
U.S. Supreme Court 163
Universal Credit Corporation (UCC) 37, 46, 58, 63, 70–72, 114, 122–123, 131

Vandenberg, Arthur 16, 21, 25, 74, 132–133, 166

Wall Street 12, 30–31, 36–37, 40, 67, 88, 103, 142; *see also* Eastern banking/money interests
Walsh, James 160, 162
Warren, Charles B. 60
Wilkin, Herbert L. 159–160, 162–163
Willys, John North 75, 104, 170
Willys-Overland Corporation 66, 100, 104
Wilson, Robert 32
Wilson, Woodrow 17–18, 41, 88, 108
World War I 67, 108
World War II 93
Wright, Orville 74

Young, DuBois 142, *153*